MINORITIES IN JUVENILE JUSTICE

MINORITIES IN JUVENILE JUSTICE

Edited by
Kimberly Kempf Leonard
Carl E. Pope
William H. Feyerherm

SAGE Publications
International Educational and Professional Publisher
Thousand Oaks   London   New Delhi

For information address:

SAGE Publications, Inc.
2455 Teller Road
Thousand Oaks, California 91320
E-mail: order@sagepub.com

SAGE Publications Ltd.
6 Bonhill Street
London EC2A 4PU
United Kingdom

SAGE Publications India Pvt. Ltd.
M-32 Market
Greater Kailash I
New Delhi 110 048 India

Printed in the United States of America

Library of Congress Cataloging-in-Publication Data

Main entry under title:

Minorities in juvenile justice / edited by Kimberly Kempf Leonard,
    Carl E. Pope, William H. Feyerherm.
        p. cm.
    Includes bibliographical references and index.
    ISBN 0-8039-7264-4 (c : alk. paper). — ISBN 0-8039-7265-2 (p :
alk. paper)
        1. Juvenile justice, Administration of—United States.
    2. Discrimination in criminal justice administration—United States.
    3. Minority youth—United States. I. Kempf Leonard, Kimberly.
    II. Pope, Carl E. III. Feyerherm, William H.
    HV9104.M57   1995
    364.3'6'08693—dc20   95-15769

This book is printed on acid-free paper.

95 96 97 98 99 10 9 8 7 6 5 4 3 2 1

Sage Production Editor: Tricia K. Bennett   Typesetter: Christina M. Hill

Contents

Preface   vii

1. The DMC Initiative:
   The Convergence of Policy and Research Themes   1
      William H. Feyerherm

2. Reflections on Race Effects in Juvenile Justice   16
      Charles E. Frazier and *Donna M. Bishop*

3. Policing Juveniles:
   Is There Bias Against Youths of Color?   47
      Madeline Wordes and *Timothy S. Bynum*

4. The Social Context of Juvenile Justice Administration:
   Racial Disparities in an Urban Juvenile Court   66
      Barry C. Feld

5. The Role of Race in Juvenile Justice in Pennsylvania   98
      Kimberly Kempf Leonard and *Henry Sontheimer*

6. Racial Disparities in the Confinement of Juveniles:
   Effects of Crime and Community Social Structure
   on Punishment   128
      George S. Bridges, Darlene J. Conley, Rodney L. Engen, and
      Townsand Price-Spratlen

7. The Overrepresentation of Minority Youths
   in the California Juvenile Justice System:
   Perceptions and Realities   153
   James Austin

8. Juvenile Justice Processing of American
   Indian Youths: Disparity in One Rural County   179
   Lisa M. Poupart

9. Equity Within the Juvenile Justice System:
   Directions for the Future   201
   Carl E. Pope

References   217

Index   227

About the Contributors   239

Preface

This book is a collection of research and policy papers on minority youths and differential processing by juvenile justice in the United States. The volume provides information about the extent and sources of disparate treatment of youths within juvenile justice and thereby helps to fill a void now present in the literature.

There is a significant, albeit inconclusive, body of published research about differential processing in criminal justice, but there is very little information about the treatment of juveniles. Previous research has focused primarily on racial disparity of adults at criminal sentencing, pretrial detention, and capital punishment. The extent of problems experienced by minority youths is unknown. This lack of information is unfortunate because there are many areas in juvenile justice that offer significant potential for unequal handling of youths. There are a variety of decision makers and stages within juvenile justice, some of which are very informal by design and occur outside of public view. There also is great variation across statutes defining delinquency and status offending. The traditional *parens patriae* philosophy of juvenile court allows even greater discretionary treatment than exists in most criminal justice systems. There are indications that juvenile justice processing is operating more in accord with criminal justice objectives, meanwhile adhering to techniques of individualized treatment consistent with the *parens patriae* doctrine. The ability of juvenile systems to deliver justice deserves greater scrutiny as youths are more often perceived accountable for their actions, deemed culpable, and treated punitively. If minority youths are more often the recipients of harsher treatment and restricted liberties, then reforms of juvenile justice are needed.

In 1988, Congress amended the Juvenile Justice and Delinquency Prevention Act to require states to investigate overrepresentation of minority youths in confinement and develop action plans to remedy problem situations. Concomitantly, a review of the literature (Pope & Feyerherm, 1990a, 1990b) identified the need for research on juvenile processing and offered many suggestions for how such studies should be conducted. As states attempt to respond to the federal mandate on minority overrepresentation in juvenile justice and research in this area is undertaken, it is important for progress that our knowledge be integrated and be a cumulative process. As such, this book is the logical next step in the sequence for understanding how juvenile justice intervenes in the lives of children and whether this intervention differs for children of color.

In Chapter 1, William Feyerherm helps to underscore how timely this volume should be in view of the convergence of research and policy developments concerning minority overrepresentation in juvenile justice. Charles Frazier and Donna Bishop share their experiences in Chapter 2 from a Florida study, including analyses of data from a statewide database, information obtained from interviews with administrators of juvenile justice, and some frustrations often associated with policy-based research. In Chapter 3, Madeline Wordes and Timothy Bynum describe the necessity of ethnographic investigation to learn about juvenile encounters with police, or the front-end of juvenile justice processing. In Chapter 4, Barry Feld encourages us to think about the conceptual requirements for studying juvenile justice decisions and the inherent problems of access to data in which those concepts can be measured. In discussing his research in Minnesota, Feld also suggests that we reconsider our expectations for observing rationality and patterns of responses in a "system" that dictates individuality in treatment. In Chapter 5, results of a study in Pennsylvania clarify the need to view juvenile justice as a series of interrelated decisions; possibly there is a cumulative process in which cases present at later stages may be systematically biased because of nonrandom attrition at earlier stages. Kimberly Kempf Leonard and Henry Sontheimer also remind us that statistical procedures evolve as tools of science and do not always prove definitive. In Chapter 6, George Bridges, Darlene Conley, Rodney Engen, and Townsand Price-Spratlen use the results of their study in Washington to explain the role of structural characteristics of communities in shaping perceptions of juvenile crime and understanding how official responses occur. James Austin also discusses social conditions in Chapter 7, particularly the need to address factors external to juvenile justice to alleviate problems of overrepresentation he observed at sequential stages from detention to confinement in California. In Chapter 8, Lisa Poupart encourages us to look beyond African American and Latino youths to other minorities who also might be negatively affected by differential treatment but require special research strategies to observe. She identifies Native Americans as recipients of harsher dispositions throughout stages of juvenile justice, and especially early at intake, from which they are apt to be cumulatively disadvantaged. In Chapter 9, Carl Pope insists that we not be overwhelmed by the problems of the past, but encouraged by the prospects of the future. He outlines strategies for research and observation of overrepresentation and steps to help overcome racial bias in juvenile justice processing.

In sum, these collected works identify the unique research concerns in studying juvenile justice, such as greater difficulty in gaining access to data because of the private and informal nature of the systems and the tradition of expunging juvenile records. Different techniques of investigation, sampling, and analysis are explained. Both qualitative and quantitative methods are used. Several racial minority groups and a diverse group of states are represented. The unique methodological features of particular studies are discussed and the corresponding advantages and disadvantages associated with the procedures are outlined. Findings are presented and their implications for policy reforms are made throughout the book. Despite great variation in the methods of inquiry, there is remarkable consistency in the findings of race problems in juvenile justice. There also is tremendous creativity, practicality, and insight among the suggestions for improving equity in the process. We hope that this volume will be of value to many researchers, students, and administrators who are interested in the welfare of America's youths, preserving public safety, and ensuring fair and equal treatment.

Kimberly Kempf Leonard
Carl E. Pope
William H. Feyerherm

1

The DMC Initiative
The Convergence of Policy and Research Themes

WILLIAM H. FEYERHERM

The 1988 conference of the National Coalition of State Juvenile Justice Advisory Groups focused almost entirely on the issues of minority youths in the juvenile justice system—the first time that a national policy and advocacy body focused with such emphasis on this problem area. In *A Report on the Delicate Balance,* the coalition reported that

> disparate juvenile and criminal justice rates for minorities are not a new phenomenon. Yet until recently we have not been sufficiently concerned to ask the important questions: Why do these rates exist? What can we do about them? How can we avoid this continued problem in the future? These questions are not easy ones to ask, particularly for those of us who are participants in the operation or management of juvenile justice at the state or national level. (National Coalition of State Juvenile Justice Advisory Groups, 1989, p. 2)

It is my contention that one reason that policymakers avoided asking such difficult questions is that the mechanisms for achieving the answers were not available. In other words, the development of

1

a sufficient body of research knowledge and capacity was a prerequisite for moving these issues beyond the stage of ongoing rhetoric into a stage of policy development and action.

In the reauthorization of the Juvenile Justice and Delinquency Prevention Act (JJDPA), Congress added the issue of overconfinement of minority youths to the set of mandates that states must address to continue receiving federal resources under the JJDPA. That action generally may be seen as substantial progress in what is termed the DMC (disproportionate minority confinement) initiative. That action also creates a mandate that is substantially different in scope and nature from the earlier mandates contained in the JJDPA. It is the thesis of this chapter that the DMC mandate represents a convergence of research and policy developments and could not have occurred without the current state of development in each area. It is my belief that continued attention to this mandate (let alone actual progress) is necessarily dependent on an interrelationship between policy and research activities in ways that are, at least in the juvenile justice arena, previously nonexistent. To explore this thesis, several areas will be combined. I will begin with a review of the past mandates of the JJDPA, move to a brief consideration of the DMC mandate, and then to an examination of some of the salient differences between them. A brief review of policy development follows, with a somewhat more extensive review of the research development in the area. Finally, some concluding remarks offer speculations as to the nature of a possible ongoing relationship between policy and research related to DMC.

JJDPA— THE POLICY CONTEXT FOR DMC

The past policy initiatives of the Office of Juvenile Justice and Delinquency Prevention (OJJDP) have included a variety of areas and projects that occasionally have brought notoriety to the agency, as well as provided for the exploration of a wide range of juvenile issues. However, the three mandated areas in the JJDPA have received much attention.

1. *Sight and sound separation* is the effort to ensure that juvenile defendants and delinquents are maintained separately from adult defendants and criminals. This has frequently led to the development of separate facilities (Mandate 3), but minimally requires that some form of separation be maintained to prevent "contamination" of juveniles from their presumed more worldly and dangerous adult counterparts.

2. *Deinstitutionalization of status offenders* is designed to separate those whose conditions (e.g., in need of supervision) require judicial attention from those who have committed specific delinquent acts. It flows in part from the growing concern with the protection of the rights of juveniles and in part from attention to the perceived deleterious effects of labeling youths as having been in an institution.

3. *Jail removal* is the effort to ensure that juveniles are held in facilities separated from adult facilities. The premise is not only that contamination be prevented but that juveniles by their nature have different needs, require different forms of supervision, and need greater attention to programming than do their adult counterparts. The design of facilities thus becomes a concern, as well as their simple separation.

Each of these three mandates has achieved a relatively high degree of success. Although there are occasions where exceptions are allowed, most states have achieved general compliance with these requirements, and indeed many have put into place forms of compliance monitoring to ensure the continued achievement of these mandates. These monitoring efforts basically involve a counting and auditing function to determine the numbers of juveniles held in contact with adults, to verify the separation of adults and juveniles, and to verify that all confined juveniles are held pursuant to delinquency allegations and not, for example, for protection as status offenders. Whether states would have achieved this degree of compliance on a completely voluntary basis is not clear, because the JJDPA contains provisions that all federal OJJDP "formula" (block grant) funds going to a state must be directed to meeting these mandated areas, until compliance is achieved. Once a state is in compliance with the mandates, these federal funds continue to be available to the state, but basically at the discretion of the recipient agency and a gubernatorially appointed state advisory group. As a result, there is some considerable incentive to reach a condition of compliance in order to have available federal funds with relatively few conditions.

CURRENT STATUS OF DMC

Within the reauthorization of the JJDPA in 1988 was contained an amendment that required states to begin to study overrepresentation of minority youths:

> In accordance with regulations which the Administrator shall prescribe, [the state plan] shall . . . address efforts to reduce the proportion of juveniles detained or confined in secure detention facilities, secure correctional facilities, jails, and lockups who are members of minority groups if such proportion exceeds the proportion such groups represent in the general population. (Juvenile Justice and Delinquency Prevention Act of 1974, as amended [Public Law 93-415], Section 223[a][23])

As a result of that amendment, several state advisory groups, and the state juvenile justice agencies with which they work, began efforts to determine the extent of overrepresentation. Many of the research efforts reported in this volume are the result of those activities. However, although that amendment made each state address the issue within its state plans (required to receive federal funds under the JJDPA), it was not until the most recent reauthorization of the JJDPA that planning to reduce overrepresentation became required to continue receipt of federal funds. With that reauthorization, what was an amendment to the act became one of the four major requirements of the act. States must make progress and show at least a good-faith effort, or be at risk of losing one fourth of their federal funds, with the accompanying requirement that the remaining three fourths must be directed toward achieving compliance with all JJDPA mandates, including the DMC mandate (speech by J. Wilson to the Florida Conference on Minority Over Representation, Tallahassee, May, 1993).

ISSUES IN THE
IMPLEMENTATION OF THE DMC MANDATE

As state and local groups have come to deal with the issue of overrepresentation, several critical issues have emerged. These have come primarily from the effort to understand overrepresentation from a systems perspective, arising from the observation that overrepresentation appears to represent the combined effects of several decision processes in juvenile justice.

The first issue may be termed an issue of *confinement versus penetration*. Congressional language deals with confinement, the holding of juveniles in secure settings such as detention centers, juvenile institutions, and so on. However, with any form of systems perspective on the juvenile justice area, it is clear that the real issue starts well before the decision to place a youth in a training school. That is, the "supply" of youths available to be potentially placed in a training school environment is dependent on earlier decisions by law enforcement as to which youths to bring into the system, by intake workers who decide which youths will be handled with informal counseling, and by workers who decide which youths are in need of child welfare services (in need of supervision) or in need of mental health services. Thus the end condition of secure confinement is the result of decisions made about which youths go furthest into the juvenile justice system. Understanding that this penetration is the key factor leads to a much wider range of possible policy changes and research issues and, in general, enormously complicates the issue. On the other hand, without dealing with the penetration issue there is no hope of addressing the confinement issue. Parenthetically, it appears that the primary sources of information used to propel Congress into concerns for DMC were based on the Children in Custody studies, which ignore the factors leading to custody, focusing instead on the numbers, conditions, and legal rationale for custody. It is thus understandable that the issue of penetration was understated in the congressional action.

A second critical issue is somewhat more subtle. The issue raised in the DMC initiative is essentially *correlational rather than descriptive.* By this, I mean that it raises the question of the relationship of a youth's racial and ethnic identification to that youth's processing by the juvenile justice system. This is different from asking how many youths of various groups are in the system. We cannot measure overrepresentation by simple counting. Nor can the issue be addressed by eliminating a certain type of treatment. Most practitioners and policymakers agree that there are some youths who require secure confinement. The issue is not to eliminate secure confinement, but to ensure its equitable usage. That requires consideration of the comparative conditions of potential inhabitants of secure confinement. It also creates a mandate that cannot be met by the simple elimination of a type of treatment or confinement, nor one that for which success (compliance) can be measured in a simple counting operation. In that respect, this is a much more complex undertaking than the previous JJDPA mandates.

A related issue is understanding the system nature of the problem, and the *tendency of most systems toward homeostasis.* As recognized by the authors of the *Delicate Balance* report, the issue is one of the "convergence of a number of unseen forces that permits isolated decision makers of substantially different backgrounds to produce consistent systemic behavior that is racist in its consequence, if not intent" (National Coalition of State Juvenile Justice Advisory Groups, 1989, pp. 10-11). This, of course, carries an understanding that effecting one set of decision makers in a positive direction may cause another set to react in an opposite direction. Most systems have some form of quasi-stationary equilibrium around which they fluctuate. An effort to change a system in one area is likely to produce a counterbalancing reaction, even though that reaction may not be consciously intended as racist. Thus movement toward achieving compliance with the DMC mandate is likely to require the cooperation of a large number of agencies, officials, and advocates. It is not enough to achieve the cooperation of one state agency, or one piece of legislation such as that which might remove the authority to incarcerate status offenders.

Former House Speaker Tip O'Neill is attributed with having said that "all politics are local politics." That saying applies to justice systems as well, at least in this instance. In earlier analyses of the juvenile justice systems in California and Florida, it was abundantly clear that each county within those states behaved very differently with respect to its juvenile justice system. Some had tendencies toward high rates of incarceration; others, very low usage. Some had very strong differences in the processing of youths from different racial groups, from the beginning of the court systems. Others had differences occurring at other stages of court processing, and some showed no differences in processing by racial group. Thus, although federal leadership has provided impetus for this mandate, it can only be achieved by careful examination of the idiosyncratic operations of each local juvenile justice system.

Taken together, the differences noted above between the DMC mandate and the earlier mandates included in the JJDPA lead to the conclusion that achieving measurable change in this area will be more difficult than in the previous initiatives. Moreover, because of the increased complexity of that change effort, the information needs of those engaged in the change process are much greater. It really is necessary to have a comprehensive understanding of the reasons for that consistent, systemic behavior in order to develop a strategy for overcoming that behavior and for establishing some level of permanency for that change.

THE DEVELOPMENT
OF THE DMC MANDATE

Although research regarding the relationship of race and juvenile court processing has been conducted for several decades (see Zatz, 1987, for a review), the first discernible reference in legislative annals to the issue of minority overrepresentation is found in the June 1986 testimony of Ira Schwartz (Center for the Study of Youth Policy) before the House Subcommittee on Human Resources. In that testimony, based on studies of the Children in Custody data conducted at the Hubert Humphrey Center in Minnesota, he informed the subcommittee that "minority youth now comprise more than half of all the juveniles incarcerated in public detention and correctional facilities in the United States" and that despite widely held perceptions to the contrary, there is recent research showing that minority youth do not account for a substantially disproportionate amount of serious crime. However, minority youth stand a much greater chance of being arrested than white youth, and once arrested, appear to be at great risk of being charged with more serious offenses than whites who are involved in comparable levels of delinquency. (Schwartz, 1986, p. 5)

In 1987, Congressman Tauke, in setting the stage for hearings on the reauthorization of the JJDPA, cited several key issues that "must be considered during reauthorization." Third among these "is minority incarceration. Data in this area is alarming. It indicates that minority juveniles are disproportionately incarcerated and we need to determine if a dual juvenile justice system is emerging" (Tauke, 1987, p. 3). In that same hearing, Barry Krisberg (1988) of the National Council on Crime and Delinquency (NCCD) cited the same studies that Schwartz had during the previous year, concluding that "minority youth are more likely than white youth to end up in public versus private facilities and more likely to end up at the deep end of the custody system" (p. 12).

The same studies are cited in a number of subsequent congressional hearings, for example, the testimony of William Bogan, Director of the National Coalition of Hispanic Mental Health and Social Service Organizations, in February 1988: "The Hubert H. Humphrey Institute has pointed out, that in 1979 the rate of incarceration for Hispanic males was about 2.3 times higher than the rate for non-Hispanic white males. And that rate, in fact, has increased to about 2.6 times higher by 1982. So, you see those rates shifting. There's more disproportionate . . . incarceration of Hispanics over time" (Bogan, 1988, p. 115). Bogan went on to raise substantial issues with the research capacity at that time, indicating that "the next step doesn't happen, where you go from the national data down to the state or individual institutions and look at that overrepresentation, look at the reasons the kids are in there, the length of sentencing, other data that would start to explain why that overrepresentation is taking place." And then he raised a very interesting perspective: "If OJJDP is going to continue the requirements for state plans, put some language in there that increases their accountability for minority issues" (Bogan, 1988, p. 116).

Congress was not the only policy arena in which these issues were addressed. The National Coalition of State Juvenile Justice Advisory Groups, in its 1987 report to Congress, urged regional hearings on the issues of differential incarceration rates, leading to action to "reduce inappropriate practices within the juvenile justice system" (p. 17). That recommendation was followed by the coalition choosing to focus nearly the entirety of its 1988 meeting and its subsequent report (1989) on issues related to DMC. The National Council of Juvenile and Family Court Judges likewise began to inquire as to the research findings in the area, to establish procedures for ensuring consideration of equity issues in its deliberations and recommendations, and to highlight DMC issues in a special edition of the *Juvenile and Family Court Journal*.

It would be a mistake to believe that the juvenile justice field was alone in recognizing the issues posed by diverse racial, ethnic, and cultural backgrounds among the nation's youths. Other service systems, including education, child welfare, and mental health, were undergoing similar issues simultaneously. For example, in the arena of children's mental health, the newly emerging CASSP initiative (Children and Adolescent Service System Projects) has as one of its guiding principles the provision of culturally appropriate services for youths in need of mental health services, a category that includes many youths in the juvenile justice system. What does distinguish the juvenile justice field was the emphasis on involuntary placement in custodial institutions, leading to the Children in Custody data, the basic source for the Minnesota analyses.

It would also be a mistake to leave this topic without recognition of a critical piece of information, referenced at several points in the discourse. As Schwartz (1986) noted, one common (mis)perception was that higher rates of incarceration were a direct result of higher rates of criminal misbehavior by minority youths. The most often-cited pieces of contrary evidence were the results of the National Youth Survey, conducted by Elliott and colleagues (Elliott & Agetan, 1980) at the University of Colorado. Krisberg (1988) summarizes those results for Congress: "Elliott and his colleagues found that if black and white youth reported equal levels of serious delinquency in a survey, that the black youth were twice as likely to be arrested and much more likely to be charged with serious offenses" (p. 12).

THE RESEARCH REQUIREMENTS OF DMC

To understand what types of research were necessary to support the DMC initiative, it is useful to return to the statement of the National Coalition of State Juvenile Justice Advisory Groups in the *Delicate Balance* report. Essentially, three types of research questions are stated there: Why is there overrepresentation? What can be done about it? How can it be prevented in the future? The answers to these research questions are available to different extents, but some preliminary answers are available to each.

To understand the research addressing the first issue—why there is overrepresentation—it is first necessary to understand the inability of researchers to answer adequately the question until relatively recently. Zatz (1987), in a well-documented history of research efforts, argues that four waves of research have occurred, characterized by differences in methodologies as well as findings. The earlier waves, suffering from few controls and poor methods of analysis, found overt discrimination. As methods of control and comparison became more sophisticated, these findings of discrimination were replaced by general findings that differences were due to behavioral differences (higher levels of serious crime). A third wave began to use even more sophisticated analysis and discovered subtle forms of bias. A fourth wave, relying on data from determinate sentencing jurisdictions, continued to find evidence of subtle disparities. Overall, as studies have become more sophisticated they have involved sufficient control variables to address the issue of higher levels of criminal conduct and have involved multiple decision points in order to assess the total, dynamic effects of the juvenile justice system. As a result, forms of bias that previously were undetectable are now more readily discerned.

In a previous work, Pope and Feyerherm (1990a) reviewed most of the research conducted on the relationship of race to juvenile justice processing between 1970 and 1988. In the more sophisticated and methodologically sound studies, we found the following set of possible explanations for overrepresentation.

1. *Indirect effects.* Justice decision makers use variables that are race related, thus producing racially aligned effects through decision variables such as family status, gang status, school participation, and so on. Zatz (1987) describes this by saying that "researchers conceptualize discrimination more broadly to include indirect and interaction effects of race/ethnicity, operating through other variables. These disparities reflect more subtle institutionalized biases, but still fall within the purview of discrimination if they systematically favor one group over another" (p. 70).

2. *Cumulative effects.* These are the aggregation of small but consistent differences in justice processing. This means that differences that might be viewed in isolation as not too discriminatory may accumulate to have a marked effect on minority youths.

3. *Justice by geography.* This refers to the differences in justice philosophy and resources that occur from place to place. For example, if most of a state's minority juveniles reside in places that either have relatively few community options or in which the justice system is particularly oriented toward community safety (through removal), then on a statewide basis there will be a decided issue of overrepresentation, even though minority and majority youths may be treated with similar sanctions within specific counties.

In addition, the work of Howard Snyder and colleagues at the National Center for Juvenile Justice points to the need to examine justice policies. In brief, Snyder argues that the effect of the war on drugs was to markedly increase the confinement of minority youths but had substantially less effect on majority youths, this despite evidence that drug use and trafficking is not primarily a minority behavior (Snyder, 1990).

The importance of this overall question is underscored by its place in the OJJDP instructions and requirements for all states in order to continue receiving JJDPA formula funds (Feyerherm, 1993). First among the requirements are two stages: identification and

assessment. In the identification stage, states are required to determine the extent to which overrepresentation occurs, both at the
statewide level and for the three major metropolitan areas. Assuming that overrepresentation is found (which is the case for all states
reporting thus far except Vermont), the next stage is assessment, in
which the analyst is supposed to examine the stages of processing
within the juvenile justice system, as well as differences between
jurisdictions, to begin determining the explanations for overrepresentation. This process of continually narrowing and defining the
target should eventually lead to targeted areas for intervention,
which is the intent of the OJJDP process.

The second major question posed by the authors of the *Delicate
Balance* report was, essentially, what can we do about it? In part, all
of the studies in this book were designed to provide some guidance
on that issue, as they have derived in major part from the efforts of
states and communities to understand the nature of overrepresentation in their juvenile justice systems. OJJDP has funded a number
of state juvenile justice agencies that currently are involved in both
the assessment process to determine the nature of the causes of
overrepresentation and intervention processes to attempt to change
that overrepresentation. Five states in particular have received special emphasis grants in this area (for more information, see Rhoden,
1994). In Oregon, those resources currently are being used to create
additional treatment resources that are culturally appropriate
within the three most populous counties of the state. In Iowa, a
major emphasis on community-based prevention efforts has led to
concentration on one community, Cedar Rapids, and intensive prevention efforts through an integrated services provider, the Jane
Boyd House. In Florida, a state-of-the-art juvenile assessment center
has been developed and teamed with a coalition of community
service providers to find appropriate community programs for minority defendants. In North Carolina, a somewhat different approach has been used that focuses on helping community groups in
10 targeted counties to understand the data available in their counties and then to structure locally appropriate solutions. In Arizona,
a range of minority-serving services have been developed in areas
that previously had nothing available for those youths in terms of
community alternatives accessible for use by the justice system.

Other states are engaged in additional activities, along with training programs developed by the American Correctional Association and the National Council of Juvenile and Family Court Judges. In addition, private foundations have become involved. For example, the Annie B. Casey Foundation has devoted substantial resources to their Juvenile Detention Alternatives Initiative, emphasizing that objective use of detention criteria should reduce the disparate numbers of minority youths currently subject to juvenile detention. Their work in five major U.S. cities should provide concrete evidence of the effectiveness of that strategy. However, few of these programs have yet been subjected to much rigorous evaluation, and so the question of "what works" is still unanswered.

About the third question, what can we do to prevent it in the future? even less is known. Clearly, the comments of Bogan to Congress were instructive. One chief way in which problems are prevented is to make someone accountable for their identification and prevention. This essentially raises the role of monitoring, which has been successfully used in previous OJJDP initiatives. What is interesting about the DMC issue is that the monitoring must take into account the relationships of variables to one another, not just the frequency of some event. In that light, the review that Zatz performed is particularly instructive, because it suggests either that the form of discrimination itself has changed over time in this country or that the ability to detect forms of discrimination has changed. Either conclusion is important, because it adds a dynamic quality to a monitoring function.

FUTURE ROLES
OF RESEARCH AND POLICY

Given the convergence of research and policy that has occurred in the DMC initiative and the apparent dependence on research results for the initiative to continue on its current track, a number of issues and concerns arise. Some of these are briefly mentioned below as topics for future concern.

First, cynics (realists?) in the area of research utilization argue that research is used by policymakers only when it is convenient and supportive of their chosen positions. If so, then we will have a problem; policy success in the DMC arena depends on ongoing quality of information—the sources of overrepresentation will change over time and will change from area to area. No quick universal fix nor any permanent fix appears possible. This means that policy progress will require ongoing access and use of quality information and analysis.

Second, researchers must be aware of the need for quality information and not be satisfied with just providing some information. Information must be examined and presented in a decision-impelling fashion. Researchers throughout the country are being asked to provide information that is relevant to policymakers. They have an obligation to understand the constraints on those policymakers and to form a viable partnership. The question is, what motivates and drives the two groups? Is the convergence simply a matter of accident, or does it represent a realization that research, even academic research, needs to be useful—needs to have value? If so, will those involved in such research find it professionally rewarding, as well as intellectually stimulating, to remain engaged in this type of research effort? In part, this will be a challenge to academic institutions to create new partnerships with state and local agencies, as well as to find ways of making those partnerships long standing, rather than simple raids on available data sources for the purposes of getting another scholarly article.

Third, there is a need to avoid the "street-light phenomenon," which describes the inebriate who is looking for his car keys under the street light because that is where the light is best, not where he lost them. Decent data sets are available to describe some juvenile justice decisions, particularly those that occur once a juvenile is within the court process, under supervision, and/or institutionalized. Although improvements could be made in those data, as well as increases in the coverage to be able to describe a greater proportion of the juvenile courts in the United States, we know relatively little about other decisions that are critical to the juvenile justice system, including the decisions of victims and observers to invoke the justice system (as opposed to informal socializing methods); the decisions of police, schools, and others to bring juveniles into the courts; and the decisions to treat some juveniles as delinquent rather than needful of treatment, supervision, mental health services, special education, and so on.

Fourth, will policymakers understand that last decade's research is not sufficient to describe this year's juvenile justice system? If so, will they understand that the success of a mandate such as DMC requires continual, high-quality information and continually improving information and analysis? Will they be willing to commit the resources needed for that information? Some hope in this regard is found in the position paper of the National Coalition of State Juvenile Justice Advisory Groups (1989):

> It is clear . . . that disparities do occur within the juvenile justice system . . . that are prompted, either consciously or unconsciously, by ethnicity and race. It is not the disparate decisions that should concern us but rather the convergence of a number of unseen forces that permit isolated decision makers of substantially different backgrounds to produce consistent systemic behavior that is racist in its consequence, if not intent. (pp. 10-11)

CONCLUSIONS

In the 9 years since Ira Schwartz's testimony at a congressional subcommittee, there has been an explosion of data surrounding the DMC issue. Some of the better pieces of analysis and information have been selected for inclusion in this volume. At issue for the moment is whether this is really a chance convergence of research and policy interests, which, like an explosion, will soon dissipate, or alternatively, whether the juncture of research and policy interests will continue to build on the mutual needs of each arena in ways that continue to improve both. Some hope in this respect is offered in the experiences of the North Carolina project, in which community groups have clamored for more information and in which counties outside of the original 10 have stepped forward asking for similar assistance in gathering and using information about their local justice systems. Given interest of citizens' groups and communitywide coalitions, it will be difficult for the issue to fade into oblivion.

2

Reflections on Race
Effects in Juvenile Justice

CHARLES E. FRAZIER

DONNA M. BISHOP

This chapter reports and discusses a study we conducted for the Florida Supreme Court's Commission on Race and Ethnic Bias in 1990. The commission was impaneled for one year and given the mandate to determine whether and to what extent Florida's civil and criminal justice systems were affected by racial and ethnic bias. Most of the commission's modest budget was to be used to pay salaries for support staff and to pay costs of commission members' travel to several regional public hearings.

We were contacted after the first regional hearing because some members of the commission and the commission staff considered us experts on the Florida juvenile justice system.[1] We were asked to conduct a study of race effects in juvenile justice decision processes.[2] A verbal agreement was reached by phone on a second or third contact, and we were told to begin planning the project.

A reader may wonder why this history is important. The answer is not simple, but it is important. First, a few phone calls followed our initial verbal agreement with the commission director. These calls seemed to have the purpose of subtly reminding us of the general drift of the testimony that previously had been presented in the first public hearing called by the commission.

We were told by the commission's executive director that the testimony presented by the attendees made one thing glaringly clear: Evidence of racial and ethnic bias in Florida's justice system was incontrovertible. Furthermore, we were informed that testimony indicated that racial and ethnic bias operates at all levels and in all aspects of court and justice practice. At least that is the sense of what was communicated to us by commission staff.

Our response, we thought naturally and appropriately, was that the information was interesting but essentially irrelevant for the study we had agreed to do. Relevant or not, good data or not, the testimony the commission heard became an increasingly frustrating and confusing part of many subsequent phone calls. By this time, we were already well into the design of our project, but the phone calls continued.

At some point after several more calls from the commission's director and/or the associate director, we saw at least the outline of a complex situation developing. Not altogether naive, we both had worried that the commission might be giving us a loyalty or an ideology test. We tried hard to resist this conclusion, despite the fact that it became clearer each day that the commission and its staff were more than a little concerned about what we might find. We knew that, for them, it was already established that racial and ethnic bias permeated Florida's courts and agencies of justice. Many distinguished witnesses had stated this in public, and the commissioners' sense was that more witnesses at future regional conferences would say the same things.

This information still meant little to us. So, we both continued to labor through long conversations with commission staff about the canons of science, the importance of good research designs and samples, good instruments, and careful interpretations of data—all the while trying to take the high road and not yield to suspicion of the commission director's motives. We were always careful in our conversations to explain how social scientists approach research. We tried to explain why the public hearing testimony was not what we considered good data. All our efforts in this regard seemed only to produce more phone calls and more questions about the quality of the official data we would use and what we thought we would find.

Although we had found race effects in Florida's juvenile justice processes with different data covering different time frames (Bishop & Frazier, 1988; Frazier & Cochran, 1986), we could not say what we would find this time nor did we consider it appropriate to approach a study with such concerns. Conversations eventually became more strained and phone calls became less frequent, and always they ended in a way that was unsatisfactory for us and for them. As time wore on, we grew less polite and less patient. Finally, however, a contract was signed and the research was completed on schedule.

When we reflect back on the experience now, we ask ourselves why it was so difficult to reach closure on an agreement to conduct what, for us, was a straightforward research project. Several reasons come to mind. We were aware (although perhaps too little aware) all along that there was concern about the political difficulty the commission would have if our study showed that race was not a factor in justice decision making. Such findings would be especially difficult because we are both white.

For the commission staff, this was an interesting but not a happy prospect. The commission, after all, might find itself in the position of having funded a study of race and justice processing (by two white researchers) that produced empirical evidence that race is not a factor. We are sure this was a consideration for the commission staff. We are also sure, however, that it was not the only reason for their reticence and the laggardly pace they took in formally contracting for our research.

Several other reasons were surely involved. One centers around the lack of understanding we had of each other, they with not knowing how social science researchers think and us in not knowing and/or not fully appreciating the concerns and agendas of a commission operating in a politically charged environment. Still, another reason is that the commission heard strong voices at the hearings that genuinely convinced them that racial bias was pervasive in the justice system. They had heard this time and time again from witnesses who spoke emotionally and forcefully of their experiences and their perceptions. They also heard all this in a language that was easy to understand.

In contrast, the data and research design that we proposed to use was discussed in language that was foreign to them. We spoke of "quantitative analyses," "multivariate models," "misspecification," "sociodemographic variables," "outcomes at several processing points," and "reliable estimates." Furthermore, we admonished that bivariable associations between race and case outcomes (e.g., higher rates of incarceration among blacks) could not be taken as firm evidence of bias. Indeed, "controls" for relevant legal variables like offense seriousness and prior record might reduce or even eliminate such associations between race and justice outcomes.

Despite the difficult start to our study, we did not break our resolve to enter it with open minds and to report whatever the findings indicated. But at the same time, we were persuaded by discussions with the commission staff to think more carefully about the testimony the commissioners had heard. We ultimately decided that data on personal experiences and perceptions might indeed help flesh out analyses of the large quantitative data set we had. As will become clear in the following pages, our study was very much improved by formal interviews we conducted with juvenile justice officials throughout the state.

OVERVIEW OF THE RESEARCH

Once all the talking was done, our study proceeded in two parts. Phase 1, which is reported here in brief, consisted of analyses of all cases of juveniles processed by Florida's juvenile justice system between 1985 and 1987.[3] From this data set, we attempted to identify the influence of race at several points in processing, including decisions of intake officials, decisions of judges on detention, decisions of state attorneys to file formal charges, and judicial decisions regarding final dispositional outcomes. Because of the way race is coded in the data we used, we can distinguish only white and nonwhite. Effectively, the nonwhite category is made up almost exclusively of African Americans.

This focus on multiple stages in processing has several advantages. First, it acknowledges that the salience of race as a factor in decision making may vary at different points in processing and sheds light on the contexts that are likely to permit racial considerations to enter decision-making processes. Second, it recognizes that although the impact of race on case processing may be small at any one stage, the cumulative effect of even small race differentials may be quite substantial. Third, it allows us to consider the indirect as well as direct effects of race on case processing. If, for example, race were to affect detention decisions, and detention decisions were to affect final dispositional outcomes, there would be an indirect effect of race on final dispositional outcomes even in the absence of a correlation between race and final disposition. Multistage analyses are imperative given that the impact of race on late-stage outcomes may be masked by failure to consider the effect of race on earlier decision points.

We viewed the Phase 1 research as the "hard data" of our study, because these analyses would reveal whether, and to what extent, nonwhites and whites are treated differently in the juvenile justice system. If controls for crucial variables measuring offenses and offense histories did not eliminate race effects on processing outcomes, then we would proceed cautiously to consider racial bias as a possible explanation for the findings. Then it would be our task to speculate about theoretical and other ways in which racial bias might operate. Our quantitative analyses, despite the large sample and sophisticated methods, would provide no clear picture of why racial differences exist.

This is why, after all the torturous talk with the commission, we planned and carried out Phase 2. Phase 2 had the explicit purpose of tapping the insights of knowledgeable "insiders" to the system. To do this, we drew a stratified random sample and conducted systematic interviews with juvenile judges, state attorneys, public defenders, and Department of Health and Rehabilitative Services (DHRS) intake supervisors. We hoped that hearing about their experiences might shed light on the racial differences our quantitative analyses identified. We came to see the two phases of the study as integrally interconnected. Ultimately, they were both necessary parts that informed our policy recommendations. We turn first to the Phase 1 quantitative research.

ANALYSES OF
STATEWIDE PROCESSING DATA

This first phase of our study involved analyses of quantitative data on statewide referrals to the juvenile justice system. We wished to determine whether nonwhites are handled differently than whites by juvenile justice officials. We accomplished this by examining juvenile delinquency referral records maintained by DHRS for a 3-year period.

Our analyses involve the estimation of multivariate models that include controls for important legal and extralegal factors commonly thought to influence processing decisions. It is necessary to include these controls because without them, we might easily misspecify the role of race considerations in case processing. For example, we might find that at judicial disposition, nonwhite youths are more likely to be incarcerated than their white counterparts. Such a finding might well be explained away, however, if the data also indicate that nonwhite offenders tend to commit more serious offenses or have more lengthy and serious prior records than their white counterparts.

The Data

The data for this study include records of the total population of cases referred to juvenile justice intake units in Florida over the period January 1, 1985, to December 31, 1987.[4] The case records were organized in such a way as to permit us to trace the movement of youths through several stages in the system from initial intake through judicial disposition. We restricted our analyses to the last referral in 1987, a procedure that allowed us to capture at least 2 full years of prior-offense information for each youth in the data set. The total number of youths in the data set is 137,028.

Dependent Variables

Intake screening is the first of four stages in the processing of delinquency cases. We classified intake screening outcomes to differentiate between recommendations for case closure without action or informal handling (coded 0) and those recommendations for formal processing (coded 1). Decisions regarding detention status are made shortly after delinquency referrals are received. Cases that were detained between initial referral and disposition are coded 1; those that were released prior to disposition are coded 0.

Whether a delinquency case proceeds to formal court processing in Florida is a decision made by state attorneys after reviewing intake recommendations, examining the evidence, and in most instances, interviewing witnesses. In this study, we classified prosecutorial decisions regarding court referral to distinguish between cases in which a petition was not filed or, if filed, a petition was subsequently withdrawn (coded 0), and cases in which a petition was filed that resulted in formal court processing (coded 1).

Youths who are formally adjudicated delinquent by the court receive dispositions ranging from community-based sanctions and services (e.g., community control, community work service) to commitment to residential facilities (e.g., youth camps, training schools) and waiver to adult court. Judicial disposition is coded to distinguish between youths ordered into some kind of community treatment program (coded 0) and those committed to a residential facility or transferred to criminal court (coded 1).

Independent Variables

The independent (or predictor) variables examined in this research include social characteristics of offenders and attributes of the current offense and offense history. The offender characteristics are race (coded white = 1; nonwhite = 0), gender (coded male = 1; female = 0), and age (coded in 1-year intervals, from 7 to 18).

A measure of offense seriousness was constructed by scoring the most serious offense for which each youth was referred. The scoring is as follows: felony offense against persons = 6; felony property offense = 5; felony offense against public order = 4; misdemeanor person offense = 3; misdemeanor property offense = 2; misdemeanor offense against public order = 1.

Another aspect of the case that is important to consider is whether it involved a contempt charge. State law allowed judges to place juveniles found in contempt in secure detention for up to 5 months and 29 days at the judicial disposition of their cases. In our analyses, contempt status is introduced as a variable to distinguish between those cases that were referred for contempt (coded 1) and all other delinquency cases (coded 0).

Prior record is measured in terms of the severity of prior referrals to the juvenile justice system. This variable takes account of both the frequency and severity of prior offending and was constructed by summing the severity of all prior offenses (using the same severity values as those described above with regard to offense seriousness), then dividing the sum by the number of prior referrals. In cases where a youth's offense history included a status offense, the status offense was assigned a value of 1.

Finally, where appropriate, we include case-processing outcomes as independent variables in the analyses. That is, we explore the effects of decisions made at earlier stages in processing on subsequent stage outcomes (e.g., the effect of being held in secure detention on judicial disposition). This procedure allows an assessment of possible indirect effects of race on case outcomes.

ANALYSIS AND FINDINGS

Because each of the processing outcomes to be examined has been defined in terms of a dichotomous contrast, we chose logistic regression as the method of estimation. In Table 2.1, we show the bivariate correlations among each of the variables in our models. Inspection of the table reveals that race is weakly but significantly related to each of the four case-processing outcomes. Nonwhites are more likely than whites to be referred by intake for formal processing, to be held in secure detention facilities, and to be petitioned to court by prosecutors. Once adjudicated delinquent, nonwhites are

TABLE 2.1 Zero-Order Correlations, Means, and Standard Deviations

	Race	Age	Gender	Offense Severity	Prior Record	Contempt Status	Intake Screening	Detention Status	Court Referral	Judicial Disposition	$\overline{X}$	SD
Race	1.00	.09*	.02*	-.10*	-.05*	-.00	-.10*	-.08*	-.06*	-.14*	.71*	.45
Age		1.00	.02*	-.04*	.12*	.03*	.16*	.15*	.12*	.20*	15.11	2.08
Gender			1.00	.12	.12*	-.03*	.14*	.08*	.11*	.10*	.76	.43
Offense Severity				1.00	.12*	-.09*	.40*	.29*	.26*	.14*	2.97	1.70
Prior Record					1.00	.04*	.30*	.21*	.24*	.22*	1.85	4.28
Contempt Status						1.00	.03*	.10*	.05*	.03*	.01	.09
Intake Screening							1.00	.29*	.61*	.14*	.45	.51
Detention Status								1.00	.29*	.32	.17	.39
Court Referral									1.00	—	.36	.48
Judicial Disposition										1.00	.22	.42

*Coefficient significant at the .001 level.

also more likely than whites to be incarcerated or transferred rather than ordered into community-based treatment. Even though they are in the same direction, these bivariable relationships fall short of supporting the sense of the testimony heard during commission hearings.

We also note that the bivariate results indicate that nonwhites are significantly more likely than whites to be referred for more serious offenses and to have significantly higher scores for previous offending. It is important, then, to examine the results of multivariate analyses to determine whether differences in the handling of whites and nonwhites remain after these offense and prior record differences are controlled.

Column 1 in Table 2.2 presents results of logistic regression analyses in which we have modeled outcomes for intake screening. Our findings show that seriousness of the current offense weighs heavily in intake decision making, being the strongest predictor of outcomes at this stage. As also might be expected, intake officers consider youths' prior records of offending and are more likely to recommend for formal processing youths with lengthy and serious prior records. In addition, nonwhites, older youths, and males are significantly more likely to be recommended for formal processing than whites, younger adolescents, and females.

Because logistic regression coefficients have no clear interpretation, we illustrate with the case of a typical youth referral.[5] In these data, the typical youth referred to intake is a 15-year-old male arrested for a misdemeanor against person (e.g., simple battery), with a prior record score consistent with having one prior referral for a misdemeanor against property (e.g., criminal mischief). The probability that a white with these characteristics will be recommended for formal processing is 47%. For a similar nonwhite youth, the probability of a recommendation for a formal processing is 54%, reflecting a rather substantial difference of 7 percentage points.

The second column in Table 2.2 presents logistic regression results for detention outcomes. The findings indicate that detention decisions are influenced to a modest degree by race when other important variables are controlled. For the typical case, the probability of being held in secure detention is 12% for a white youth, compared with 16% for a nonwhite youth.

TABLE 2.2 Logistic Regression Results

	Intake Screening	Detention Status	Court Referral	Judicial Disposition
Intercept	–4.818	–7.272	–3.202	8.0147
Race	–311*	–360	–118	–645
	(.015)	(.017)	(.014)	(.025)
Gender	.338*	.243	258	.455
	(.155)	(.020)	(.015)	(.038)
Age	.175*	.256	.087	.340
	(.003)	(.005)	(.003)	(.009)
Prior Record	.288	.085	.123	.090
	(.003)	(.002)	(.002)	(.002)
Offense Severity	.507*	.467	.254	.128
	(.004)	(.005)	(.004)	(.008)
Detention Status			.973	1.283
			(.017)	(.025)
Contempt Status	1.178*	3.006	1.095	.913
	(.142)	(.068)	(.070)	(.099)
$\bar{Y}$	.451	.175	.36	.22
N	137,028	137,028	137,028	47,747
–2 Log likelihood	140,602	105,438	155,701	41,126
Model χ^2	42,031	21,553	23,582	9,345
	$df = 6$	$df = 6$	$df = 7$	$df = 7$

*Coefficient significant at the .001 level. Standard errors are shown in parentheses.

In column 3 of Table 2, we see that, as was the case with the initial two processing stages, offense seriousness and seriousness of the prior record each have significant effects on prosecutorial decision making. Also worthy of note is the finding that, net of controls for other variables in the model, being detained increases the likelihood of court referral. Gender and age each exert significant effects. The race effect is very modest at this decision stage. A typical white youth has a probability of court referral of 32%, compared to a probability of 34% for the typical nonwhite youth. Some portion of the total effect of race is hidden here, subsumed by the effect of detention status. Note, for example, that nonwhites are more likely than whites to be detained, and youths who are detained are more likely to be prosecuted. Thus racial inequality at the court referral stage is more pronounced than the race coefficient in this model would suggest.

In column 4 of Table 2, results are presented for judicial disposition. The model indicates that severity of the current offense and prior record each have significant, although fairly modest, effects on dispositional outcomes. As would be expected, those charged with more serious offenses and those with more weighty prior records are more likely to be committed or transferred. Those who are detained and those whom the judge finds in contempt also are more likely to receive severe judicial dispositions. At this stage in processing, each of the sociodemographic characteristics also has a significant effect on case outcomes. The effect of race is quite substantial. The typical white delinquent has a probability of being committed or transferred of 9%, compared to a probability of commitment for nonwhites of 16%, a difference of 7 percentage points.

In sum, our quantitative analyses indicate that nonwhite juveniles referred for delinquency offenses in Florida receive more severe (i.e., more formal and/or more restrictive) dispositions than their white counterparts at each of the four stages in processing. Specifically, after controls are introduced for age, gender, seriousness of the referral offense, and seriousness of their prior records, we find significant race effects. The magnitude of the race effect ranges between 4 and 7 percentage points at four decision points, with some indirect effects working through detention decisions.

ANALYSES OF INTERVIEW DATA

In the second phase of the research, we designed and administered a telephone survey.[6] Interviews with a total of 31 juvenile court judges, prosecutors, public defenders, and DHRS intake supervisors were completed. As described earlier, this part of the study was designed to help us understand how and why the racial differences we found in the quantitative analysis came to be. Our sampling technique and interview design were structured in every way possible to avoid the kinds of potential for error we saw in the commission's interviews at public hearings.

The telephone survey began with the researchers reading a two-paragraph description of the findings from the quantitative portion of the study. Respondents were then asked whether they thought the findings were consistent with their experiences in Florida's juvenile justice system between 1985 and 1987.[7] Most (64%) indicated that the findings were consistent with their experiences. Immediately after asking respondents this question, we asked them to explain their observations and views. That is, if their perceptions were that racial differences did influence treatment decisions, we asked if they had opinions regarding how best to explain or make sense of such practices. This follow-up question was open ended and was designed both (a) to give respondents an opportunity to indicate whatever explanations they might have for the findings and (b) to avoid suggesting explanations the respondents may not have imagined otherwise.[8] Finally, we followed up with another open-ended question inquiring whether there were still other factors that might help explain the indicated race differentials. Throughout the interview, we moved back and forth between open- and closed-ended questions as well as from general to specific questions. When answers were off the point of the question or were not altogether clear, we followed up with more questions.

Race Is a Factor and the
Quantitative Findings Are Accurate

Nearly two thirds of the interview respondents indicated that they believed juvenile justice dispositions were influenced by race. As might be expected, however, perceptions of racial differences varied by the functional role of respondents in the system (Farnworth, Frazier, & Neuberger, 1988), their years of experience, age, gender, and ethnicity.

Virtually all intake supervisors and public defenders said that their experiences and perceptions were consistent with the quantitative findings we described to them. To these professionals, non-whites were almost invariably treated more harshly than were similarly situated whites. A much smaller proportion of prosecutors and judges (25% and 33%, respectively) believed race influenced juvenile justice processing decisions.

Beyond functional role, respondents with more years of experience in the juvenile justice system, those who had worked in more than one circuit, and male respondents were more likely to report that our findings of racial differences in juvenile justice processing were consistent with their experiences. Respondents who identified themselves as Hispanic, Jewish, or African American were also more likely to perceive racial differences in processing (75%) than were majority group white respondents (60%).[9]

Below, we discuss in more detail the substance of the views of respondents who perceived racial differentials in processing. For purposes of presentation and discussion, we have grouped the responses to reflect the different interpretations that emerged. Where respondents offered more than one interpretation, we excerpted the material and included it where it seemed to fit best.

Racial Differences Attributable to Racial Bias

A number of survey respondents indicated a firm belief that racial bias accounted for racial differences in juvenile justice processing. They were not, however, specific about what the sources of bias were nor did they imply that anyone should expect otherwise.

[State attorney:] Any fool knows that there is some racial and ethnic bias.

[Judge:] There is no question that there is a degree of bias remaining [in the system].

[Public defender:] Yes, I find that [the findings are consistent with my experiences]. Especially, this happens with final dispositions. And with direct files [prosecutorial transfers of juveniles to adult court], it's also clear there too. Almost all juveniles direct filed are black. I can remember only one white youth who was transferred.

[Intake supervisor:] I think more blacks get arrested and that [view of blacks as more problematic] carries forward in the system.

[Public defender:] Direct-file cases are influenced by race at the state attorney stage.

[Public defender:] When it gets to court, I do notice bias especially in direct-file cases. Nonwhites with weapons are more likely to be direct filed than whites with weapons.

Racial Differences Attributable to Prejudiced Individuals

Several of our respondents noted the existence of racial bias and indicated that the source was racially prejudiced individuals. Some respondents imply that individual bias is rare, others suggest it is systemwide, and still others attach the likelihood of bias to functional roles such as judges or the police.

[Intake supervisor:] Police arrest blacks and refer them to DHRS in situations where they would not refer whites. Police and state attorneys are more likely to recommend detention and judicial action when blacks are involved. All of this is due to racial discrimination, some of which is intentional.

[Intake supervisor:] These results reflect bias and prejudice against nonwhites. We do not have an unbiased system.

[Public defender:] They [juvenile justice officials generally] think, you know, if you have a minority in front of you that they are more likely to be poor, more likely to have failed on probation before, more likely to have a family in crime. Judges have these biases.

[State attorney:] A police officer, because of fear and ignorance, will probably see blacks as more of a problem.

[Intake supervisor:] There is racial bias in the court system. Nonwhites are filed on earlier [at younger ages and for less severe infractions] by prosecutors. Their first inclination is to say: "This kid needs help" or "This kid needs punishment," where a middle-class white kid would not get this kind of handling.

The first two comments offer no interpretation as to why some officials are discriminatory in their decisions, but the remaining three quotes suggest that some officials or some categories of officials simply assume that minority youths are more in need of official attention. Racial bias in this sense is grounded in the assumption that any member of a group possesses the worst traits and/or tendencies stereotypically attributable to the whole group.

Racial Differences and Economic Factors

Although most respondents in the study indicated that race differentials did exist in the dispositions received by whites and nonwhites, some were quick to point out that there were reasons other than individual racial prejudice that account for most of these differences. These respondents suggested that race was a factor mostly because it was correlated with other factors in a juvenile's case that were appropriate considerations. In the excerpts below, respondents identify not only what the factors were that accounted for harsher treatment of nonwhite youths, but they also explain why they believe economic, family, and organizational factors are reasonable considerations.

Several respondents indicated that nonwhite youths and their families were less likely to possess the social and economic resources that were commonly available to whites. They also perceived that juvenile justice decisions were affected by youths' access to such resources. One prosecutor noted, for example, that "socioeconomic status is more important than anything else." The ability to retain private counsel or to know about and be able to afford the services of a private mental health provider were identified specifically as important ways whites were advantaged in the system. In this view, bias against racial minorities was a product of differential treatment based on socioeconomic status.

[Intake supervisor:] Nonwhites do receive more severe sentences. Whites are able to have private counsel and get favorable plea bargains [often involving treatment in private agencies paid for by parents].

[Public defender:] If a rich kid from [respondent names subdivision known to be occupied by white, affluent families] comes downtown with mommy and daddy, there is a low probability of a petition.

[Intake supervisor:] Their families [minority group families] can't afford to purchase alternatives that middle-class families can afford . . . so they go [deep] into the system.

[Judge:] Minorities or low-income kids get more [juvenile justice system] resources. If parents can afford [names expensive private treatment facility], he [the child] gets probation. If not, he gets committed. Income is significant in that a lot of early interventions are directed to middle-income groups. As income decreases, the ability to afford these programs lessens. If a child needs constructive activity, a middle-class family can afford a band instrument, for example. Maybe there is institutional bias.

[State attorney:] The biggest problem is the lack of money and resources. Blacks don't have the resources. Whites are more likely to have insurance to pay for treatment. Blacks don't have the jobs that pay benefits like insurance to pay for treatment. The poor I saw were always poor, but the black poor were poorer yet.

[Public defender:] There is economic discrimination. If parents can afford a private attorney or if they can afford this or that private counseling, they get the best treatment.

As might be expected, some respondents were very critical of practices that resulted in the economically disadvantaged receiving harsher treatment. Others, however, offered the view that such practices were not only defensible but enlightened. In the view of this latter group, justice officials were wisely using their knowledge of the system to provide helpful services to the economically disadvantaged that they could not otherwise afford. To make them eligible for these needed services (e.g., counseling that the more well-to-do could purchase on their own), given the laws and policies within which they were required to operate, justice officials had first to formally process youths from lower socioeconomic groups through the juvenile justice system. That is, poor juveniles had to be adjudicated delinquent before the court could order the kind of services for them that affluent families could acquire for their children while avoiding formal court action.

Another way economic resources were said to influence juvenile disposition processes and to disadvantage nonwhite youths has to do with rules, policies, and practices of the justice system. For example, children from families without telephones or access to transportation were seen to receive more formal and more harsh dispositions.

> [Intake supervisor:] Our manual told us to interview the child and the parent prior to making a recommendation to the state attorney. You are less able to reach poor and minority clients. They are less responsive to attempts to reach them. They don't show. They don't have transportation. Therefore, they are more likely to be recommended for formal processing. Without access to a client's family, the less severe options are closed. Once it gets to court, the case is likely to be adjudicated, primarily just because it got there. . . . It's a self-fulfilling prophecy.

> [Intake supervisor:] Class is important. Lower classes have no phone [and] no transportation, so they tend to be ineligible for diversion. Also, there are some lesser sanctions that are not available to minorities because of no transportation to a work site or because they can't write [good] essays, etc.

Racial Differences and Family Considerations

Many respondents indicated that juvenile justice officials make decisions influenced in part by considerations involving the youth's family. Respondents frequently reported, for example, that youths from single-parent families and those from families incapable of (or perceived to be incapable of) providing good parental supervision were referred to court and placed under state control in situations in which youths receiving (or thought to be receiving) adequate parental supervision were diverted from the juvenile justice system. Several respondents noted that these distinctions were fair and appropriate. When justice officials perceive that there is family strength and support, they tend toward less intrusive treatments and sanctions. All respondents agreed that this practice affects minority youths more harshly. To some degree, the respondents believed this was the case because minority youths are more apt to come from broken and dysfunctional homes. It was also clear, however, that the family systems of racial and ethnic minorities were generally perceived in a more negative light than were the family systems of white youths. Some negatively valued attributes were presumed to be characteristic of minority youths and their families because the group to which they belong has higher rates of broken homes, poverty, and so on. This is clear in the following excerpts.

[State attorney:] [Minorities get harsher sanctions] because judges see these [nonwhite] kids as having less of a support system.

[Judge:] Minority folks believe differently and get treated differently.

[Judge:] Inadequate family and bad neighborhood correlate with race and ethnicity. It makes sense to put kids from these circumstances in residential facilities.

The minority family seems to be generally suspect. As with the judge quoted above, the basic conclusion for some respondents was that in most instances the minority family unit is somehow unacceptably deficient. Others expressed the same view.

[State attorney:] Yes. From my experience, the family, school, culture of black kids is more likely to generate future crime because the support groups don't care about school or getting into trouble, etc.

[State attorney:] Yes, social and economic status are important. Programs are geared toward family involvement. More blacks and Hispanics seem to suffer family and economic deficiencies.

[State attorney:] Detention decisions, for example, are decided on the basis of whether the home can control and supervise a child. So minorities don't get home detention because, unfortunately, their families are less able to control the kids. If family stability was not a prerequisite to admission to less severe program options, racial differences would be less.

Interestingly, nonwhite families were perceived as being less adequate than white families even when both families were broken. The tendency seemed to be to consider the broken minority family as "more broken" than its white counterpart. As one prosecutor put it:

> [Prosecutor:] It might be more common in black families . . . that the dad is unknown, while in white families even when divorced, Dad is married or something else. The choices are limited because the black family is a multigenerational, nonfathered family. You can't send the kid off to live with Dad.

Taken individually or together in various combinations, these views about minority families indicate racial bias, attitudes that feed on and support racial bias, and they ultimately operate to justify the system's bent toward treating youths from minority families more formally and more harshly.

Institutional Racism

Some of the comments above imply that the bias that causes racial differentials in juvenile justice is embedded in institutional structure and practice. That is, they suggest that the system is structured in a way that generally disadvantages minority racial and ethnic groups. Although some respondents believed that most discriminatory juvenile justice decisions reflected racial prejudice on the part of individuals, more saw the real problem as endemic to the system. The way the system is structured and the ways officials are conditioned to think about delinquency make discrimination hard to avoid. Empey (1983), Platt (1969), and others have observed that the juvenile justice system, from its inception, has focused on considerations that ensure differential treatment and discrimination against minorities and the lower classes.

When decisions to process juveniles formally as opposed to informally, or harshly as opposed to leniently, hinge on evaluations of the social circumstances in which juveniles live, officials are in a precarious position. They must somehow evaluate comparatively perceived differences in family structure, neighborhood reputation, demeanor of juveniles and their families—indeed the culture of various groups from which juvenile defendants come. Almost invariably, there is a reliance on common stereotypes of the nonwhite community, family, and interpersonal styles to support differentials in dispositions received by whites and nonwhites. Several of our respondents observed this pattern directly in their years of juvenile justice practice.

> [Judge:] There are racial differences that are not a result of any kind of discrimination, and there is some institutional racism. Institutional racism is particularly seen as relating to the myths held [by juvenile justice officials] about families of blacks, their culture, etc.

> [Intake supervisor:] Yes. There are more matriarchal families and parents gone during the day; this is more common among blacks. But there is also the fact that law and justice don't take into account racial and cultural differences, just like IQ tests don't.

> [Intake supervisor:] It becomes almost routine to recommend [a petition for] black juveniles for drugs because it is so associated with the black community. There is an undercurrent of racism that naturally happens.

> [Intake supervisor:] There is the perception all through the system that the nonwhite community needs more cleaning up. The perception that crime is black becomes a kind of self-fulfilling prophecy. People expect black neighborhoods to be crime ridden.

> [State attorney:] Also, inner-city kids experience a more violent way of life. They see violence as a way to resolve differences. It's a community problem. More kids [i.e., more delinquents] come from those blighted, bad areas.

First-Hand Experience With Racial/Ethnic Bias in Juvenile Justice

The interviews also focused on respondents' personal observations of and experiences with racial or ethnic bias. Respondents were asked whether they had witnessed or were aware of racial or ethnic bias influencing official decisions and, if so, at what stages in processing racial bias was most likely to play a role in decision making. Because most respondents indicated that they had little or no basis for assessing the extent of bias in jurisdictions other than their own, the discussion and excerpts below generally refer to single jurisdictions.

Respondents were about evenly split (48% said yes, 52% said no) in their responses to a direct question about whether they had personally witnessed decisions made by juvenile justice officials that they believed to reflect racial or ethnic bias. When the question was modified to inquire as to whether respondents were aware of or had reason to believe that racial and/or ethnic bias influenced decisions by professionals in their jurisdictions, 77% said yes. Later, when asked how common they thought racial and ethnic bias was in the juvenile justice system today, only one respondent said that it did not occur at all. Sixty percent believed that it was uncommon or very uncommon, 33% believed it to be common, and 7% indicated that it was very common. At the very least, these responses and the excerpts below suggest that the vast majority of professionals in Florida's juvenile justice system believe that minority clients encounter some amount of discrimination. It is also interesting that most, although certainly not all, respondents who perceived bias found it to be most likely among professionals working in other agencies of the system, not their own. This is a finding that opens a troubling possibility. It is possible that respondents who believed bias was present attributed it to others even when they had no good reason to do so. For this reason, we have focused our analysis on those respondents who indicated they had directly observed racial discrimination.

> [Intake supervisor:] Law enforcement and judges are most likely to be biased. These I have witnessed, but I don't think there is any reason to believe that one group is more unblemished than the rest. Attorneys, though, are pretty fair. For example, one judge spoke down to a black defendant in a flagrantly derogatory way. I was floored by it. That judge is obviously prejudiced. Contempt powers are sometimes used by judges in a racially influenced way.

> [Public defender:] Bias is most likely at the law enforcement stage and least likely at prosecutors' decisions to petition and judges' sentencing. I used to get a lot of "loitering and prowling" cases.

These only came from the black and ethnic neighborhoods. They [police] can't get them [blacks] on drugs, so they go after them on loitering and prowling. I also saw that victims were more likely to report petty thefts by minorities than by whites.

[Public defender:] Kids that don't speak English are treated differently and I see it as bias. Law enforcement is very likely to do this. Also the state attorney at filing, DHRS in detention screening. It is least likely at DHRS intake. A lot of times I hear from black kids that law enforcement officers called them names, like "nigger." They do illegal stops in black areas. They [police] don't stop groups of whites for standing around in their neighborhoods. This just doesn't happen to whites.

[Public defender:] Yes. I've witnessed it. It's most likely at the early and middle stages. It's least likely at disposition because a lot of times judges just follow DHRS recommendations. I've experienced people downgrading a kid and enjoying being able to sanction minorities severely. There is a mood that the person wants to get from the kid. For example, . . . a judge said "You're a bad dude," then imposed a severe sanction. Sometimes judges will say, "Isn't your father so and so?" which is some felon they know of from cases involving minority [defendants]. I don't think these are hard, biased individuals, but they really do believe that these kids are worse by race and the nature of their circumstances.

[Intake supervisor:] Yes, I've witnessed bias—mostly from police, less so from state attorneys. Most intake officers are black and are sensitive to this issue—they don't allow race to enter. They follow the matrix pretty well. I see bias in the hallways [of the court] mostly. The public defenders and state attorneys get together and work out arrangements for the child to plead guilty. Blacks are encouraged to plead guilty more often than whites even when arrested for the same crimes. Then the [black] child is adjudicated and that has severe consequences.

[Judge:] Yes, no doubt, I see it all day. First, it's most likely among police and second at the judicial level. Police, the authoritarian personality thing is involved, I guess. Judges are more apart, [more] unchecked. I have heard judges and police make racial slurs in my presence. There is more subtle stuff too. Some believe that black and Hispanic parents [because of their low socioeconomic status] are less likely to be able to successfully nurture their children to make it into the mainstream.

[State attorney:] Yes, I have seen it. But it is isolated and certainly not pervasive. It depends on individuals, not stages, for decisions.

[Intake supervisor:] Yes, sure I've witnessed racial and ethnic bias. It's most likely in the final stages and least likely in the beginning. That's because [in the beginning stages] you don't know what the state attorney will be doing yet. Yes, I can give examples. I've seen judges come in from rural counties and bring their [prejudicial] views with them. Also, every time there is a cocaine case, non-whites are treated more harshly than whites. School fights too. Whites come with their private attorneys and get off better.

[Intake supervisor:] Yes, bias is there through all stages. It is most likely at earliest stages beginning with the police. They use stereo-typed responses. Bias is least likely at final disposition, but some-times the court tends to accept the biased recommendations from others from the earlier stages. Here is a situation that is an exam-ple. In detention, a juvenile acts out. Minorities are seen as more difficult to reason with so they get the harshest response. Coun-seling efforts aren't even tried with minorities.

[Public defender:] Probably [I have seen it] most with prosecutors. It's most likely at arrest, however. The race factor is dramatic there. It is not very likely at the judicial disposition stage. An example is two kids at arrest, one is black and the other is white. They both break into a car. The white kid gets a notice to appear. The black kid gets secure detention.

[Intake supervisor:] Yes, I know one judge that would let race come into play. Bias is even throughout the system, though. Consider secure versus nonsecure detention of equal petty theft cases. The white gets nonsecure and the black gets secure detention.

[State attorney:] Yes. It is most likely in DHRS. It's least likely with public defenders and state attorneys. DHRS generally employs locals who operate on stereotypes. At the dispositional stage, DHRS staff [line case workers] have made racial slurs in their comments.

[Judge:] Yes, I am aware of it occurring. Probably it is most likely at law enforcement and at state attorney levels.

What Does All This Mean?

Our data leave little doubt that juvenile justice officials believe race is a factor in juvenile justice processing. Perhaps more important, it is clear from our findings that professionals working in the system believe race discrimination contaminates both the appearance and reality of justice. Some officials see race as a substantial problem, whereas others see it as a relatively minor problem. Some regard race prejudice and discrimination as having direct and major effects on juvenile justice dispositions, and others see the effects operating indirectly and subtly to the disadvantage of nonwhites.

This suggests that some amount of race prejudice and de facto discrimination is deeply entrenched in the organization and practice of juvenile justice and that policies aimed at eradicating discrimination must focus both on individual racism and racism in its most subtle institutional forms. Policy must address prejudiced viewpoints that facilitate unintentional, unconscious, and/or institutional discrimination. With these ideas in mind, we offer general policy recommendations.

POLICY RECOMMENDATIONS

Making policy recommendations under any circumstance is risky business. Problems tend to be entrenched, multifaceted, complex, and resistant to change. Policies seldom match the problems they are designed to solve on any one of these dimensions. This is certainly the case with issues of race discrimination in justice processing and the recommendations that follow. We have tried to the extent possible, however, to tie the recommendations to particular aspects of what justice officials in this study perceived to be problematic. That is, we focus on the kinds of bias justice officials perceive and the reasons they believe prejudice and discrimination exist in juvenile justice processing. Four recommendations are offered. Each one is designed to address problems the respondents identified.

With Regard to Individual
Prejudices and Misconceptions

Some of our respondents regarded individual prejudice as an important source of racial bias. That there were and that there are now prejudiced persons working at various levels in any state's juvenile justice system should surprise no one. This view was expressed many times and a number of different ways. Respondents implied that this is a form of bias about which little or nothing can be done. There is both an element of truth and an indefensible fatalism in this view.

As a partial truth, no social scientist would likely dispute a link between individual race prejudice and general cultural precepts relating to race. This link, however, takes on more importance than it deserves when it becomes a justification for inaction. For example, one respondent remarked that "as long as racial bias exists in the general culture, it will operate through individuals in the juvenile justice system." The implication here is that the general culture is too big a target for reform or that it is a problem that others should address.

It is unrealistic to assume that agencies of the juvenile justice system could somehow wall themselves off from the influence of racist patterns of thought that are deeply rooted in culture. It is not, however, unreasonable to expect that an atmosphere could be created in which race discrimination is not tolerated.

Our first recommendation, then, is that states should establish procedures for all the agencies comprising the juvenile justice system to require reporting, investigating, and responding to professionals whose decisions appear to have been influenced by racial or ethnic bias. When juvenile justice professionals observe others in their own or other agencies responding toward racial and/or ethnic minorities by ridiculing physical or cultural characteristics, customs, or manners of speaking, just requiring reporting is not enough. Means also must be available for them to initiate an investigation. It is also important that agency personnel be supported when they do this and when they apply informal sanctions against persons engaging in racial discrimination. If ultimately there is a finding of impropriety against an employee, formal redress should follow. Severe cases should result in termination of employment and initiation of a civil rights suit by the state's justice department.

We suggest that states legislate reporting requirements and that the agencies themselves establish internal procedures for receiving and responding to complaints of racial or ethnic bias. The mere creation of such laws, formal complaint procedures, and a schedule of appropriate sanctions are important first steps toward bringing about change. The establishment of procedures to initiate an inquiry, when indications of bias are observed, may be thought by some to be ineffectual. We are encouraged, however, by the impact of sexual harassment grievance procedures in government agencies and by laws and policies prohibiting smoking in public places. The immediate effect of both sexual harassment and smoking policies in government agencies appears to have produced very significant changes, in part, by increasing awareness of and sensitivity to the issues involved and, in part, by carrying out appropriate formal sanctions when rule infractions or improprieties are determined.

With Regard to Prejudice and Discrimination Based on Myths and Misperceptions

Interview data from this study led us to believe that substantial numbers of juvenile justice professionals may be influenced frequently by misperceptions or misinformation about minority racial and/or ethnic groups. One of the respondents to the telephone interview, for example, believed that blacks are much more likely to use illegal drugs than are whites and that therefore a greater focus on and harsher treatment of black offenders is entirely appropriate. Contrary to this common belief and some official statistics, however, social science data do not support a conclusion that the prevalence and incidence of unlawful use of any controlled substance is predominantly a problem of blacks (Akers, 1992). Furthermore, even if it was the case that one particular racial group had a drastically higher rate of drug use than another, American constitutional and

criminal law would not support differential treatment of individuals on the basis of group rates.[10]

Other respondents saw nonwhite families as less interested in
their children because they showed distrust of the system or lack of
respect and disdain for some of the officials. Our data do not provide
an adequate basis for determining to what extent minority families
encountered by Florida officials did have and did display more
negative feelings for the system and its officials. The data do suggest, however, that some court officers insisted on white or middle-
class styles of response even when dealing with lower income
minority families. Respondents also reported that uncooperative
and disrespectful behavior by minority youths brought stiffer sanctions than similar behavior by white youths.

Based on these findings, our second recommendation is that
state legislatures mandate the development of a race, ethnic, and
cultural diversity curriculum that personnel at every level of the
juvenile justice system should be required to complete through state
university continuing education credits. The curriculum should be
directed toward debunking myths about racial and ethnic minorities, and it should address the forms and effects of bias.

With Regard to Official Policies and Practices That Differentially Affect Minorities

In the course of our formal interviews, several intake supervisors indicated that current policies and practices in their agencies
inadvertently resulted in organizational practices that generally
disadvantaged minority youths. For instance, they reported that
youths referred to intake for delinquency were ineligible for diversion programs unless their parent(s) appeared for a formal interview. These same intake supervisors observed that minority parents
or guardians were generally less likely than were majority group
families to have telephones, permanent addresses, access to transportation, and/or the ability to take leave time from work without
loss of pay. As a result, minority youths and their families were
considerably less likely to comply with official intake policies than
were whites. In turn, minority youths were defined as ineligible for
programs such as diversion, which enable youths to avoid the full

measure of official stigmatization. Such organizational policies have the effect of making the official records of minority youths look worse than those of majority youths even when there were no differences in their behavior.

On the basis of these findings, we offer a third recommendation. Intake policies and practices should be altered so that youths referred for screening are not rendered ineligible for diversion and other front-end programs if their parents or guardians (a) cannot be contacted, (b) are contacted but are unable to be present for an intake interview, or (c) are unable to participate in family-centered programs. Every effort should be made by intake workers to interview and work with parents/guardians, but it is discriminatory for it to be a prerequisite to admission to one of the more informal options in juvenile justice.

Another practice that negatively and disproportionately affects minority youths is the use of more lenient dispositions for those who seek private treatment. Parents from middle and upper socioeconomic status backgrounds commonly arrange for their children to receive counseling offered by private mental health providers when their children become involved in the juvenile justice system. As a result, they often are given less severe dispositions than otherwise would be the case. Juvenile justice officials often use the formal system to obtain what they believe are comparable services for low socioeconomic status youths. To do this, however, youths must first be petitioned to court and then, as a part of a formal court action, are committed to a state-run program or to one of a variety of quasi-official agencies that provide treatment under a contract with the state.

These treatments are not comparable. Lower socioeconomic status youths (who are more apt to be racial or ethnic minorities) receive the stigma of being a committed delinquent, whereas their more well-to-do counterparts are considered less serious offenders because their treatment occurred outside the official justice system. This occurs even when the offending behavior does not differ in any demonstrable way. As one prosecutor we interviewed suggests, such policies constitute institutional bias: "Minorities do not have the same opportunities to focus on constructive activities. I think the way the system sets up programs shows some institutional bias."

Equal justice would dictate that this same emphasis be present in the response to any serious offender regardless of economic and social circumstances. Furthermore, to ensure equal justice for minor offenders, all those authorized for diversion should receive the same treatment by the same agencies. That is, the economically advantaged and disadvantaged should go to the same agencies.

In light of these considerations, we offer a fourth and final recommendation. In any situation in which persons with economic resources (e.g., income or insurance benefits) are allowed to arrange for private care as a means of diversion from the juvenile justice system or less harsh formal dispositions, precisely the same treatment services should be made available at state expense to serve the poor—whether minority or majority race youths. Such a funding structure would enable those with financial need to access the same private service providers as the affluent. Such a system would provide the same quality of sanctions and treatments to youths regardless of socioeconomic resources, and it would reduce the chances of differential levels of social stigma.

We are not entirely naive about the likelihood that these recommendations will be adopted or, if they are, that observable reductions in racial bias will result. They are, after all, fairly modest proposals, and we are mindful that race discrimination has survived for generations in a legal environment that expressly forbids it. We are at the same time, however, cautiously optimistic about these recommendations. Our sense is that most justice officials would welcome such policies. If that is so, and if implemented with a genuine interest in their success, such policies will both help reduce discriminatory actions and promote equal justice.

NOTES

1. This designation of "experts" flowed mainly from the fact that the commissioners knew that we were two of a relatively small number of people to ever take the time to decipher and then to effectively use data from a statewide computer information system.

2. We had done research on juvenile justice and were familiar with the data in a statewide client information system managed by the DHRS. In fact, at the time we had nearly readied for analysis a large data set on all juveniles referred as delinquents or status offenders for 1985-1987, and we had already examined data on race effects on processing in the same state for an earlier time period (1979-1981) (see Bishop & Frazier, 1988; Frazier & Bishop, 1985; Frazier, Bishop, & Henretta, 1992; Henretta, Frazier & Bishop, 1986).

3. The details of the sample and a full discussion of all the quantitative analyses are reported in Bishop and Frazier (1994).

4. Florida law requires that all juvenile complaint reports be processed through intake offices located in each county. Consequently, we have records of all police contacts other than those that resulted in informal field adjustments, as well as referrals from parents, school officials, and other nonpolice sources. The data set is quite comprehensive: It includes cases closed without action, cases disposed of informally (e.g., through diversion to a community agency), and cases formally petitioned to and processed in court.

5. We do this by calculating predicted proportional change in the probability of an intake recommendation for formal processing for a one-unit change in the independent variables. This change in probability varies depending on where the effect of the variable is evaluated, that is, the level of the other independent variables as well as any specific independent variable being considered. This same process is used in the interpretation of the logistic regression coefficients for all dependent variables.

6. We have done telephone interviews previously and had found them useful (see Bishop & Frazier, 1988; Frazier & Bishop, 1990).

7. The phrasing of the question was, "Based on your experience . . . do these findings sound reasonable; . . . do they reflect a reality present in the system between 1985 and 1987?"

8. At a later point in the interview, we did ask several direct questions about the possibility that findings of racial differences in processing might be explained by a correlation between race and other social and economic factors. In this regard, we asked specifically about the role of income, social class, family structure, education, neighborhood, and institutional bias.

9. That this pattern exists raises the question as to whether minority officials are more sensitized to and thus more able to discern racial differences or whether they are just more likely to report observed differences.

10. Interestingly and ironically, the Supreme Court has affirmed its need to apply law to individuals in its ruling on the constitutionality of the death penalty. The view is that regardless of the evidence of discrimination against a minority racial group, a decision stands unless individual discrimination is shown (*McClesky v. Kemp*, 481 U.S. 279, 1987).

3

Policing Juveniles
Is There Bias Against Youths of Color?

MADELINE WORDES

TIMOTHY S. BYNUM

The decisions of police officers regarding encounters with juveniles are often highly discretionary. Officers typically have a great amount of flexibility in dealing with juvenile offenders, and a large proportion of cases are handled informally. Many believe the apprehension phase is the most important stage of juvenile justice processing because it marks the entry point to the juvenile justice system (National Council of Juvenile and Family Court Judges, 1990). If youths of color are overrepresented within the juvenile justice system, the initiation of overrepresentation may lie in police decisions. Specifically, the important police decisions entail contacting, apprehending, referring to court, and requesting secure detention.

Contrary to the proceedings in juvenile court, where ordinarily a record of decisions exists on all referred cases, many police decisions are informal and thus not a part of the formal record-keeping system. Therefore, it can be difficult to conduct research on police decisions and to determine the effect of race on these decisions. Although there are fewer studies of police decisions compared to

47

court decisions, the existing literature documents that youths of color are more likely to be arrested and referred to court than white youths (Bishop & Frazier, 1988; Fagan, Slaughter, & Hartstone, 1987; Thornberry, 1979).

It is important to place the impact of race in context with other factors that police officers may deem important. We must examine not only the direct effects of race on police decisions but also the indirect effects. Observational studies, most notably Piliavin and Briar (1964), have found that demeanor and appearance were associated with police decisions. Furthermore, black youths were perceived by officers to have a more negative demeanor and to be dressed less appropriately. In addition, more recent research has noted the impact of the complainant's desire for formal court involvement on the police decision to further the case. Some complainants may be more likely to request such action for offenses involving youths of color (Black & Reiss, 1970; Smith & Visher, 1981). Complex indirect relationships involving such factors as demeanor and social and family situation appear to exert an influence on police decisions along with legal issues of offense seriousness.

The Present Study

In this chapter, the direct and indirect effects of the race of the juvenile on police processing will be examined. Two main questions will be addressed. First, what was the extent of disproportionate representation of youths of color in law enforcement agencies? Second, was differential treatment a contributing factor to overrepresentation? To adequately address this issue, both qualitative and quantitative data were used. Given that entry into the law enforcement system is highly discretionary and most often not documented, qualitative data were collected. These early discretionary decisions are not part of the written records in most departments. Because there were not written records of contacts with juveniles, entry into the system was examined qualitatively. Once in the written records, however, the data were analyzed quantitatively.

METHOD AND DATA SOURCES

Setting

Data were collected from nine jurisdictions across Michigan. These jurisdictions differed in size, racial composition of the population, types of offenses handled, and philosophy of juvenile justice. A wide variety of jurisdictions were purposefully sampled to increase the generalizability of the findings.

Police Case Files

Data were collected from case files in the records in each jurisdiction. Each coded case file represented the most serious charge for an individual youth (17 years of age or under) in 1990. A disproportionate random sample was taken from the population of juveniles in each law enforcement agency. In most sites, the population was stratified on race, gender, and offense type. The purpose of this sampling strategy was to be able to represent small categories of individuals, such as Latino female status cases, and still represent the large categories, such as white male misdemeanor cases. A total of 2,845 case files were coded from the police records across all sites.

Interviews With Juvenile Officers/Detectives

Two types of interviews were conducted. A more formal interview procedure was conducted with juvenile officers and detectives, and a less formal procedure was used for interviews with patrol officers. The principal purpose of the interviews was to learn about the important factors in the decision-making process and the decision maker's perceptions and recommendations regarding disproportionate representation.

Juvenile officer or detective interviews were conducted with almost all key personnel in each law enforcement agency ($N = 17$). In some sites, juvenile officers make referral decisions, and in others, certain detectives are specifically assigned to juvenile cases. In some departments, no positions are assigned specifically to juvenile cases. The interviews were approximately 1 hour in length.

In the second type of interview, observers rode with law enforcement officers during their patrol shifts. Observers would informally ask a specific set of questions throughout the ride-along. The questions centered on police encounters with juveniles and disproportionate representation. Also, any interactions with juveniles during the ride-along were documented. Patrol observations were sampled on an availability basis. Most of the 59 police ride-alongs were conducted on the second shift (approximately 3:00 p.m. to midnight). Observers generally rode with officers on one or two shifts. During ride-alongs, observers took notes of their conversations with the officers and any interactions with juveniles if this could be done unobtrusively. Otherwise, impressions were recorded after the event or shift.

Data Analysis Strategy

Several analytic strategies were used to explore the issues of disproportionate representation and differential treatment. For the quantitative data, three main sets of analyses were conducted. First, disproportionate representation was assessed for each site as a whole and for each major decision point within the site. Second, descriptive statistics were used to describe the cases in the files. Third, multivariate relationships were explored using logistic regression. Because the disposition variables were coded dichotomously (e.g., detained or not detained), it was necessary to use logistic regression techniques. All offense-related characteristics were entered into a multivariate equation for each general offense category.

In assessing disproportionate representation and bivariate relationships, a weighted sample was used to approximate the population. For the multivariate analyses, however, the original sample was used because these techniques rely on correlations that can be inflated by weighting adjustments.

The qualitative responses to the questions were content analyzed using Ethnograph. The qualitative findings were analyzed for each site separately, then synthesized to give a holistic picture of the law enforcement system across counties.

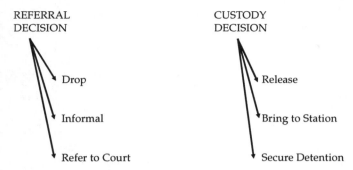

Figure 3.1. Flow of Police Department Cases

Decision Points

Figure 3.1 is a basic model of the dispositional choices in law enforcement. The first decision was made by the patrol officer on contacting the youth. Did the officer choose to make the juvenile part of the official record? Because many departments did not keep any record of contacts, it was difficult to ascertain how many youths were handled informally with no establishment of a record. Once the case was put in the official system, there were two decisions to be made: referral and custody. The referral decision normally consisted of three choices: drop the case, handle it informally (possibly divert), or refer the case to court. The custody decision involved releasing the juvenile at the scene (or never taking him or her into custody), bringing the youth to the station, or bringing the youth to secure detention.

FINDINGS

Extent of Disproportionate Representation

Blacks were disproportionately represented in almost all law enforcement agencies studied. Table 3.1 shows the percentage of youths of color at each stage in the law enforcement process. Disproportionate representation was assessed by comparing the per-

TABLE 3.1 Percentage of Youths of Color in City Populations and in
Law Enforcement Agencies

	Dept. 1		Dept. 2			Dept. 3	
	Black	Other	Black	Latino	Arab	Black	Latino
City population	83.1	6.3	0.5	4.1	2.9	5.0	3.6
All offenses							
In police records	96.0	0.7	48.9	1.1	9.7	9.6	0.8
Brought to station	97.0	0.5	49.0	1.3	12.4	11.3	—
Held secure	98.8	—	53.0	6.1	6.1	53.5	—
Referred to court	98.1	0.4	53.2	1.2	14.8	15.8	1.5
Felony offenses							
In police records	98.5	—	33.6	0.9	12.1	12.8	—
Brought to station	98.3	—	26.0	—	14.3	15.6	—
Held secure	98.6	—	50.0	8.3	8.3	50.0	—
Referred to court	98.6	—	33.8	1.5	13.8	30.4	—
Misdemeanor offenses							
In police records	95.3	1.8	54.0	1.2	9.8	9.6	1.3
Brought to station	94.8	2.0	58.8	1.7	13.0	11.0	—
Held secure	100.0	—	50.0	—	—	100.0	—
Referred to court	95.1	2.5	62.2	1.1	16.6	12.1	2.2
Status offenses							
In police records	94.8	0.8	7.1	—	—	7.8	—
Brought to station	97.3	—	3.8	—	—	10.1	—
Held secure	100.0	—	100.0	—	—	20.0	—
Referred to court	100.0	—	25.0	—	—	18.6	—

centage of youths of each race in the community population with the population in the agency records.

As can be seen in Table 3.1, the extent of disproportionate representation was substantial in communities with small black populations. For instance, 6% of the general youth population in one small jurisdiction, Department 6, was black, compared to 20% of juveniles in the police records. In cities where the population was predominantly black, there was little overrepresentation. Cities with a racially mixed population showed disproportionate representation, but not to the extent of the almost exclusively white communities. For example, one moderate-sized city had a juvenile population that was 50% black. The police records from Department

TABLE 3.1 Percentage of Youths of Color in City Populations and in Law Enforcement Agencies (continued)

Dept. 4		Dept. 5		Dept. 6	Dept. 7	Dept. 8	Dept. 9
Black	Latino	Black	Latino	Arab	Black	Nat. Amer.	Black
50.3	13.8	34.7	4.9	6.2	96.5	24.5	15.7 [a]
63.6	11.4	55.3	2.8	20.3	98.3	14.3	57.1
60.8	11.8	56.3	0.6	30.0	100.0	28.6	—
61.5	23.1	76.9	3.2	—	100.0	—	—
68.2	13.6	57.4	2.5	23.7	99.2	16.7	66.7
70.0	13.3	58.5	2.0	13.8	98.2	—	—
63.6	9.1	66.3	—	20.0	100.0	—	—
75.0	25.0	86.5	6.7	—	100.0	—	—
81.8	18.2	59.6	1.9	23.1	100.0	—	—
66.7	12.0	55.4	3.5	28.6	99.2	—	57.1
72.7	9.1	50.0	1.2	50.0	100.0	—	—
—	100.0	72.8	—	—	100.0	—	—
50.0	25.0	57.3	3.3	30.0	98.3	—	66.7
51.4	8.6	51.1	2.5	7.7	85.7	18.8	—
44.4	16.7	60.0	—	—	100.0	50.0	—
50.0	—	58.3	—	—	100.0	—	—
57.1	—	54.3	1.9	—	100.0	100.0	—

a. Law enforcement agency was county sheriff's department; thus county population was used.

4 in that city, however, indicated a 64% representation. In Department 2, there was a statistically sufficient population of Arabs, and they were also overrepresented in the law enforcement agency records.

It is important to recognize, however, that although Latinos and Native Americans were not usually overrepresented in the records as a whole, they were disproportionately represented at the more formal intervention stages in the law enforcement process. For instance, Table 3.1 shows that in one city (in Department 4), Latinos comprised only 14% of the youth population, yet 23% of those youths were brought to secure confinement by the police.

The extent of disproportionate representation increased as cases were forwarded further through the system. In other words, over-representation of youths of color was most severe for youths referred to court and those taken to secure detention. As an example (Department 5), blacks comprised 35% of the city's youth population, 55% of youths in the police records, 57% of youths referred to court, and 77% of those brought to secure detention.

These findings clearly demonstrate that disproportionate representation is an issue for these law enforcement agencies. To explore the contributing factors to this problem, it is first necessary to describe the findings from interviews and observations of patrol and juvenile officers.

QUALITATIVE FINDINGS

Juvenile Officers

Juvenile officers reported complex reasons for disproportionate representation. The responses have been organized into six conceptual categories and are listed here in the order of frequency mentioned: (a) lack of parental supervision, lack of discipline, broken homes, single-parent families; (b) low socioeconomic status, poverty, lack of employment, high-crime neighborhoods, high-density population areas; (c) personal problems, poor school performance, substance abuse issues; (d) racial prejudice and bias by law enforcement officers, and community members are more likely to report minorities; (e) minorities commit more serious crimes and are more likely to be involved in criminal behavior; and (f) lack of concern by city officials, and more formal urban police practices (blacks are more likely to live in the city).

Approximately one half of the juvenile officers stated that race does not play a role in the decision to refer a youth to court. Of those noting disparity in referral practices, the reasons stated were racial bias or prejudice, class bias—"poor kids get less breaks," nonlocal resident status, seriousness of crime, and victim characteristics. Most officers did not indicate any personal racial or class bias, yet said they were aware of it by colleagues or in other departments.

Most respondents stated that the wishes of the victim and the seriousness of the offense were more important than family factors in their decisions. Of those respondents citing family issues as relevant, parental control over the juvenile was the most common response. Whether the child was remorseful was also mentioned as an important consideration in their decisions.

Patrol Officers

In response to "Why do you initiate contact with a juvenile?" the three main replies were seriousness of offense; response to calls; and investigation of youths who look "suspicious," "funny," "out of place," or were "hanging out on street corners." One officer defined suspicious as a "black kid in a white neighborhood."

In almost all sites, family issues were reported as important in the police decision of whether to handle a case formally (arrest, refer to juvenile officer). The most frequently stated family issues were extent of cooperation from the parents, parental supervision and control over the youth, and attitude of parents. In all sites, officers reported that the juvenile's attitude and demeanor strongly influenced the decision to proceed formally.

Stated above are the reasons why a youth is contacted by police and why a particular youth may become part of the official record. Although officers usually did not directly exhibit racial bias, the factors that influence decisions such as "suspiciousness" and "no male at home to enforce discipline" can be related to race.

Description of Juveniles

Prior to an official police report, the characteristics of the juveniles contacted are unknown. Once the youth had a formal record in the system, however, those juveniles can be described. There were no consistent differences across sites between youths of color and white youths in terms of age, age at first offense, and number of prior offenses. The mean age of juveniles at their first law enforcement agency record ranged from 11.3 to 14.9 years old. On the average, juveniles had very few prior offenses on record. Only one department reported youths with an average of more than one prior offense on record. In three of seven sites that kept records of priors, white youths had more prior offenses on record. Youths of color had more priors in three sites.

Characteristics of the Current Offense

Table 3.2 lists the various offense types (i.e., property, personal, drug, and miscellaneous misdemeanors and felonies) by racial/ ethnic group for each department. The most common offenses across sites were status offenses and property misdemeanors. Although the high number of status offenses may seem surprising, in some jurisdictions every reported runaway was entered into the record-keeping system.

The offense types of each racial/ethnic group was considerably different depending on the department. However, one consistent trend emerged. Although the number of drug felonies is a small proportion of all offenses, black youths were more likely than white youths to be charged with drug offenses.

Table 3.3 reveals the more specific offense behavior of the incidents in the records. In the sites with Latino and Arab populations, these youths were most likely to be charged with using a weapon. In four of eight sites, there was no difference between white and black youths in the use of a weapon, in three sites blacks were more likely to use a weapon, and in one site whites were more likely. For example, in Department 4, blacks and whites used a weapon in 11% of the cases, whereas Latinos used a weapon in 44% of the cases. There were also differences in the number of co-offenders and the number of concurrent charges. Youths of color were more likely to have co-offenders in the incident in most sites. Latino and Arab youths were more likely than other youths to be charged with multiple offenses.

In sum, there was some evidence suggesting youths of color were charged with more serious offenses. However, the pattern was not the same in every site. To begin exploring the complex relationships between race, offense characteristics, and disposition, the findings from the multivariate analyses will be presented in the following section.

TABLE 3.2 Percentage of Each Racial/Ethnic Group With Particular Offense Types by Law Enforcement Agency

Sites	N	Status Offense	Misc. Misd.	Property Misd.	Personal Misd.	Misc. Felony	Property Felony	Drug Felony	Personal Felony
Department 1A									
Black	1,554	51.3	1.1	8.8	4.3	2.8	21.3	4.2	6.2
White	79	70.5	0.0	9.7	3.0	0.0	9.5	0.0	7.3
Department 1B									
Black	956	57.1	0.5	7.7	2.6	5.6	17.9	4.5	4.1
White	8	100.0	0.0	0.0	0.0	0.0	0.0	0.0	0.0
Department 2									
Black	339	0.6	0.0	83.8	5.0	0.3	7.4	0.3	2.7
Arab	67	0.0	2.6	54.3	23.3	0.0	7.6	0.0	12.2
White	278	9.3	3.1	60.4	6.7	0.4	16.9	0.4	2.9
Department 3									
Black	108	18.1	5.6	33.5	25.1	0.9	10.5	0.1	1.8
White	1,000	23.0	3.6	50.8	9.6	0.6	10.2	0.0	6.5
Department 4									
Black	89	20.2	13.5	38.2	4.5	1.1	12.4	3.4	6.7
Latino	16	18.8	18.8	31.3	6.3	18.8	6.3	0.0	0.0
White	35	40.0	11.4	34.3	0.0	2.9	8.6	0.0	2.9
Department 5									
Black	517	21.7	4.7	19.7	23.2	1.2	14.7	4.6	10.1
Latino	27	20.8	3.8	22.6	32.1	0.0	17.0	0.0	3.8
White	390	26.0	9.6	22.7	14.4	0.3	20.4	0.0	6.7
Department 6									
Black	28	8.3	12.5	62.5	0.0	0.0	16.7	0.0	0.0
White	106	25.8	16.1	21.5	9.7	1.1	22.6	0.0	3.2
Department 7									
Black	234	2.6	14.5	21.8	15.4	1.3	27.4	4.3	12.8
White	4	25.0	0.0	0.0	25.0	0.0	0.0	0.0	50.0
Department 8									
Native American	3	100.0	0.0	0.0	0.0	0.0	0.0	0.0	0.0
White	18	72.2	5.6	16.7	5.6	0.0	0.0	0.0	0.0

TABLE 3.3 Percentage of Each Racial/Ethnic Group With Particular Offense Characteristics by Law Enforcement Agency

Sites	N	Suspect Had Weapon	Fight Occurred	Had Co-offenders	Damage/Theft > $500	Victim Needed Medical Attention	Victim Was Female	Victim Was Black	Victim Knew Suspect
							If There Was a Victim		
Department 1A									
Black	1,554	14	3 (1,378)[a]	44 (1,393)	17 (1,478)	2 (1,489)	44 (338)	66 (265)	38 (415)
White	79	2	3 (76)	29 (74)	5 (74)	3 (77)	63 (8)	33 (6)	87 (10)
Department 1B									
Black	956	14	3 (901)	33 (920)	15 (942)	2 (941)	41 (162)	81 (116)	41 (171)
White	8	0	0	0	0	0	0	0	0
Department 2									
Black	339	3	3	67 (337)	3 (334)	1	10 (39)	11 (39)	9 (39)
Arab	67	22	10	68 (66)	5	5	28	0 (62)	12 (22)
White	278	10	4 (277)	71	8	2	23 (53)	0 (19)	3 (58)
Department 3									
Black	108	16	4	63	4	0	55 (42)	10 (42)	71 (45)
White	1,000	8	4 (999)	53	3 (999)	2	41 (281)	2 (281)	65 (287)
Department 4									
Black	89	11	7 (87)	48 (87)	5 (85)	6 (87)	50 (20)	74 (19)	68 (19)
Latino	16	44	13 (15)	60 (15)	0	0	100 (1)	0 (1)	100 (1)
White	35	11	3	37	3	0	33 (3)	0 (3)	33 (3)
Department 5									
Black	517	10	29 (512)	51 (513)	6	5 (516)	51 (262)	48 (257)	69 (263)
Latino	27	26	36	49	4	0	30 (12)	0 (12)	92 (12)
White	390	12	22	42	5	2	37 (175)	11 (167)	60 (179)
Department 6									
Black	28	0	0	84	0	0	0 (15)	62 (15)	0 (16)
White	106	1	12	69	2	2	53 (43)	3 (43)	50 (43)
Department 7									
Black	234	15	27	61 (228)	11 (228)	8	46 (148)	92 (122)	67 (154)
White	4	0	25	50	0	50	100 (3)	0 (3)	100 (3)
Department 8									
Native American	3	0	0	0	0	0	0	0	0
White	18	6	0	22	0	0	100 (1)	0 (1)	0 (1)

a. Numbers in parentheses represent the cases on which data were available. If no number is present, data were available on all cases.

FACTORS RELATED TO DISPOSITION:
LOGISTIC REGRESSION ANALYSIS

Logistic regression was used to determine the importance of race on disposition after accounting for prior offenses and specific offense behavior. Logistic regression analysis allows for the consideration of several factors simultaneously. Separate analyses were conducted for each offense type due to the overwhelming effect of offense type on disposition.

Table 3.4 lists the significant factors influencing referral and custody decisions for felony, misdemeanor, and status cases. The specific regression weights for each variable in the three logistic regression analyses are listed in the appendix tables. The variables in the model for felony cases included race, gender, age, number of priors, number of concurrent charges, whether there was a weapon involved, amount of victim injury, drug charge, and specific police department. Because the department that handled the case was a significant factor in determining disposition in every analysis, this finding will not be stated for each analysis. However, it is important to recognize the crucial impact of the particular department that was handling the case in the determination of outcome.

For felony offenses, several variables were significantly related to the referral decision. Juveniles who were dropped were more likely to be white, have fewer prior offenses on record, have co-offenders, not have a drug charge, and not have a weapon. Hence having a less serious offense, having a less serious prior history, and being white were related to being dropped or handled informally. Conversely, juveniles who were referred to court were more likely to be black, have more prior offenses on record, act alone in the incident, be charged with a drug offense, and have a weapon. Thus more serious offense behavior, more serious prior history, and being black were related to referral to court. Black youths were more likely to be referred to court, controlling for offense-related behavior and priors.

For the custody decision, race was again a factor in determining who was brought to secure detention. Being a youth of color had an independent effect on being securely detained. Other factors related to secure detention included having more prior offenses, being

TABLE 3.4 Factors Significantly Influencing Law Enforcement Referral and Custody Decisions for Felony, Misdemeanor, and Status Cases[a]

	Felony[b] (n = 691)	Misdemeanor[c] (n = 961)	Status[c] (n = 516)
Referral decision:			
Drop or divert	White Fewer priors Co-offenders Not drug charge No weapon Department	White Younger Department	White Younger Department
Refer to court	Black More priors No co-offenders Drug charge Weapon Department	Black Latino and other minorities Older Department	Black Older Department
Custody decision:			
No custody	Younger Fewer priors Department	White Younger Department	Female Younger Department
Bring to station	Older Not drug charge No weapon Department	Black Older Fewer priors Department	Male Older Department
Secure detention	Black Latino and other minorities More priors Drug charge Weapon Department	More priors Department	Female Black

a. All factors listed were significant at $p < .05$.
b. The factors simultaneously entered into the logistic regression equations for felonies were race, gender, age, number of prior offenses, department, number of co-offenders, drug charge, weapon involved, and amount of victim injury.
c. The factors simultaneously entered into the logistic regression equations for misdemeanor and status cases were race, gender, age, number of prior offenses, and department.

charged with a drug offense, and having a weapon. Those youths who were not taken into custody were younger and had fewer priors. Those youths who were brought to the station, but were not taken to detention, were older and charged with less serious offenses (i.e., no drug charge and no weapon).

For misdemeanors, the findings were similar. In analyzing misdemeanors, however, specific offense behavior was not included in the analysis because the incidence of serious injury, drug charges, and weapon possession was rare. Included in the analysis were the variables of race, gender, age, number of priors, number of concurrent charges, and department. Again, the department that handled the case had a significant impact on every category of disposition.

Similar to felonies, being white, along with being younger, was related to being dropped or handled informally for a misdemeanor charge. Juveniles who were older and youths of color, however, were more likely to be referred to court. Race was also a factor in the custody decision for misdemeanor offenses. Being white and being younger were related independently to being released at the scene or to no custody. Conversely, being black, older, and having fewer priors were related to being brought to the station. The only variable besides department related to being held in secure detention was having more priors. This finding is likely due to the small number of youths with misdemeanor charges who were securely detained.

The same variables used in the misdemeanor analysis were used for status offenses. The factors associated with referral decision were very similar. Being white and being younger were related to the informal processing of the case. Being black and being older were related to court referral. The logistic regression results for status offenses also revealed that the custody decision was related to race. For status offenses, being black was related to being brought to secure detention. Gender was also a significant factor in the custody decision for status cases. Being released at the scene was related to being female and being younger. Conversely, being brought to the station was associated with being male and being older. However, placing a youth in secure custody was related to being female. It is not simply that female status offenders were treated more leniently or more harshly, because they were more likely to be both released and securely detained.

In summary, the findings from the logistic regression analysis of law enforcement decisions strongly suggest that there was differential treatment by race/ethnicity for felony, misdemeanor, and status offenses. Whites were more likely to receive less intervention for similar offenses and similar offense behavior.

CONCLUSION

The findings are complex, but all support the notion of differential treatment dependent on racial or ethnic group. First, the extent of the problem of overrepresentation of youths of color in these jurisdictions was documented. Blacks were disproportionately represented in almost all police jurisdictions. Moreover, the further a youth was processed into the system, the greater the extent of disproportionate representation.

The qualitative findings suggest that some patrol officers made decisions of whether to contact a youth based on race or race-related factors (e.g., hanging out of the street, in the wrong neighborhood). Also, many juvenile officers suggested that their perception of the ability of the family to control the youth was weighed into their decisions of how to process the case. Many stated that a boy needs a male influence and a mother alone cannot control delinquent behavior. Thus black youths, who are more likely to live with their mother as the sole household provider (Bynum, Wordes, & Corley, 1993), may be adversely affected by the officers' perceptions.

The quantitative data further suggested differential treatment. Logistic regression techniques revealed that race/ethnicity played a significant and independent role in the referral and custody decisions made by police officers. White youths were more likely than black youths to be dropped, diverted, or released at the scene, controlling for offense seriousness and prior offenses. Similarly, black youths were more likely to be referred to court, and to be detained.

Racially biased entry into the juvenile justice system can have far-reaching effects, including further sanctioning by the juvenile courts. Given the indications of differential police processing, it is imperative that policymakers as well as police officials attend to this serious problem.

TABLE 3A.1 Logistic Regression Findings for Law Enforcement Referral and Custody Decisions: Felony Cases ($n = 691$)

| | Referral Decision | | | | Custody Decision | | | | | |
| | Drop or Divert | | Refer to Court | | No Custody | | Bring to Station | | Secure Detention | |
Variable	B^a	SE^b	B	SE	B	SE	B	SE	B	SE
Gender	.11	.25	-.12	.25	.05	.34	-.13	.24	.00	.29
Race	**		**		**				*	
Other minority	-.95	.59	1.08	.59	-1.54	1.09	.12	.57	1.28*	.66
Black	-1.09**	.29	1.13**	.29	-.24	.34	-.28	.31	1.02*	.46
Age	-.07	.05	.05	.05	-.15**	.06	.14**	.05	-.05	.07
Number of priors	-.12**	.05	.13**	.04	-.14*	.06	-.03	.04	.17**	.05
Co-offenders	.35**	.17	-.34**	.10	-.10	.14	.16	.10	-.21	.12
Victim injury	-.12	.11	.14	.11	-.08	.14	.05	.10	-.01	.11
Drug charge	-1.32**	.46	1.00**	.39	-.80	.68	-1.04**	.33	1.29**	.33
Weapon	-.33*	.14	.32*	.14	.19	.19	-.64**	.14	.64**	.15
Department	**		**		**		**		**	
1	.02	.20	.15	.19	-3.39**	.52	.59**	.20	2.07	1.85
2	.38	.23	-.18	.23	1.46**	.26	-.65**	.24	.07	1.88
3	-.43*	.22	.63**	.22	-.52	.28	1.06**	.23	.75	1.87
4	1.01**	.39	-1.17**	.39	.53	.41	-.03	.38	.91	1.89
6	-.32	.37	.53	.37	1.36**	.40	-.63	.38	-4.76	9.19
7	-.66	.27	.04	.25	.56*	.28	-.33	.26	.95	1.86
Constant	1.16	.96	-1.00	.94	1.53	1.18	-1.84*	.97	-2.88	2.22

a. Standardized regression coefficient.
b. Standard error for regression coefficient.
*$p < .05$; **$p < .01$.

TABLE 3A.2 Logistic Regression Findings for Law Enforcement Referral and Custody Decisions: Misdemeanor Cases ($n = 961$)

	Referral Decision				Custody Decision					
	Drop or Divert		Refer to Court		No Custody		Bring to Station		Secure Detention	
Variable	B[a]	SE[b]	B	SE	B	SE	B	SE	B	SE
Gender	-.01	.16	.06	.16	-.22	.16	.16	.16	.65	.60
Race	**		*		**		**		*	
Other minority	-.77**	.31	.64*	.31	-.51	.29	.29	.30	2.44	1.63
Black	-.54**	.21	.47*	.21	-.77**	.19	.63**	.19	2.46	1.32
Age	-.15**	.04	.11**	.04	-.14**	.04	.11**	.04	.25	.20
Number of priors	-.04	.05	.04	.05	.06	.05	-.12*	.06	.22*	.10
Department	**		**		**		**		*	
1	.16	.19	.21	.20	-7.66	6.80	2.27**	.26	2.44	3.03
2	-.61**	.19	.88**	.20	1.11	1.37	.04	.18	1.69	3.10
3	.31*	.15	.03	.16	1.10	1.37	.28*	.13	.25	3.07
4	1.56	.36	-2.15**	.51	1.33	1.38	-.49*	.24	-.16	3.23
6	-.10	.24	.15	.26	2.19	1.39	-1.17**	.27	-4.34	14.99
7	-1.32**	.21	.87**	.21	1.94	1.37	-.93**	.20	.12	3.13
Constant	3.34**	.69	-3.07**	.69	1.57	1.51	-2.35**	.66	-12.29**	4.49

a. Standardized regression coefficient.
b. Standard error for regression coefficient.
*$p < .05$; **$p < .01$.

TABLE 3A.3 Logistic Regression Findings for Law Enforcement Referral and Custody Decisions: Status Cases ($n = 516$)

	Referral Decision				Custody Decision					
	Drop or Divert		Refer to Court		No Custody		Bring to Station		Secure Detention	
Variable	B[a]	SE[b]	B	SE	B	SE	B	SE	B	SE
Gender	-.42	.28	.29	.29	-.86**	.20	1.01**	.20	-1.69**	.62
Race	*		*							
Other minority	4.55	11.74	-4.41	11.73	-.19	.80	.38	.79	-6.20	54.02
Black	-1.28**	.46	1.29**	.47	-.33	.37	.15	.37	1.81*	.88
Age	-.31**	.11	.32**	.11	-.18**	.06	.16**	.06	.03	.18
Number of priors	-.07	.07	.07	.07	-.02	.07	-.04	.06	.12	.13
Department	**		**		**		**			
1	1.84**	.37	-1.94**	.39	.09	.33	.14	.30	-.44	5.09
2	-.97**	.32	1.15**	.33	.51	.31	-.38	.28	.96	5.09
3	-.09	.53	.33	.54	-3.02**	.88	2.57**	.66	1.63	5.15
4	.32	.49	-.15	.49	-.12	.42	.17	.39	.74	5.12
6	-.36	.49	.33	.52	2.14**	.48	-1.88**	.46	-4.83	25.29
7	-.74	.72	.27	.77	.41	.71	-.62	.70	1.95	5.16
Constant	7.41**	1.72	-7.61**	1.81	3.70**	.98	-3.92**	.97	-3.06	5.76

a. Standardized regression coefficient.
b. Standard error for regression coefficient.
*$p < .05$; **$p < .01$.

4

The Social Context of Juvenile Justice Administration
Racial Disparities in an Urban Juvenile Court

BARRY C. FELD

Although the same statutes and court rules of procedure apply in Minnesota's 87 counties, there is substantial variation in juvenile justice administration that relates consistently to urban, suburban, and rural differences in social structure (Feld, 1991). Juvenile courts in different types of locales appear to pursue different substantive ends, as reflected in their detention and sentencing practices, and to use different procedural means, as reflected in procedural formality and the presence of lawyers (Feld, 1989, 1991). The more procedurally formal urban courts sentence more severely than do their rural counterparts (Feld, 1991, 1993). The impact of structural differences in juvenile justice administration is especially problematic in Minnesota, because minority youths reside disproportionately in the urban counties (Minnesota Supreme Court Task Force on Racial Bias in the Judicial System, 1993).

Urban Juvenile Justice

Minnesota's urban juvenile courts operate in a milieu that pro-vides fewer mechanisms for informal social control than do rural ones; consequently, they place greater emphasis on formal social control. For example, a larger proportion of urban households are female headed with children than in other parts of the state (Feld, 1991, 1993). To the extent that family disruption weakens informal social controls, urban counties may rely more heavily on formal controls.

Urban juvenile courts also confront a larger proportion of delin-quent youths, because serious crime is primarily an urban phe-nomenon. More than half of all FBI Part I offenses are committed in Minnesota's two urban counties, and almost one half of all juveniles arrested in 1986 for FBI Part I and Part II offenses (45.6% and 44.5%, respectively) resided in its two urban counties (Feld, 1991). Control-ling for population differences, urban youths of all races appear to be both quantitatively and qualitatively more criminally active than their suburban or rural counterparts (Feld, 1991, 1993).

Urban courts also spread a broader, more encompassing net of control that includes proportionally more and younger youths than do suburban or rural courts. Although prosecutors filed petitions against 29.32 juveniles per 1,000 youths aged 10 to 17 years through-out the state, in the two urban counties, they charged 34.12 juveniles per 1,000, as contrasted with 29.72 in rural counties and only 24.24 in the suburban counties (Feld, 1991). Moreover, urban courts charge more and younger offenders with status offenses than do courts in other settings, and they receive larger proportions of referrals in all offense categories from nonpolice sources (Feld, 1991).

Procedural Formality

The presence of defense counsel is central to a procedurally formal model of juvenile courts and provides one indicator of social-structural and contextual variation in juvenile justice admin-istration. Although the Supreme Court in *In re Gault* (387 U.S. 1, 1967) held that all juvenile offenders were entitled to the assistance of counsel in delinquency proceedings, in Minnesota less than half of the juveniles adjudicated delinquent receive the assistance of counsel (Feld, 1984, 1988a, 1989, 1991). However, attorneys appear in urban courts more than twice as often as they do in rural courts (Feld, 1989, 1991, 1993). In 1986, only 45.3% of juveniles in Minnesota were represented, including about two thirds (66.1%) of youths charged with felonies, less than half (46.4%) of those charged with misdemeanors, and about one fourth (28.9%) of those charged with status offenses. In the urban courts, 62.6% of all juveniles are represented, whereas only one fourth (25.1%) of rural youths have counsel. Of those charged with felonies, in the urban settings 82.9% had counsel, whereas in the rural counties less than half (49.6%) had lawyers. There was an even sharper drop-off in rates of representation in rural counties for juveniles charged with misdemeanors (23.5%) and status offenses (14.3%). Similar findings are reported by Kempf, Decker, and Bing (1990) in Missouri, where 41.5% of urban black youths and 39.0% of urban white youths charged with violent offenses had counsel as contrasted with only 1.1% of rural black youths and 11.5% of rural white youths. Because the presence of counsel is the most obvious indicator of procedural formality, the urban courts are the most legalistic and due process oriented, whereas the rural courts adhere most closely to the traditional, informal model.

Procedural Formality
and Sentencing Severity

There also appears to be a relationship between social structure, procedural formality, and sentencing severity. The more formal, urban courts hold more than twice as many youths in pretrial detention and sentence similarly charged offenders more severely than do the suburban or rural courts. For nearly every offense category, the more formal, urban judges sentence more severely than do either the suburban or rural judges. For example, of delinquents adjudicated for felonies, urban judges incarcerate one third (33.3%) as contrasted with about one fifth (20.4%) of those in the rural counties (Feld, 1991). Regression analyses reveal that after controlling for other legal variables, being tried in an urban court is an aggravating factor (Feld, 1991, 1993).

Pretrial Detention

Whereas only a small proportion (7.6%) of all formally charged juveniles in Minnesota receive a detention hearing,[1] the seriousness of the present offense and the length of the prior record both appear to alter substantially a youth's likelihood of being detained (Bailey, 1981; Cohen & Kluegel, 1979a; Feld, 1988a, 1989; McCarthy, 1987). Although the vast majority of delinquents are not detained, including even those youths charged with the most serious offenses and with the most extensive prior records,[2] urban counties detain proportionally two to three times as many youths as do suburban or rural counties. For example, for youths charged with felony offenses, urban courts detain about 1 of 4 (25.9%) as contrasted with about 1 in 10 (10.2%) in the rural counties (Feld, 1991, 1993).

Because of the relationship between social-structural characteristics and juvenile courts' procedural and substantive orientations, there is "justice by geography." Where youths live affects how their cases are processed and the severity of the sentences they receive (Feld, 1991, 1993; Kempf et al., 1990). This relationship is crucial to understanding aggregate racial disparities in juvenile justice administration, because in states like Minnesota, racial diversity is primarily an urban phenomenon (Minnesota Supreme Court Task Force on Racial Bias in the Judicial System, 1993).

Racial Disparities and
Sentencing Discretion in Juvenile Courts

The traditional juvenile court's emphasis on rehabilitating offenders rather than punishing for offenses fostered judicial discretion, procedural informality, and organizational diversity (Feld, 1988b; Rothman, 1980). The broad legal framework associated with "individualized justice" allows judges to apply the same law very differently to ostensibly similar juvenile offenders. The wide frame of relevance associated with individualized justice raises concerns about the impact of discretionary decision making on lower class and nonwhite youths who are frequently overrepresented in the juvenile justice system (Dannefer & Schutt, 1982; Fagan et al., 1987; Krisberg et al., 1987; McCarthy & Smith, 1986; Pope & Feyerherm,

1990a, 1990b). When practitioners of individualized justice base discretionary judgments on social characteristics that indirectly mirror race, rather than on legal variables, their decisions frequently result in differential processing and more severe sentencing of minority youths relative to whites and raise issues of fairness and equality.

Juvenile court judges answer the question, "What should be done with this child?" in part by reference to explicit statutory mandates (Feld, 1988b). However, practical and bureaucratic considerations influence their discretionary decision making as well (Bortner, 1982; Cicourel, 1968; Emerson, 1969; Matza, 1964). Juvenile justice practitioners enjoy greater discretion than do their adult process counterparts because of their presumed need to look beyond the present offense to the "best interests of the child" and paternalistic assumptions about the control of children.

An obvious question, then, is to what extent legal factors such as the present offense and prior record or social characteristics such as race, sex, family status, or social class influence dispositional decision making. Juvenile justice personnel make dispositional decisions throughout the process. Police officers may refer a case to intake for formal processing, adjust it informally on the street or at the station house, or divert it (Bittner, 1976; Black & Reiss, 1970). Intake, in turn, may refer a youth to the juvenile court for formal adjudication or dispose of the case through informal supervision or diversion (Bell & Lang, 1985). Finally, even after formal adjudication, a juvenile court judge may choose from a wide array of alternatives, ranging from a continuance without a finding of delinquency to probation or commitment to a state training school. Moreover, the dispositional decision-making process is cumulative; decisions made by initial participants—police, intake, or detention—affect the types of decisions made by subsequent actors (Barton, 1976; McCarthy & Smith, 1986; Phillips & Dinitz, 1982). Thus assessing judicial sentencing decisions implicates decisions made by other juvenile justice personnel.

Matza (1964) describes the "principle of offense" as a principle of equality, treating similar cases in a similar fashion based on a relatively narrowly defined frame of legal relevance such as present offense and prior record. Evaluations of dispositional practices suggest that, despite the nominal commitment to individualized justice, the principle of offense pervades practical decision making throughout the process (Feld, 1987, 1988b). Traditionally, juvenile courts pursued substantive justice in which individual characteristics of the offender, rather than circumstances of the offense, determined the disposition. Such substantive decision making is supposed to achieve the best decision in the individual case rather than to apply abstract legal principles or guidelines to recurring factual situations. The juvenile court's "rehabilitative ideal" mandates consideration of various social background variables and not simply legal factors (Horowitz & Wasserman, 1980).

Recent evaluation research of dispositional practices suggests that, despite the juvenile court's nominal commitment to individualized justice and the best interests of the child, the principle of offense pervades practical decision making as characteristics of the offense increasingly determine sentences (Feld, 1987, 1988b). As a corollary of the procedural formality imposed by *Gault*, juvenile courts increasingly seek formal rationality by using general rules applicable to categories of cases rather than pursuing individualized substantive justice.

The elevation of the principle of offense receives practical impetus from bureaucratic imperatives. One is the desire of juvenile and criminal justice agencies to avoid "scandal" and unfavorable political and media attention (Bortner, 1982; Cicourel, 1968; Emerson, 1969, 1974; Matza, 1964). This organizational imperative encourages courts to attach more formal and restrictive responses to more serious forms of juvenile deviance. "Whether a juvenile goes to some manner of prison or is put on some manner of probation . . . depends first, on a traditional rule-of-thumb assessment of the total risk of danger and thus scandal evident in the juvenile's current offense and prior record of offenses" (Matza, 1964, p. 125).

In addition, juvenile courts necessarily develop bureaucratic strategies to cope with the requirements of contradictory formal goals and highly individualized assessments (Marshall & Thomas, 1983). Because the present offense and the prior record of delinquency are among the types of information routinely and necessarily collected by juvenile courts, they often provide the basis for decision making. As the juvenile court balances its internal, clinical,

and administrative concerns with external public relations considerations, it restores the principle of offense, at least in part, as a form
of decisional rule (Matza, 1964).

A basic issue of equal justice in juvenile courts is whether
individualized, discretionary sentences based, at least in part, on
social characteristics result in more severe sentencing of similarly
situated minority youths (Fagan et al., 1987; Krisberg et al., 1987;
McCarthy & Smith, 1986); whether, despite a nominal commitment
to individualized justice, sentences are based on offenses and the
racial disproportionality results from real differences in rates of
offending by race (Hindelang, 1978; Huizinga & Elliott, 1987;
Wolfgang, Figlio, & Sellin, 1972); or whether the structure of juvenile justice decision making itself acts to the detriment of minority
juveniles (Pope & Feyerherm, 1990a, 1990b). In short, to what extent
do legal offense factors, social variables, or justice system processing
variables influence juvenile court judges' sentencing decisions?

One possible nondiscriminatory explanation for the disproportionate overrepresentation of minority youths in the juvenile justice
process is that dispositional decisions are based on the principle of
offense (i.e., legal variables, rather than on an assessment of individual needs), and that minority and lower class youths commit more
and serious crimes. Thus their overrepresentation in the juvenile
system may result from real differences in their rates of delinquent
activity rather than discrimination by decision makers. Wolfgang
et al. (1972) observed that "official delinquents," youths whose
contacts with law enforcement personnel resulted in official records,
are disproportionately concentrated in poor and minority communities and that in every socioeconomic category, black youths
engaged in delinquency to a greater extent than their white counterparts. Similarly, Hindelang (1978) concluded that racial differentials in the criminal justice system probably reflect real differences
in rates of behavior rather than the effects of discriminatory decision
making. On the other hand, Huizinga and Elliot (1987) concluded
that "it does not appear that differences in incarceration rates between racial groups can be explained by differences in the proportions of persons of each racial group that engage in delinquent
behavior" (p. 212). Krisberg et al. (1987) also argued that "differ-

ences in incarceration rates by race cannot be explained by the proportions of each racial group that engage in delinquent behavior" (p. 196).

Recent research notes that some of the racial differences in the sentencing of juveniles cannot be accounted for by the legal variables (Fagan et al., 1987; Krisberg et al., 1987; McCarthy & Smith, 1986). Although evaluations of juvenile court sentencing practices are sometimes contradictory (Fagan et al., 1987; McCarthy & Smith, 1986), two general findings emerge. First, the present offense and prior record account for most of the variance in sentencing that can be explained (Barton, 1976; Clarke & Koch, 1980; Horowitz & Wasserman, 1980; McCarthy & Smith, 1986; Phillips & Dinitz, 1982). In those multivariate studies, legal variables typically account for about 25% of the variance in sentencing.

A second finding is that after controlling for legal offense variables, individualized discretion is often synonymous with racial disparities in sentencing juveniles (Fagan et al., 1987; Krisberg et al., 1987; McCarthy & Smith, 1986; Pope & Feyerherm, 1990a, 1990b). Many of these studies report that minority or lower class youths receive more severe dispositions than do white youths, after controlling for legally relevant variables (Arnold, 1971; Carter, 1979; Carter & Clelland, 1979; Dannefer & Schutt, 1982; Thomas & Cage, 1977; Thomas & Fitch, 1975; Thornberry, 1979).

Examining the effects of race or social class only at the time of sentencing may mask the more significant effect that these personal characteristics have in the initial screening stages of juvenile justice administration. Frazier and Cochran (1986) and Bortner and Reed (1985) reported that race influenced initial detention decisions, with black youths more likely to be detained than white youths, and that detained youths were more likely to receive more severe sentences. Frazier and Bishop (1985) reported that race, as well as legal factors, influenced detention and dispositional decisions and that black youths were more disadvantaged than white youths as they proceeded further into the system. McCarthy and Smith (1986) reported that although screening, detention, charging, and adjudication decisions are strongly influenced by the principle of offense, as cases penetrate further into the process, race and class directly affect dispositions, with minority youths receiving more severe sentences. Fagan et al. (1987) reported that initial screening decisions were not overtly discriminatory but that decisions made at six points in the juvenile process amplified racial effects as minority youths moved through the system, and as a result, "minority youth receive consistently harsher sentences" (p. 252). In sum, prior research indicates that the principle of offense is the most significant factor influencing juvenile court dispositions of juveniles. However, an additional amount of the variance in sentencing appears to be related to a juvenile's race, either because race correlates with other disadvantageous social characteristics (such as family structure, socioeconomic status, or school performance, which affect individualized sentencing), or as a result of conscious or unconscious racial discrimination.

DATA AND METHODOLOGY

This study uses data collected by the Minnesota Supreme Court's Judicial Information System (SJIS) in each county for delinquency and status offense cases processed in 1986.[3] The SJIS sample consists of all individual juveniles against whom delinquency or status offense petitions were filed in 1986. It excludes juvenile court referrals for abuse, dependency or neglect, and routine traffic violations. Only formally petitioned delinquency and status cases are analyzed; the SJIS does not include cases referred to juvenile courts but disposed of informally without a petition.

Unfortunately, the SJIS does not collect data on a juvenile's family, school, or socioeconomic status. Although the SJIS data do not include the prior record of offenses, adjudications, or dispositions, each youth processed in a county's juvenile court receives a unique identifying number that is used for all subsequent purposes. A youth-based data file was created and a prior record of petitions, adjudications, and dispositions was constructed by merging 1984, 1985, and 1986 annual data tapes and matching the county/youth identification numbers across years.[4] The data reported here reflect a youth's most current juvenile court referral as well as all petitions, adjudications, and dispositions for at least the preceding 2 years or more.

The offenses recorded by the SJIS were regrouped into six analytical categories.[5] The "felony/misdemeanor" distinction provides one indicator of offense seriousness. Offenses are also classified as being against person or property, other delinquency, or noncriminal status offenses, such as truancy, runaway, incorrigibility, or alcohol consumption (Minn. Stat. Ann. § 260.015 [19]-[24], 1982). Combining person and property with the felony/misdemeanor distinction produces a six-item offense severity scale.[6] When a petition alleges more than one offense, the youth is classified on the basis of the most serious charge.[7] The study uses two indicators of severity of dispositions: out-of-home placement and secure confinement.[8]

Hennepin County

The present study provides a limited opportunity to analyze the relationships between a juvenile's race, juvenile justice decision making, and sentences. Although the SJIS code forms include the variable "race," racial information is the only variable consistently omitted by court personnel in most counties in the state. In part, this reflects the Minnesota reality that racial diversity is almost exclusively an urban phenomenon.[9] Fortunately, Hennepin County (Minneapolis), the largest urban county and the one with the largest proportion of minority youths in Minnesota (U.S. Bureau of the Census, 1982, pp. 25-198), records a juvenile's race more routinely.[10] Thus the following analyses report the effects of race on juvenile justice administration only in Hennepin County, an urban setting.

The Minnesota Supreme Court Task Force on Racial Bias (1993) conducted a study, similar to this one, that analyzed 1991 SJIS data.[11] The racial bias results are very consistent with this study, and its findings are reported as well.

RACE AND JUVENILE JUSTICE ADMINISTRATION IN AN URBAN COURT

Based on the 1980 census, there were approximately 116,000 youths aged 10 to 17 living in Hennepin County, of whom slightly more than 105,000 were white and about 5,400 were black (U.S.

Bureau of the Census, 1982, pp. 25-198). The next largest urban racial grouping was Native American youths (almost 2,300), with a smaller smattering of Latino and Asian American youngsters (U.S. Bureau of the Census, 1982, pp. 25-246).

Although blacks and other racial minorities made up about 8.7% of Hennepin County's youth population in 1980, they constituted about one third (34.0%) of the clientele of the Hennepin County juvenile court in 1986. Table 4.1 indicates that almost one of four (23.6%) youths against whom petitions were filed were black, and about 1 in 10 (10.4%) were Native American or other minorities. In 1991, 39% of all delinquency petitions were filed against minority juveniles (Minnesota Supreme Court Task Force on Racial Bias in the Judicial System, 1993, p. 98). Thus the disproportionate overrepresentation of minorities regularly reported in other studies appears in Hennepin County as well.

An examination of juveniles' race, present offense, and prior record suggests that at least part of the overrepresentation of minority youths may be attributed to differences in their offense patterns. As a group, a larger proportion of blacks and other minorities are charged with felony offenses and offenses against the person than are whites. Compared with whites, 3.6% more black youths are charged with felony offenses, as are 3.0% more other minority youths. Much of the disparity may be attributed to offenses against the person, with proportionally twice as many black youths as white youths charged with felony (3.1% vs. 7.8%) and misdemeanor (4.0% vs. 10.1%) crimes against the person. Similarly, in 1991, more minority youths than white youths were charged with felony (9.3% vs. 4.2%) and misdemeanor (9.3% vs. 7.7%) offenses against the person (Minnesota Supreme Court Task Force on Racial Bias in the Judicial System, 1993). Black and other minority youths are significantly underrepresented relative to whites only in the category of other delinquency—public order offenses, minor drug possession, and probation violations. Significantly, a much larger proportion of urban Native American youths appear in juvenile courts for status offenses (40.8%) than for any other type of offense or than either of the other racial groups.

Black and other minority youths also had more extensive records of prior delinquency involvement than did their white coun-

TABLE 4.1 Race, Present Offense, and Prior Record: Hennepin County

	White	Black	Other
Delinquents			
%	65.9	23.6	10.4
n	2,232	800	353
Felony			
%	16.5	20.1	19.5
n	369	161	69
Felony offense against person			
%	3.1	7.8	4.5
n	70	62	16
Felony offense against property			
%	13.4	12.4	15.0
n	299	99	53
Misdemeanor			
%	55.9	55.8	39.7
n	1,248	446	140
Minor offense against person			
%	4.0	10.1	4.8
n	89	81	17
Minor offense against property			
%	27.5	31.1	24.9
n	613	249	88
Other delinquency			
%	24.5	14.5	9.9
n	546	116	35
Status			
%	27.5	24.0	40.8
n	613	192	144
Prior record			
0	70.6	58.1	59.8
1–2	23.6	31.3	29.5
3–4	4.5	8.0	8.8
5+	1.3	2.6	2.0

SOURCE: Feld (1989). Reprinted by special permission of Northwestern University School of Law, *Journal of Criminal Law and Criminology, 79*(4), pp. 1185-1346.

terparts. Approximately 10% more whites than blacks and others appeared in juvenile court for the first time. Conversely, blacks and other minorities were nearly twice as likely as whites to have records of chronic recidivism. Feld (1991) reported that Minnesota's urban juveniles had higher rates of recidivism than did delinquents in other locales and that urban courts threw a wider net of formal social control than did courts in other settings. Thus the extensive prior records reflect that these youths were charged in an urban county and also every previous discretionary decision made by every juvenile justice operative. Although the more extensive record of prior referrals may reflect real differences in rates of behavior by race similar to those reported for the present offenses, it may also indicate cumulative differential selection of juveniles by race over time (Fagan et al., 1987; McCarthy & Smith, 1986).

Race and Representation by Counsel

The overall rates of representation for the Hennepin County sample containing information on juveniles' race were as follows: private attorneys, 10.3%; public defenders, 37.5%; and unrepresented, 52.1%.[12] Thus, even in the most populous county in Minnesota with a well-established public defender system, the majority of juveniles still appeared without the assistance of counsel.

Table 4.2 reports the relationship between race, offense, and rates of representation and reveals that larger proportions of blacks and other minorities than white juveniles were represented. Compared with white juveniles, 15.4% more black youths and 10% more youths of other racial minorities, overall, had counsel. Of course, a serious present offense and prior record increases the likelihood of representation (Feld, 1988a, 1989). The greater presence of counsel is consistent with black and other minority youths' somewhat more extensive and serious delinquency involvements. Because Table 4.2 controls for the present offense, however, some differences in rates of representation by race remain. In 1991, lawyers represented 57.0% of minority youths as compared with only 35.5% of white juveniles (Minnesota Supreme Court Task Force on Racial Bias in the Judicial System, 1993).

Earlier research reported that private counsel represented only 5.1% of all Minnesota's delinquents and only 8.0% of those appearing in urban courts (Feld, 1991). Although 10.4% of all juveniles in Hennepin County retained private counsel, a larger proportion of white youths had private counsel, whereas public defenders were more likely to represent black and other minority youths. Other studies report that youths charged with serious crimes were more likely to retain private counsel (Feld, 1988a, 1989). Comparing the

TABLE 4.2 Representation by Counsel and Race: Hennepin County (in percentages)

	White			Black			Other		
	Private	Public Defender	None	Private	Public Defender	None	Private	Public Defender	None
Overall attorney	11.5	31.7	56.7	7.9	50.7	41.3	8.1	45.2	46.7
n	245	674	1,205	59	378	308	26	145	150
Felony	22.7	51.0	26.3	10.4	68.8	20.8	13.8	65.5	20.7
Felony offense against person	30.3	51.5	18.2	10.2	72.9	16.9	28.6	71.4	0.0
Felony offense against property	20.9	50.9	28.2	10.6	65.9	23.5	9.1	63.6	27.3
Misdemeanor	12.5	29.9	57.6	9.1	55.0	35.7	10.9	55.8	33.3
Minor offense against person	12.5	51.1	36.4	12.8	64.1	23.1	5.9	58.8	35.3
Minor offense against property	15.1	35.6	49.3	7.4	56.6	36.0	10.5	58.1	31.4
Other delinquency	9.5	19.8	70.7	10.1	45.9	44.0	14.3	48.6	37.1
Status	2.4	23.4	74.2	2.9	24.6	72.5	2.4	24.0	73.6

SOURCE: Feld (1989). Reprinted by special permission of Northwestern University School of Law, *Journal of Criminal Law and Criminology*, 79(4), pp. 1185-1346.

uses of private counsel by race reveals that when charged with felony against the person, white youths are almost three times more likely than black youths to have private counsel (30.3% vs. 10.2%) and, when charged with a felony involving property, twice as likely to have private counsel (20.9% vs. 10.6%). Conversely, blacks are most likely to be represented by the public defender. The few Native American and other minority juveniles charged with a felony offense against the person are nearly as likely as white youths to retain private counsel, but less likely than black youths to retain private counsel when charged with a felony involving property.

The SJIS data do not include information on juveniles' family status or socioeconomic status. However, black and other minority delinquents' greater use of public defenders rather than private attorneys may be an indirect indicator of their relatively lower socioeconomic status than white delinquents. The only other study to examine the relationship between race and type of representation reported that "Anglo youth are more likely to have private counsel . . . whereas minority youth are more likely to have public defenders or court-appointed attorneys, . . . an artifact of the race/social class interaction" (Fagan et al., 1987, p. 242). Some research suggests that private attorneys are marginally more successful than public attorneys in avoiding the most severe sentences for their clients (Feld, 1989). Fagan et al. (1987) reported a relationship between counsel and rates of dismissal—25% for white youths versus 19% for black youths—which resulted in more minority offenders being adjudicated.

Race, Present Offense, Prior Record, and Disposition

Although the SJIS data lack information on social variables such as family structure, socioeconomic status, or school achievement that would be useful to a full understanding of juvenile court dispositions, the data do lend themselves to explorations of the relationship between legal variables, race, and dispositional decision making. Table 4.3 uses two measures of juvenile court dispositions: out-of-home placement and secure confinement. Table 4.3 examines the dispositions received by juveniles of different races on

TABLE 4.3 Race, Offense, and Disposition (home/secure): Hennepin
County (in percentages)

	White	Black	Other
Overall			
Home	21.0	25.8	23.5
Secure	13.3	18.5	15.0
Felony			
Home	42.5	52.8	52.9
Secure	34.3	46.5	39.7
Felony offense against person			
Home	45.7	57.4	33.3
Secure	34.3	49.2	26.7
Felony offense against property			
Home	41.8	50.0	58.5
Secure	34.3	44.9	43.4
Misdemeanor			
Home	18.5	23.1	24.6
Secure	12.8	15.6	17.4
Minor offense against person			
Home	22.5	30.8	29.4
Secure	11.2	14.1	17.6
Minor offense against property			
Home	23.4	20.2	27.9
Secure	17.8	15.8	19.8
Other delinquency			
Home	12.3	23.9	14.3
Secure	7.5	16.2	11.4
Status			
Home	13.8	10.4	9.1
Secure	2.1	2.6	1.4

SOURCE: Feld (1989). Reprinted by special permission of Northwestern University School of
Law, *Journal of Criminal Law and Criminology, 79*(4), pp. 1185-1346.

the basis of their present offense. In the aggregate, about 5% more
black youths and 2% to 3% more youths of other minorities than
whites received out-of-home placement and secure confinement
dispositions.

The racial differences in sentencing are most conspicuous for
black juveniles charged with felony offenses and offenses against
the person, the offense categories in which black youths predomi-
nate relative to whites (Table 4.1). For those charged with felony
offenses, 10.3% more blacks than whites were removed from their
homes, and 12.2% more were institutionalized. Of first-time delin-

quents charged with a felony against the person in 1991, 30.1% of minority youths were removed from their homes as compared with only 19.9% of white juveniles (Minnesota Supreme Court Task Force on Racial Bias in the Judicial System, 1993). For juveniles of other races, the pattern is more complicated, with less severe sentencing than whites for those charged with felony offenses against the person, but higher rates for those charged with felony offenses against property (i.e., burglary). Although "other delinquency" was the only offense category in which minority youths were underrepresented compared to whites (Table 4.1), proportionally more minority youths in this category received out-of-home and secure confinement dispositions as well. It was only for status offenses that white youths consistently received more severe sentences than did minority youths. Although the largest proportion of youths charged with status offenses were Native American and other minority youths (40.8%; Table 4.1), they also experienced the least juvenile court intervention.

The apparent racial differences in sentencing may be the result of differences in the white and minority juveniles' prior records. The more extensive prior records of delinquency of black and other minority juveniles than their white counterparts (Table 4.1) may account for some of the apparent differences in their dispositions.

Table 4.4 summarizes juveniles' dispositions—out-of-home and secure confinement—while controlling for the seriousness of the present offense and the prior record. Even with controls, larger proportions of black juveniles charged with felony offenses against the person and property and other delinquency received out-of-home placement and secure confinement dispositions than did similarly situated white offenders. These differences are most conspicuous for black juveniles charged with felony offenses who receive sentences of secure confinement. Of the juveniles charged with a felony offense against the person, 12% more black juveniles than white youths with no prior record, 24.2% with one or two priors, and 11.4% more of those with three or more prior petitions were incarcerated. Similarly, 4.8%, 7.2%, and 15.1% more blacks than whites charged with felony offenses against property received secure confinement sentences. For youths charged with "other delinquency," 1.6%, 8.3%, and 12.9% more blacks than whites were

TABLE 4.4 Race, Offense, Priors, and Disposition (home/secure): Hennepin County (in percentages)

	White (no. of prior offenses)			Black (no. of prior offenses)			Other (no. of prior offenses)		
	0	1–2	3+	0	1–2	3+	0	1–2	3+
Felony offense against person									
Home	44.4	27.3	100.0	55.6	50.0	85.7	20.0	16.7	75.0
Secure	35.2	18.2	60.0	47.2	44.4	71.4	20.0	16.7	50.0
Felony offense against property									
Home	32.1	48.0	89.7	41.2	45.2	87.5	42.9	72.2	85.7
Secure	28.5	34.7	72.4	33.3	41.9	87.5	32.1	44.4	85.7
Minor offense against person									
Home	16.7	29.4	66.7	13.3	48.0	75.0	10.0	50.0	100.0
Secure	6.1	17.6	50.0	6.7	16.0	50.0	—	33.3	100.0
Minor offense against property									
Home	19.9	31.5	36.8	8.1	27.1	61.5	23.4	28.6	45.5
Secure	15.3	24.4	23.7	5.9	23.5	42.3	14.9	17.9	45.5
Other delinquency									
Home	9.4	19.5	33.3	12.5	35.0	46.2	13.6	12.5	20.0
Secure	4.7	13.8	33.3	6.3	22.5	46.2	13.6	—	20.0
Status									
Home	9.7	20.2	29.7	7.0	14.3	28.6	6.2	16.7	10.0
Secure	1.0	3.6	8.1	0.8	4.1	14.3	1.0	2.8	—

SOURCE: Feld (1989). Reprinted by special permission of Northwestern University School of Law, *Journal of Criminal Law and Criminology*, 79(4), pp. 1185-1346.

incarcerated. There were no consistent patterns in the sentencing of youths of other races or in other categories of offenses.

Race and Detention

The heavier reliance on detention in urban settings probably stems from the greater availability of detention facilities in urban settings (Feld, 1991). A primary determinant of a state's or county's detention rate is the availability of detention bed space (Bookin-Weiner, 1984; Frazier & Bishop, 1985; Krisberg & Schwartz, 1983). Each urban county in Minnesota has its own detention facility, which provides an inducement to use those facilities. The greater availability and use of detention in urban settings reflect the presence of a critical mass of eligible juveniles, greater reliance on formal mechanisms of control, and a more formal, punitive orientation (Feld, 1991).

Other analyses of the effects of detention on dispositions indicate that pretrial detention exerts an independent influence on a juvenile's ultimate disposition (Bailey, 1981; Clarke & Koch, 1980; Cohen & Kluegel, 1979a; Frazier & Bishop, 1985; Krisberg & Schwartz, 1983; McCarthy, 1987). Some of the racial disparities in sentencing black juveniles reported in Tables 4.3 and 4.4 may result from differences in rates of pretrial detention (Krisberg et al., 1987; Krisberg, Schwartz, Litsky, & Austin, 1986).

Table 4.5 reports the overall rates of detention for Hennepin County as well as separately for white youths, black youths, and other minority youths. In 1986, 7.6% of all Minnesota youths and 12.9% of all urban juveniles were detained (Feld, 1991, 1993). In Hennepin County, 14.1% of formally charged juveniles received one or more detention hearings. This rate of detention is nearly double the state average and reflects a higher rate of detention for every offense category except status offenses (Feld, 1991).

Although 14.1% of all youths referred to juvenile court are detained, the detention rates differ substantially by race: Only 10.6% of white juveniles are detained as compared with 22.6% of black and 17.3% of other minority youths. More than twice as many black and half again as many other minority youths as white juveniles are detained. Youths charged with more serious present offenses and those with prior referrals have higher rates of detention, and somewhat larger proportions of minority youths were charged with serious offenses and had prior records than did their white counterparts (Table 4.1). Thus it is necessary to control for the effects of the present offense and prior record on the decision to detain before attributing the racial disparities in sentencing to differential rates of detention.

TABLE 4.5 Race, Offense, Priors, and Detention: Hennepin County (in percentages)

	White (no. of prior offenses)			Black (no. of prior offenses)			Other (no. of prior offenses)			County
	0	1–2	3+	0	1–2	3+	0	1–2	3+	Total
Overall detention		10.6			22.6			17.3		14.1
Felony offense against person	24.1	27.3	60.0	52.8	72.2	71.4	40.0	33.3	50.0	42.6
Felony offense against property	15.0	30.1	54.7	33.3	42.0	75.0	25.0	33.3	100.0	27.9
Minor offense against person	9.1	35.2	66.7	17.8	28.0	50.0	10.0	50.0	—	23.2
Minor offense against property	7.1	20.4	23.7	18.4	24.7	38.4	19.1	14.3	45.5	15.8
Other delinquency	5.2	9.3	20.0	9.4	22.5	15.4	4.5	25.0	—	7.9
Status	3.9	5.4	18.9	2.4	10.2	14.3	5.1	8.4	20.0	5.4

SOURCE: Feld (1989). Reprinted by special permission of Northwestern University School of Law, *Journal of Criminal Law and Criminology*, *79*(4), pp. 1185-1346.

Table 4.5 reports the rates of detention for juveniles of different races while controlling for the seriousness of the present offense and prior record. Thus 42.6% of all Hennepin County juveniles charged with a felony offense against the person are detained. Although a larger proportion of black youths than white youths commit felony offenses against the person (Table 4.1), it is readily apparent that proportionately more black and minority youths than white youths are detained for the same offense. For juveniles charged with a felony offense against the person appearing in juvenile court for the first time, more than twice as many blacks as whites are detained, 52.8% versus 24.1%. For juveniles charged with a felony offense against the person with one or two prior referrals, again more than twice as many black youths as white youths are detained, 72.2% versus 27.3%. Even for youths with three or more prior referrals charged presently with a felony offense against the person, 11.4% more black youths than white youths are detained. Similarly, the Minnesota race bias study (Minnesota Supreme Court Task Force on Racial Bias in the Judicial System, 1993) found a significant relationship between race and detention in three offense categories and reported that "minority youths are detained at nearly two and one-half times the rate of whites in each of these [offense] categories" (pp. 101-102). This finding is consistent with other evaluations of the effects of race on pretrial detention and disposition (Fagan et al., 1987; Frazier & Bishop, 1985; McCarthy & Smith, 1986). Perhaps most directly on point, Kempf et al. (1990) analyzed the interaction of race and geography on detention and concluded that "within nearly every category, black youths were detained more often than white youths, overall. This outcome was accentuated in urban courts [where 31% of black youths and 21% of white youths were detained]" (pp. 81-82). Similarly, Wordes, Bynum, and Corley (1994) controlled simultaneously for the effects of legal and social variables and found that "race continued to exert an independent effect on the detention decision" (p. 162). Comparisons of rates of detention across races while controlling for the present offense and prior record suggest that at least some of the differences in the sentencing of minority youths charged with felony offenses against person and property probably result from the variations in rates of pretrial detention.

Regressing Appointment of Counsel, Pretrial Detention, and Dispositions for Independent Variables, Including a Juvenile's Race

Tables 4.1 through 4.5 report bivariate analyses of race. The following ordinary least squares (OLS) multiple regression equations were computed for Hennepin County and include a juvenile's race—white, black, and other—as an additional independent variable.[13] Race was dummy coded separately for black and Native American juveniles (1 = *not black*, 2 = *black*; 1 = *not Native American*;

TABLE 4.6 Regression Model of Factors Influencing Appointment of Counsel, Including a Juvenile's Race: Hennepin County

Independent Variable	Zero-Order r	Standardized Beta Coefficient	Multiple R	R^2
Offense severity	.370*	.336*	.370	.137
Prior home removal disposition	.171*	.051*	.395	.156
Home removal	.217*	.102*	.406	.165
Prior record	−.144*	−.082*	.412	.170
Black	−.097*	−.065*	.415	.173
Native American	−.031***	−.051**	.418	.175

SOURCE: Feld (1989). Reprinted by special permission of Northwestern University School of Law, *Journal of Criminal Law and Criminology*, 79(4), pp. 1185-1346.
*$p < .001$; **$p < .01$; ***$p < .05$.

2 = *Native American*) to permit an assessment of a youth's minority status on juvenile justice decision making.

Counsel

Table 4.6 reports the regression factors influencing the appointment of counsel. As in other analyses (Feld, 1989, 1991), the seriousness of the present offense is the principal determinate of the decision to appoint counsel (beta = .336). The seriousness of the present offense carries substantially more weight relative to other variables (beta = .336 vs. .270). In addition, the regression equation confirms the observation that being a black or Native American juvenile increases the likelihood of representation relative to their white counterparts (Table 4.2). The regression equation controls for the fact that minority youths are involved somewhat more often in serious offenses and have more extensive prior records, which, in turn, increase their likelihood of representation (Feld, 1989). The beta weights for race (black, beta = −.065; Native American, beta = −.051) are comparable to those for a prior record and a prior home removal disposition, suggesting a small but significant residual relationship between minority racial status and the appointment of counsel.

TABLE 4.7 Regression Model of Factors Influencing Detention Decision,
         Including a Juvenile's Race: Hennepin County

Independent Variable	Zero-Order r	Standardized Beta Coefficient	Multiple R	R^2
Home removal	−.297*	−.266*	.297	.088
Offense severity	−.235*	−.176*	.341	.117
Prior record	.168*	.081*	.361	.131
Black	.113*	.090*	.371	.138
Prior secure confinement disposition	−.195*	−.069*	.375	.141
Native American	.029	.046**	.378	.143
Secure confinement disposition	−.235*	.063***	.380	.144

SOURCE: Feld (1989). Reprinted by special permission of Northwestern University School of
Law, *Journal of Criminal Law and Criminology, 79*(4), pp. 1185-1346.
*$p < .001$; **$p < .01$; ***$p < .05$.

Detention

Table 4.7 reports the regression factors influencing the detention
decision in Hennepin County. An eventual home removal disposition, the seriousness of the present offense, and the presence of a
prior record dominate both decisions. However, the fourth variable
to enter the regression equation is a juvenile's race (black, beta =
.090). This confirms the observation that, after controlling for the
present offense and prior record, black juveniles in Hennepin
County were being detained at higher rates than their white counterparts (Table 4.5). Indeed, comparing the betas indicates that a
youth's race has a greater impact on the detention decision than
does having a prior record of offenses or a prior training school
commitment. The influence of being a Native American juvenile on
the detention decision is about half of that for black youths (beta =
−.046), but still significant. Moreover, any residual influence of a
juvenile's race on the detention decision after controlling for the
present offense and prior record raises further troubling questions
about the administration of this practice.

TABLE 4.8 Regression Model of Factors Influencing Out-of-Home Placement and Secure Confinement Dispositions, Including a Juvenile's Race: Hennepin County

Independent Variable	Zero-Order r	Standardized Beta Coefficient	Multiple R	R^2
Out-of-Home Placement				
Prior home removal disposition	.347*	.287*	.347	.120
Detention	−.297*	−.200*	.417	.174
Offense severity	.239*	.125*	.448	.200
Attorney	.217*	.094*	.455	.207
Number of offenses at disposition	−.103*	−.051**	.458	.210
Black	−.016	.056**	.461	.212
Native American	−.006	.037***	.462	.214
Secure Confinement				
Prior secure confinement disposition	.354*	.284*	.354	.126
Offense severity	.312*	.186*	.446	.199
Detention	−.235*	−.118*	.460	.212
Gender	.191*	.085*	.478	.219
Attorney	.213*	.066*	.472	.223
Number of offenses at disposition	−.118*	−.057*	.475	.226
Age	−.099*	.053**	.478	.229

SOURCE: Feld (1989). Reprinted by special permission of Northwestern University School of Law, *Journal of Criminal Law and Criminology, 79*(4), pp. 1185-1346.
*$p < .001$; **$p < .01$; ***$p < .05$.

Dispositions

The final set of regression equations examines the effect of a juvenile's race on the dispositional decisions—out-of-home placement and secure confinement (Table 4.8). The regression equations for Hennepin County juvenile court sentencing decisions account for 21.4% of the variance in home removal and 22.9% of the variance in institutionalization. A previous sentence removing a juvenile from the home is the most powerful determinant of the present decision to remove from the home (beta = .347). Similarly, a previous secure confinement sentence is the most powerful determinant of the present decision to incarcerate (beta = .354).

Two recent studies examined the effect of prior juvenile court sentences on the present one. Thornberry and Christenson (1984) reported that prior dispositions exert a strong influence on the current dispositions and that repeat offenders receive the same type of disposition for subsequent offenses; that is, there is stability in sentencing. By contrast, Henretta et al. (1986) analyzed the effects of previous sentences on the present disposition while controlling for other variables and report evidence of progression or escalation, rather than stability, in sentencing. They conclude that

> prior dispositions exert a fairly strong influence on the disposition of new offenses. . . . Only severity of the current offense proved to be a stronger predictor of case outcomes. . . . We did not find only stability in dispositional outcomes over repeat offenses. In our data, there is evidence of progression or escalation in the severity of disposition of subsequent offenses. (Henretta et al., 1986, p. 561)

Although this study was not designed to replicate those earlier studies, it provides evidence of the strong influence of prior dispositions on later sentences. The zero-order correlations (r) between prior home removal and present home removal and between prior secure confinement and present secure confinement show the strong relationship between the two decisions. A previous sentence of the same type as the current sentence is the first variable to enter the regression equation, has a beta weight that is double or triple that of the next variables, and explains about two thirds to three fourths of the total explained variance in sentencing.

The relationship between the previous disposition and the present one is consistent with the traditional, rehabilitative juvenile court sentencing philosophy. If sentencing decisions are individualized to fit the offender rather than the offense, then regardless of the present offense, a repeat involvement calls for similar, if not greater, intervention, absent a significant change in individual circumstances. Recidivism provides strong evidence that a juvenile has failed to "learn a lesson" or respond to "treatment." The previous disposition serves as a minimum constraint on the severity of the present sentence. To the extent that minority youths have more extensive prior involvements with juvenile courts, however, they may be somewhat more at risk for later sanctioning as well.

The next three variables to enter the regression equations for home removal and secure confinement, albeit in somewhat different order, are pretrial detention, the presence of an attorney, and the seriousness of the present offense. A relationship between the seriousness of the offense and the severity of the sentence reflects a modicum of proportionality in individualized dispositions. A comparison of the beta weights for the present offense (home, beta = .125; institutionalize, beta = .186) and the previous dispositions indicates that the latter are substantially more powerful determinants of the present sentence.

Pretrial detention exerts a significant influence on both of the sentences imposed (home, beta = −.200; institutionalize, beta = −.118). The presence of detention in the regression equations means that after controlling for the effects of the present offense, prior record, and other variables that detention and dispositions may share in common, detention per se exerts an independent effect on sentences. And this urban court detained the largest proportion of juveniles (Feld, 1991). A juvenile's pretrial detention status is comparable to the present offense in the decision to confine (beta = −.118 vs. .186) and more influential in the decision to remove a juvenile from home (beta = −.200 vs. .125).

Other studies have noted the deleterious effect of pretrial detention on postadjudication dispositions (Clarke & Koch, 1980; Frazier & Bishop, 1985; Krisberg & Schwartz, 1983; McCarthy, 1987). The presence of detention in the regression equations indicates that detention has a substantial impact on the sentences that youths receive. It is possible that the association is spurious and that both detention and dispositions share common factors other than those for which this study can control but which explain the relationship between the two. It is just as plausible that the initial detention decision is "irrational," in the sense of having no formal legal rational basis, but that it then strongly influences subsequent decisions (Frazier & Bishop, 1985).

The presence of an attorney appears to be an aggravating factor in a juvenile's disposition, accounting for about .7% of the variance in home removal and about .4% of the variance in secure confinement. Although the overall explained variance is small, the beta coefficient indicates that the presence of an attorney has nearly as much influence on a youth's removal from home as does the seriousness of the offense (attorney, beta = .094; offense, beta = .215).

Finally, whether a juvenile is black or Native American also is associated with the decision to remove him or her from home. Although the effects of race are small compared with the other variables, they are still statistically significant. Moreover, although a juvenile's minority racial status is associated with more serious offenses (Table 4.1), higher rates of representation (Table 4.2), and the initial detention decision (Table 4.5), even after controlling for differences in offenses, representation, and detention status minority youths remain at somewhat greater risk for removal from their homes. Somewhat surprisingly, there are no racial disparities in the commitment of juveniles to secure institutions, although indirect racial differences in sentencing may be subsumed in the other variables with a racial component such as offenses, priors, detention, and representation.

DISCUSSION AND CONCLUSION

Although these data provide some evidence of disparities in the detention and sentencing of minority youths, there are other possible explanations besides racial discrimination for which this study cannot account. Historically, juvenile court judges based their decisions on a host of individual characteristics of the offender. Because the SJIS data include only legal variables, this study cannot control for many of the factors that the principle of individualized justice deems relevant—family status, socioeconomic status, clinical evaluations, "treatment needs," school progress, employment status, and the like. Indeed, the differential access of white and minority youths to private counsel provides an indirect indicator that black offenders may be somewhat poorer (Table 4.2). Although individualized social variables that correlate with race may account for some of the racial differences in detention and out-of-home placement, they simply raise under a different guise the propriety of individualizing sentences on the basis of factors other than present offense and prior record when doing so produces a disparate effect (Coffee, 1978; Feld, 1978, 1988b).

The overall findings in this study are consistent with other research on racial disparities and juvenile court sentencing practices. Marshall and Thomas (1983) reported that careful measurement of legal and extralegal variables "account for only a little more than a quarter of the variance in the judicial dispositions" (p. 57); Thomas and Fitch (1975) reported that "the levels of association between both objective and personal variables and case dispositions are of weak to moderate magnitude, suggesting that no single factor exerts a major independent influence on judicial decision making" (p. 75); and Horowitz and Wasserman (1980, p. 411) concluded that even the inclusion of social background variables with offense variables only accounts for one fourth of the variance. Although legal variables exhibit a stronger statistical relationship with dispositions than do social variables, a very substantial amount of the variation in sentencing juveniles cannot be explained. Generally, the present offense and prior record—for which a prior disposition often serves as a surrogate in this study—are the best predictors of dispositions. However, they too only account for about one fourth of the variance in sentencing (Table 4.8; home, $R^2 = .214$; institutionalize, $R^2 = .229$). Moreover, although this study could not explain the determinants of pretrial detention, its racial component coupled with its pronounced negative effect on subsequent sentences introduces another "arbitrary and capricious" factor into the dispositional process. Finally, the adverse effects of representation on subsequent sentences raise further questions about the justice of the dispositional process.

The absence of any powerful, explanatory relationship between the legal variables and dispositions may be interpreted as true individualized justice; that is, every child is the recipient of a unique disposition tailored to his or her individual needs and social circumstances without regard to the present offense or prior record. An

equally plausible interpretation, however, is that there is no rationale to dispositional decision making; it consists of little more than
hunch, guesswork, and hopes, constrained marginally by the
youth's present offense, prior record, and previous dispositions. In
such a case, individualization is simply a euphemism for subjectiv-
ity, arbitrariness, and discrimination. A system of justice in which
the most powerful explanatory legal variables—present offense and
prior record—account for only about 25% of the variance in sentencing remains a highly discretionary and perhaps discriminatory
one.[14] To the extent that the data permit inferences of bias, urban
black youths are at greater risk of pretrial detention, which prejudices later dispositions, as well as at greater risk of home removal
than are their similarly situated white colleagues. At the same time,
the large amount of unexplained variance means that there is substantial attenuation between a youth's criminal behavior and the
severity of the disposition; minor offenders can receive more severe
dispositions than serious offenders. Similarly situated offenders—
defined in terms of their present offense or prior record—receive
markedly dissimilar dispositions. The desirability of perpetuating
such subjective and idiosyncratic detention and sentencing of similarly situated offenders when doing so fosters racial differences in
justice administration goes to the heart of the juvenile court as an
institution.

NOTES

1. Detention refers to a juvenile's custody status following arrest or referral but
prior to formal court action—adjudication or disposition. Detention, as distinguished from shelter care, connotes a physically restrictive facility, that is, a detention
center, state institution, or adult jail (Minn. Stat. Ann. § 260.015 Subd. 16 and 17,
1986). Minnesota detention statutes and court rules authorize pretrial preventive
detention if the child constitutes a danger to self or others, or will not make court
appearances (Feld, 1984; Minn. R.P. Juv. Ct. 18.02 [2] [A] [i], 18.06 [5] [b] [i], 18.09 [2]
[D] [i]; Minn. Stat. Ann. §§ 260.171 Subd. 1, 260.172 Subd. 1, 1986). The offense that
a juvenile allegedly committed is not an explicit statutory criterion for detention
except insofar as a juvenile court judge may view it as evidence of "endangering"
self or others.

Minnesota's apparent low rate of pretrial detention (Feld, 1988a, 1989) results,
in part, from its restrictive definition of *detention*. Juveniles are only counted as
detained if a detention hearing is held after a juvenile was taken into custody, usually

within about 2 court days. Many juveniles who are detained pending the arrival of parents or even held for 1 or 2 days but released prior to a detention hearing are not counted as detained in Minnesota, as they are in other jurisdictions (Feld, 1988a).

2. Most of Minnesota's delinquents are not serious offenders (Feld, 1989, 1991), and in purely numerical terms, more minor offenders are detained than are felons. Indeed, for the entire state, slightly more than one third of detainees are charged with felonies (36.2%), and most are charged with misdemeanors (46.7%) or even status offenses (17.0%). In absolute terms, more shoplifters (332) are detained than are burglars (305) (Feld, 1991, 1993).

3. The SJIS compiles statewide statistical data on juvenile delinquency and status petitions filed annually, as well as dependency, neglect, and abuse cases. The data are based on the petitions filed; there is no database that includes the cases referred to intake, county probation, or juvenile courts that were handled informally. The data collected on a case-specific basis include offense behavior, representation by counsel, court processing information, entries each time a court activity occurs, any continuation or change in the status of a case, and types of dispositions. In most counties, this information is obtained from the juvenile courts' own automated computer system and is entered by court administrators in each county, who are trained by the state court administrator. Because the juvenile courts themselves rely on this computerized information for record keeping, scheduling hearings, maintaining court calendars, and monitoring cases, it is highly reliable.

The SJIS data files used in this study are housed in the National Juvenile Court Data Archive (NJCDA) at the National Center for Juvenile Justice, which is the research arm of the National Council of Juvenile and Family Court Judges. The Office of Juvenile Justice and Delinquency Prevention, U.S. Department of Justice, has supported the juvenile court data archive for the past decade. Currently, about 30 states contribute their annual juvenile court data tapes to the NJCDA.

4. The youth identification numbers are unique within a county, but not within the entire state. A youth who has delinquency referrals in several different counties will receive separate identification numbers in each county. Thus the variable "prior referrals" may be slightly inflated by a juvenile with multiple referrals in several counties, and slightly reduced by juveniles whose prior records consist of only one referral in each of several counties. Such multicounty cases are infrequent. Because Minnesota lacks a statewide juvenile information system, a juvenile court at sentencing normally has information regarding prior referrals only in its own county. Thus the variable "prior referrals" includes the information routinely available to and relied on by the courts themselves.

5. The NJCDA has developed a 78-item coding protocol that recodes the raw offense data provided by the states into a uniform format. This permits delinquency offense data from several different original formats to be recoded for analysis using a single conversion program.

6. Felony offenses against person generally correspond to the FBI's Uniform Crime Report classification of Part I violent felonies against the person—homicide, rape, robbery, and aggravated assault. Felony offenses against property generally include Part I property offenses—burglary, felony theft, and auto theft. Minor offenses against person consist primarily of simple assaults; minor offenses against property consist primarily of larceny, shoplifting, or vandalism. Other delinquency contains a mixed bag of residual offenses—drug offenses primarily involving possession of marijuana, public order offenses, and offenses against the administration

of justice such as contempt of court. Status offenses are the juvenile violations that are not criminal for adults—runaway, truancy, curfew, ungovernability, and the like (Federal Bureau of Investigation, 1987).

7. When a petition contains multiple allegations, there is no way to separate whether they are multiple charges arising out of the same offense transaction or whether they represent several offenses committed on different occasions that were simply petitioned in the same document.

8. Out-of-home placement includes any disposition in which the child is taken from his or her home and placed in a group home, foster care, in-patient psychiatric or chemical dependency treatment facility, or secure institution. Secure confinement is a substantial subset of all out-of-home placements but includes only commitments to county institutions or state training schools.

The NJCDA developed a 22-item conversion program to transform state-specific dispositions into a uniform national format. The NJCDA staff speak directly with the states' data collectors and reporters to determine how specific dispositions or programs should be classified—out of home and secure—within the national format.

9. Minnesota is almost totally white. Based on the 1980 census, all other racial groups accounted for only 3.4% of the total population (Feld, 1991). In 1980, blacks (1.3%), Spanish-Latinos (0.6%), and Native Americans (0.9%) accounted for most of Minnesota's racial diversity. Significantly, minority racial groups are concentrated almost exclusively in the two urban counties, Hennepin and Ramsey, which include the Twin Cities of Minneapolis and St. Paul. Black households accounted for more than 10 times the proportion of urban households (3.2%) as they do of suburban (0.3%) or rural (0.1%) households. All nonwhites are nearly four times more likely to reside in urban counties (6.7%) than in either suburban (1.8%) or rural (1.7%) settings (Feld, 1991).

10. In Hennepin County, of 4,243 delinquency and status petitions filed in 1986, a juvenile's race is reported in 79.8% of all petitions, or 3,385 cases, which constitutes the N in this study. The data reported here constitute a very large subset of the total cases in the county. Comparing the "race" subsample with the overall county totals suggests that it is representative, that is, the cases missing information on race do not introduce any systematic biases. For example, for the entire Hennepin County juvenile court population (4,243) and the "race" sample (3,385), the proportion of offenses are, respectively: felony against person, 4.1% and 4.4%; felony against property, 12.9% and 13.3%; minor offense against person, 5.2% and 5.5%; minor offense against property, 26.8% and 28.1%; other delinquency, 21.8% and 20.6%; and status, 29.0% and 28.0%. Similarly, for Hennepin County as a whole and for the "race" sample, the proportions of juveniles with priors are 0 = 66.7% and 66.5%; 1-2 = 26.1% and 26.0%; 3-4 = 5.6% and 5.8%; and 5+ = 1.6% and 1.7%.

11. The Minnesota race bias study's (Minnesota Supreme Court Task Force on Racial Bias in the Judicial System, 1993) analyses of juvenile justice administration were part of a large study of racial bias in the Minnesota judicial system. The race bias study used the same SJIS data source, analyzed more recent data (from 1991), and attempted to replicate earlier studies reported by Feld (1989, 1991, 1993).

The race bias study analyzed data from all counties in which racial data were present in at least 50% of all cases. In addition to urban Hennepin County, the study analyzed 15 rural counties where the predominant minority populations were Native American or Latino juveniles. The study coded offenses similarly to Feld (1989,

1991), although it was not able to reconstruct juveniles' prior records or prior dispositions as completely. Consequently, the delinquency history variable contained only two categories: no prior petitions or any prior petitions.

12. These proportions for the sample, including racial data, are nearly identical with the entire Hennepin County juvenile court population in which only 47.7% of youths had attorneys: 10.4% had private attorneys and 37.3% had public defenders.

13. OLS multiple regression procedures were used to analyze the relationships among the independent variables and to assess the relative impact of each independent variable on the dependent variable. Tables 4.6-4.8 report the standardized regression coefficient for each independent variable (beta), the zero-order correlation coefficient (r) between each independent variable and the dependent variable, the multiple regression correlation coefficient (R), and the R^2. Forward, stepwise regression equations were computed using SPSS for the following dependent variables: attorney, detention, out-of-home placement, and secure confinement. The independent variables and their coding, which affects the signs of the beta coefficients, include attorney ($1 = yes, 2 = no$); secure confinement ($1 = yes, 2 = no$); a previous secure confinement disposition ($1 = yes, 2 = no$); out-of-home placement ($1 = yes, 2 = no$); a previous out-of-home placement ($1 = yes, 2 = no$); age ($1 = 12$ *or younger* to $7 = 18$ *years of age*); gender ($1 = male, 2 = female$); detention ($1 = no, 2 = yes$); prior adjudications ($1 = none$ to $4 = 5$ *or more*); present offense ($1 = felony offense against person$ to $6 = status$); number of offenses at disposition ($1 = none$ to $6 = five$ *or more*).

14. The Minnesota race bias study (Minnesota Supreme Court Task Force on Racial Bias in the Judicial System, 1993, App. D, p. 9) concluded with a similar cautionary observation:

> Judges have a great deal of discretion to do whatever they feel is in the best interests of the juvenile. There are no rules that stipulate juveniles who are charged with similar offenses must be treated in a like manner. Any number of factors (e.g., the juvenile's family situation, treatment evaluation reports, etc.) may influence the judge's decision to detain or remove the juvenile from home. Therefore, the variations in rates of detention and removal may reflect social characteristics of juveniles for which this study could not control, and for which race was an indirect indicator. Regardless of whatever good intentions the juvenile court system may possess, it appears that it is in need of a serious policy evaluation at this time.

5

The Role of Race in Juvenile Justice in Pennsylvania

KIMBERLY KEMPF LEONARD

HENRY SONTHEIMER

The juvenile justice system is asked to meet several goals. Juvenile justice must respond to the varied needs of young people and at the same time maintain its obligation to provide for the safety of the community. And just as parents discover quickly that they must function simultaneously as caregivers, teachers, protectors, and disciplinarians, the tasks required of the juvenile justice system are diverse and multifaceted. Techniques preferred for each parenting role are time, location, and task specific. The unique requirements of individual children also must be met. The *parens patriae* objectives of juvenile justice require that administrative decisions be tailored to individual children and operate away from public view so as to shield children. Finally, the juvenile justice system is asked to function within a constrained set of resources, generally inadequate to meet fully the needs of all children under its care.

Although the tasks confronted by the juvenile justice system appear daunting, no objective can undermine the necessity of providing justice in a systematic, fair, and equitable manner. Justice must ensure a balanced arena for the youths it serves. Patterns of disparity in case processing are at odds with the principle of justice and the effectiveness of the system. Disparity may occur in many forms. This chapter reports findings of a study of racial disparity in Pennsylvania.

REVIEW OF THE LITERATURE

Previous research on racial disparity in the adult criminal justice system has concentrated on several decision points, including pretrial detention, sentencing, and the imposition of capital punishment. Relatively few studies have focused on possible bias experienced by minorities in the juvenile justice system. However, the juvenile system, by design, has the potential to practice differential handling. The juvenile court is based on a *parens patriae* philosophy that emphasizes both informal procedures and individualized justice. Juvenile court judges and probation officers have broad powers regarding detention, adjudication, and disposition decisions. Laws defining juvenile delinquency are sometimes so broad as to include acts in which almost all children engage. Although the informal operation of the juvenile court was expected originally to enhance the goal of individualized justice, current juvenile court philosophy places increasing emphasis on accountability and punishment. This new punitive focus, combined with the discretion inherent in juvenile justice processing, creates the potential for differential treatment that systematically may disadvantage certain groups. If minority children receive more punitive outcomes than similarly situated white youths, reforms are needed to ensure that juvenile justice decision making is racially neutral.

The need for further research in the area of juvenile justice processing was highlighted in a recent review of the literature by Pope and Feyerherm (1991). This review, commissioned by the Office of Juvenile Justice and Delinquency Prevention (OJJDP), included several recommendations for research on racial disparity in the juvenile justice system. Pope and Feyerherm advocate that research efforts examine multiple processing stages, including arrest, court processing, and corrections. Researchers should use both observational components and quantitative analysis, using multivariate techniques to control for relevant variables. A variety of jurisdictions (rural, suburban, urban) should be examined and minorities other than blacks should be included in future studies. From a methodological perspective, Pope and Feyerherm caution that aggregating data (e.g., by area, time frame, or offense type) may mask evidence of racial disparity. Also, they suggest that research designs control for changes in sample size as cases pass through the system.

A number of recent studies have identified race as predictive of juvenile court dispositions, even after controlling for relevant legal criteria: prior record, offense seriousness, type, and level of injury or damage (Bishop & Frazier, 1988; Bortner, Sunderland, & Winn, 1985; Fagan, Slaughter, & Hartstone, 1987; Feyerherm, 1981; Johnson & Secret, 1992; Marshall & Thomas, 1983; McCarthy & Smith, 1986; Slaughter, Hartstone, & Fagan, 1986; Thomas & Cage, 1977; Thornberry, 1979; Zatz, 1982). Other researchers have reported little or no race effect (Bailey & Peterson, 1981; Bortner & Reed, 1985; Cohen & Kluegel, 1978, 1979b; Horowitz & Wasserman, 1980; Kowalski & Rickicki, 1982), a race effect conditional on decision stage (Chused, 1973; Dannefer & Schutt, 1982; Peterson, 1988), and a race effect favoring minorities (Bishop & Frazier, 1988; Dannefer & Schutt, 1982; Pawlak, 1977; Thomas & Cage, 1977). The current body of research thus represents mixed and collectively inconclusive findings, with interpretation further complicated by the methodological shortcomings of some studies and a lack of replication efforts.

Despite the inconsistent findings of previous studies, current research should build on the existing knowledge base and attempt to ameliorate identified weaknesses of prior efforts. Research prior to the mid-1970s used bivariate contingency analysis as the principle technique of investigation, allowing for control variables to be considered only one at a time. Subsequent research incorporated more rigorous multivariate analysis to explain outcome at individual decision stages. Bishop and Frazier (1988), Kempf et al. (1990), and Leiber (1992), for example, used logistic regression and Lockhart, Kurtz, Sutphen, and Gauger (1991) used multiple regression analysis. Based on the reviewed studies, current research also should examine multiple decision stages using a more process-oriented approach in light of the knowledge that early stage decisions may affect subsequent ones. Indeed, a consistent finding since the mid-1980s regarding the juvenile justice process is that the effect of race on disposition may be masked by prior detention (Bishop & Frazier, 1990; Bortner & Reed, 1985; Johnson & Secret, 1992; Kempf et al., 1990; Leiber, 1992; Lockhart et al., 1991). Current research should control for prior record while recognizing that differential treatment of minorities may affect the accumulation of juvenile arrests (or police contacts) and thus account, in part, for the over-representation of minorities at later stages (Fagan et al., 1987, pp. 226-227). Regrettably, the possible presence of sample selection bias across multiple stages of juvenile justice has seldom been examined.

Prior research indicates that offense seriousness and type are important conditional factors in juvenile justice processing. Ferdinand and Luchterhand (1970) found no differential handling by race for youths involved in the most serious crimes and with lengthier prior records, but did observe disparate treatment among those with less serious offenses. Offense severity may itself be affected by differential treatment of racial groups. For example, Lockhart et al. (1991, p. 88) report that black juveniles are more often charged with a felony when the arresting offense could also be considered a misdemeanor. The potential for this type of charging bias suggests that simply controlling for offense seriousness as a relevant legal variable may mask possible disparity.

Minority overrepresentation also may be affected by police patrolling patterns and referral decisions. Thornberry (1973) reported harsher treatment of black youths by police in Philadelphia. Dannefer and Schutt (1982) found race to be the most important predictor of the police decision; police were more likely to intervene when suspects were black, as compared to white or Latino. Wilson (1968) identified a relationship between neighborhood context and police arrest decisions, which raises the possibility of conditional relationships between race and neighborhoods. Huff (1990) argued that urban police downplay gang-related delinquency, which may be more prevalent among minorities.

In addition to prior record and the seriousness of the referral offense(s), other youth characteristics besides race may affect court processing. Sex has been associated with both more leniency for some cases and harsher treatment for others (Johnson & Secret, 1992; Kempf et al., 1990; Leiber, 1992). Economic status also may affect how youths are processed (e.g., Byrne & Sampson, 1986; Wolfgang et al., 1972). A juvenile's family structure, such as residing in a female-headed household or sibling involvement in delinquency, is often known to the court and may influence decision making (Pope & Feyerherm, 1991). Traits such as race, family composition, and economic status may interact and influence court processing in different and subtle fashions. For example, some researchers have argued that child abuse and neglect referrals disproportionately affect poor minorities and that inappropriate placement decisions are often the result of social service workers reacting to poverty (Buriel, Loya, Gonda, & Klessen, 1979; Olsen, 1982; Reid, 1984).

Juvenile court outcomes may also differ according to court location (i.e., in rural, suburban, or urban areas). Pope and Feyerherm (1991) reported that Latino and Native American youths, in particular, are more likely to reside in nonurban areas. Many researchers have also reported higher prevalence and incidence of delinquency in urban areas (Blau & Blau, 1982; Laub, 1983; Laub & Hindelang, 1980; Sampson, 1986). The Pennsylvania Commission on Sentencing (1981) reported "the long held belief that sentences are less severe in urban areas" (p. 25). Aday (1986) described rural courts as having more centralized procedures than urban courts. In Georgia, blacks tended to be processed in relatively decentralized courts, which are also characterized by less intake discretion (Lockhart et al., 1991). Hagan's (1979) study of criminal courts found that urban courts had more uniform sentences because the bureaucratic demands of a greater volume of cases and more employees reduced the opportunities for urban judges to intervene personally in cases. Myers and Talarico (1986) reported a similar finding of more bureaucratization and formal control in urban criminal courts, which were also characterized by higher crime rates.

According to Feld (1991, pp. 156-157), Minnesota's urban counties tend to be heterogeneous and diverse, and juvenile justice intervention there is more formal, bureaucratized, and due process oriented. This formality is associated with more severe pretrial detention and sentencing practices. By contrast, juvenile courts in the more homogeneous and stable rural counties use less formal procedures and more lenient sentences. Feld (1991, p. 168) hypothesized that if racial heterogeneity decreases the effectiveness of informal social controls, then urban counties may need more formal mechanisms of control. In Missouri, racial disparity also existed within each court type, and urban courts were more formal than rural courts (Kempf et al., 1990).

Suburban juvenile courts have not been studied as separate entities from urban and rural courts. Concerning criminal courts, however, Austin reported (in McNeely & Pope, 1981, pp. 11-21) that suburban and especially rural courts sentenced nonwhite adults to prison at a higher rate than urban courts. Austin's interpretation was that urban courts adopt a more legalistic model than their rural or suburban counterparts. In a study of racial disparity in sentencing in Pennsylvania prior to the adoption of guidelines, Kempf (1982) and Kempf and Austin (1986) found the greatest disparity by race was associated with the incarceration decision in suburban courts. Urban and rural courts issued longer sentences than did suburban courts, but no race difference by urbanization was observed for sentence lengths.

The collective findings of the reviewed studies are inconclusive but raise many issues. Currently, claims of racial bias cannot be dismissed on the basis of the empirical evidence available. Even if the results allowed for greater confidence in interpretation, an analysis of this issue in a particular state and time period not examined before could add significantly to the knowledge base. The study described in this chapter will permit empirically supported statements about the effect of race on juvenile justice processing in Pennsylvania. The data for this study include a wide range of factors to be considered and adequate variation to allow simultaneous controls for the legal and extralegal criteria identified as important in the previous research. In addition, tests are made to examine and control for sample selection bias across various decision stages.

RESEARCH DESIGN AND METHODOLOGY

The research process of comparing the juvenile justice experiences of white, Latino, and black youths began by identification of the 14 counties[1] with the highest proportions of black and Latino youth residents. The 14 counties reported 20,325 delinquency cases

involving white, black, or Latino youths during 1989. These cases
constitute 70% of all Pennsylvania delinquency cases for these racial
groups during 1989. Status offenses are handled differently and
were excluded from consideration.

Sample cases (N = 1,797) were selected through a stratified
random procedure. The objective was to collect data on 2,016 cases,
equally distributed as 672 cases each in the urban, suburban, and
more rural court categories. Those cases were classified further by
race and crime type of the most serious charge (property, person,
drug, other), with the goal of identifying 56 cases per category. There
were five categories for which this was not possible because there
were fewer than 56 cases identified in the sampling frame (all
suburban Latino cases and rural blacks with drug referrals). A
standardized instrument was used for data collection from any
available documentation in individual case files. The process provided independent screening for accuracy of completed coding
forms.

Missing data were minimal (less than 5%) for most items. Legal
information was almost always available, with the exception of
items related to the youths' demeanor and victim characteristics,
such as race. Some family and school items reflect missing data rates
of 10% to 20%, and family income was not available for 24% of the
cases. However, in an effort to avoid problems posed by missing
data, variables are coded to include the missing information as
absent the trait.[2]

Techniques of Investigation

This study used logit analysis to account for the variation in the
probability of a dichotomous juvenile justice outcome. Dummy
variables were created for each category of race, sex, court type, and
for drug- and person-related offenses. The parameters in the logit
models are estimated using maximum likelihood techniques. In
these techniques, the parameter estimates are chosen such that they
maximize the probability of obtaining the observed sample distribution on the outcome variable. The models provide estimates of
the independent contributions that each criterion makes to the explanation. The variables are assessed simultaneously so their order

within the model makes no difference. Results present both coefficients (B) and the ratios of the coefficient to the standard error (B/SE). The latter, approximately t ratios, are used to test whether the variable has no effect on outcome. Values, either positive or negative, that are far from 0 (in this study greater than the absolute value of 2), reject this hypothesis of no effect.

It is important to note that the interpretation of results from logit analysis are not as straightforward as those obtained from multiple regression. First, the properties of maximum likelihood estimation are not exact, but results may be interpreted as approximations that hold reasonably well under conditions typically encountered. Second, the magnitude of the effect of each independent criterion varies with the values of all exogenous variables in the model; therefore, because the effect is conditional, description of that effect is not as simple as interpretation of the coefficient in the typical regression model. Third, there is no summary statistic associated with logit models that has an interpretation comparable to R^2 for a multiple regression model.

The best way to overcome the latter disadvantage of logit analysis is to use multiple strategies to examine the success of the model. We first use the chi-square "goodness of fit" test, which examines the hypothesis that all coefficients except that of the intercept have a value of 0, or essentially, the likelihood that the observed frequency distribution of Y could occur by chance if the model is correct. The higher the chi-square, the more likely the hypothesis of a chance distribution is rejected, and the more likely the model is correct. The probability associated with the change distribution also is reported.

Another strategy "in the spirit of R^2" involves calculation of the predicted probability of a case having an outcome of 0 or 1. The proportion of cases accurately predicted can be assessed at a predetermined level of probability. The difficulty associated with this test is the absence of an agreed on baseline. The probability level might be set at .50, for example, to test whether the model fares better at distinguishing outcome than a simple coin toss. Alternately, the probability might be set according to the actual distribution of the outcome variable. From the latter probability test, it also is possible to determine fairly well whether the model was better able to predict one of the two possible outcomes. This study adopts the second convention because juvenile justice outcomes should fare better than a coin toss. Considered together, these tests provide sufficient means for interpreting logit models. (For additional information on logit analysis and corresponding goodness-of-fit strategies, see Aldrich & Nelson, 1984; Greene, 1990; Hanushek & Jackson, 1977; Maddala, 1987.)

Sample Selection Bias

As discussed in the literature review, racial disparity in juvenile justice has recently been identified as a topic that requires consideration of potential interdependence between early and later decision stages and outcomes. For example, white youths may more often be released at intake screening than minority youths who are otherwise similar. If the youths who exit early in the system are not included in the analysis of the adjudication outcomes, then selectivity bias may be present in the sample (Killingsworth, 1983). This means that results based on the sample may not be representative of what would happen to any youth drawn at large with the same measured characteristics. As a consequence, recommendations have been made for a process-oriented research approach. No agreement on the form this type of investigation should take has been achieved, however, and few examples from prior research exist on this topic, other than inclusion of the detention outcome as an exogenous criterion in models of adjudication and disposition outcomes.

The purpose of the analysis is to identify the significant determinants of various outcomes in juvenile justice. For instance, we are interested in determining the factors that lead to cases being adjudicated. One problem with many studies to date is that they analyze the adjudication outcome using the sample of youths who have had formal petitions filed. This sample of youths may be a select group, with specific unmeasured characteristics that make them substantively different from youths who exited the system at earlier stages, but who have otherwise similar measurable characteristics. The end result is that parameter estimates of the effect of race and other independent variables on the adjudication decision are conditioned on this select sample. This study follows a technique suggested by Heckman (1979, 1980; Greene, 1981, 1990) that partially corrects for this "selectivity bias."

Heckman's technique, which yields selectivity-corrected estimates is called the Heckman two-step model. In the first step, a probit model is estimated to determine the probability of being included in the sample. Estimates from this equation are then used to create a term called *lambda*, which is also known in some literatures as the inverse Mills's ratio.[3] Lambda is then included as a regressor in a second-stage equation, where it serves to correct for selectivity bias. At least one variable from the first stage is omitted in the second model to control for potential collinearity between lambda and remaining variables in the equation (Killingsworth, 1983).

In the case above, first we estimate the probability of having a petition filed. A sample selection term, lambda, is computed and then included in the model of adjudication outcome. In the selectivity-corrected adjudication model, B provides an unbiased estimate of the effect of an increase in X on the probability of adjudication for any youth (at the petition stage) with a given set of characteristics, whereas in the original unadjusted model, B provides an estimate of the effect for a youth with the same observed characteristics, conditioned on the fact that he or she made it to the adjudication stage.

In this study, the Heckman method is applied independently to examine potential bias between three stages. We control for selectivity bias between (a) intake screening and the filing of petitions, (b) petitions and adjudication, and (c) adjudication and dispositional placement. Thus we only partially correct for sample selection bias because when we model petition, we are only considering those youths referred to court—others are not brought in by police. Similarly, when we model adjudication, we consider only those from the petition stage—others are lost at the intake stage; and the disposition model controls only for the sample at adjudication. Ideally, effects from each preceding stage would be controlled, but the multistage specification exceeds current identification capabilities of the Heckman method.

DESCRIPTIVE RESULTS

Minority youths are overrepresented in Pennsylvania courts, as shown from the comparison of the proportion of the general youth population in the 14 counties accounted for by blacks (19%) and Latinos (4%) with their representation among juvenile court referrals (46% and 7%, respectively). Within juvenile justice, minority youths are detained at a greater rate than whites (shown in Figure 5.1).[4] More restrictive outcomes for minorities also are shown at waiver, the petition stage, adjudication, and placement. Thus the original relationships indicate harsher outcomes for minority children among five decision stages of juvenile justice. No cumulative disadvantage for minorities is directly observed because their representation at subsequent stages does not increase over that shown for early detention. However, these results fail to consider type of offense, prior record, or social history, all of which may help to explain that the race difference is not due to bias on the part of probation officers and judges.

Descriptive comparisons of the cases show little race difference by age or sex; most youths were male, with an average age of 16. Nearly half of the youths—even more of the blacks—also were not identified as having personal problems.[5] Half of all youths, including 62% of the blacks, had no youth-related problems. The majority of youths also had not been suspended or left school.[6] These difficulties with school were identified at a slightly higher rate among Latino youths. Prior juvenile records were more common among minority youths and slightly higher for Latinos than blacks.[7]

Nearly half of all youths had no family problems, with only one problem noted for another 25% to 33%.[8] Minority youths of both groups were more apt than whites to have more than one family problem. Absentee fathers were more common among minority youths (68%) than whites (42%). English was their second language or not spoken by parents for 61% of suburban, 47% of rural, and 45% of urban Latino youths. Latinos (52%) more often had families who were poor,[9] followed by blacks (34%) and, much less often, by whites (12%).

Three offenses was the average number specified at referral, with a range from 1 to 29. Approximately one fourth of all cases

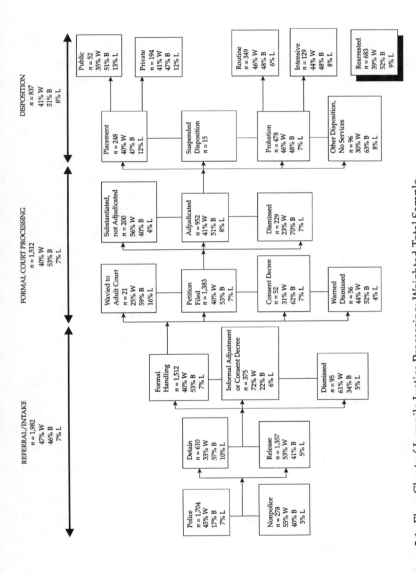

Figure 5.1. Flow Chart of Juvenile Justice Processing: Weighted Total Sample

NOTE: Population (of 14-county sample), ages 10 to 17: 77% white, 19% black, and 4% Latino. W = white youths, B = black youths, L = Latino youths.

involved drug-related offenses and 40% involved offenses against
persons.[10] Black youths were slightly less likely than others to have
injured victims or recorded circumstances connecting them with the
offense.[11] Valid measurement of offense seriousness was not possible.[12]

The main police department of the county (usually the department of the largest municipality) was the source of their referral for
most Latino youths (73%), followed by black youths (62%), and, much
less often, white youths (31%). Referral rates (number of referrals
divided by population) ranged from 0.8 in Chester County to 4.8 in
Philadelphia. Parent and/or attorney not present at the court hearing (coded as 1 = *absent*, 0 = *otherwise*) occurred for 19% of the black,
18% of the Latino, and 11% of the white youths.

The effects of several variables considered simultaneously are
presented next. As noted earlier, if delinquency case outcomes are
influenced by race when other demographic, offense, and relevant
criteria are controlled, then findings will be considered to show
differential treatment. If this disparity involves more restrictive
outcomes for black and/or Latino youths, the results will be interpreted as indications that juvenile justice is not color blind.

MULTIVARIATE RESULTS

Models for the Total Sample

Logit models were examined for the total sample and independently by race. The results for the total sample for models of four
decision stages are shown in Table 5.1.[13] This table also enables us
to compare findings from the models corrected for selectivity bias
with those from the original analyses. Significant chi-square statistics for each model suggest that the outcomes at every stage are not
random.

The approximate t values (B/SE) for intake indicate that progression beyond referral is more likely for blacks and Latinos, and
are associated with the number of offenses, suburban and urban
areas, prior records, referrals from the main police department,
school problems, drug- and person-related offenses, age, and higher
county rates of referral. The original model of filed petitions shows

TABLE 5.1 Factors Affecting Juvenile Justice Outcomes for the Total Sample: Original Models and Models Corrected for Sample Selection Bias[a]

	Intake Outcome		Petition Outcome				Adjudication Outcome				Placement Outcome			
	Original		Original		Corrected[b]		Original		Corrected[c]		Original		Corrected[d]	
Factor	B	B/SE	B	B/SE	B	B/SE	B	B/SE	B	B/SE	B	B/SE	B	B/SE
Constant	**-4.25**	**-5.09**	-.30	**-2.87**	**1.05**	**13.99**	**-1.87**	**-2.97**	**1.07**	**4.55**	**-3.57**	**-3.62**	-.90	-1.93
Number of offenses	**.50**	**7.52**	**.25**	**5.72**	-.00	-.28	**.10**	**3.21**	-.01	-1.24	**.08**	**2.51**	**.03**	**2.59**
Drug offense	**.50**	**2.40**	.23	1.41	-.01	.46	.22	1.54	.04	.97	**.57**	**2.93**	**.14**	**2.57**
Person offense	**.44**	**2.43**	**.31**	**2.19**	.01	.28	.11	.90	-.06	-1.58	.17	.95	.04	.95
Circumstances	-.11	-1.71	-.03	-.49	.01	1.51	**.12**	**2.53**	**.42**	**3.21**	.02	.28	.02	.87
Prior record	**.57**	**5.77**	**.30**	**4.40**	.00	.20	**.30**	**5.39**	.28	1.58	**.53**	**8.16**	**.16**	**4.29**
Youth problem	.20	1.95	**.26**	**3.14**	.01	.77	**.33**	**4.76**	.12	.50	**.25**	**2.72**	**.10**	**2.11**
School problem	**.49**	**3.27**	**.24**	**2.02**	-.02	-1.29	**.22**	**2.08**	.00	.13	-.05	-.35	.02	.55
Family problem	.15	1.53	.11	1.38	-.00	-.44	.08	1.25	.00	.02	.12	1.49	.04	1.69
Absent father	.09	.55	-.01	-.04	-.00	-1.11	.01	.12	-.00	-.09	-.01	-.06	-.02	-.35
Poor family	.24	1.12	.21	1.31	.02	1.24	.10	.75	-.02	-.53	**.39**	**2.16**	**.10**	**2.15**
Black	**.78**	**4.15**	**.37**	**2.38**	-.04	-1.89	.15	1.09	-.05	-1.09	**-.46**	**-2.06**	-.04	-.66
Latino	**.47**	**2.21**	.19	1.08	-.04	-1.57	-.05	-.30	-.05	-1.19	-.23	-.99	.00	.06
Sex	-.07	-0.37	.06	.39			.17	1.10			.22	.77		
Age	**.11**	**2.35**	.04	1.07			.02	.61			-.02	-.39		
Main police	**.74**	**4.39**	**.71**	**5.07**	.03	1.59	**.33**	**2.55**	**-.13**	**-2.30**	-.04	-.20	.05	.84
Urban area	**.96**	**2.20**	**.93**	**2.54**	.04	.71	**.89**	**2.56**	-.15	-1.20	-.09	-.17	.09	.57
Suburban area	**1.38**	**7.10**	**1.04**	**6.16**	-.01	-.44	**.47**	**3.08**	**-.17**	**-2.15**	-.39	-1.72	.04	.50
Referral rate	**.31**	**2.03**	-.06	-.47	**-.05**	**-2.55**	**-.32**	**-2.56**	-.02	-.56	-.14	-.78	-.04	-.74
No parent/attorney at court							.19	1.29	**-.07**	**-2.16**	-.12	-.53	.03	.55
Detained							**.82**	**6.60**	**.10**	**3.76**	**2.14**	**11.33**	**.50**	**4.57**
Lambda									**-.55**	**-2.53**			.68	1.93
Chi-square	515.90		322.54		37.50		336.66		188.95		452.93		310.54	
p	.00		.00		.00		.00		.00		.00		.00	
Log likelihood	-594.09		-847.38		-219.49		-1,034.70		-710.82		-547.42		-434.79	
n	1,752		1,752		1,406		1,738		1,279		1,738		907	

a. Significant factors appear in bold print; b. The selectivity bias term (lambda) was estimated using intake as the first-stage equation; c. Lambda was estimated using petition as the first-stage equation; d. Lambda was estimated using adjudication as the first-stage equation.

that nine of these same variables, including status of blacks, achieve significance. As shown in the corrected model, results from the Heckman method show a statistically insignificant lambda (–.091, with B/SE = –1.527), which indicates that unmeasured factors that raise the probability of intake do not lead to either a higher or lower probability of a petition. In this model, with the added control for factors associated with intake, only the rate of referral significantly affected petition outcome, with lower rates more likely to result in formal petitions.

Differences between the original and corrected models for adjudication outcome also are shown, although race did not directly affect court outcome in either model. According to the first model, delinquency was substantiated more often for youths who were detained; had prior records; had youth-related and/or school attendance problems; had multiple offenses, with circumstances that indicated likely involvement or that aggravated the offense; were referred from the main police department; were in suburban or urban areas; and/or were in courts with lower caseloads. The Heckman method for controlling selection bias from petition to the adjudication outcome shows a statistically significant lambda (–.533, with B/SE = –2.525), which indicates that the unobserved factors that lead to petition have a negative effect on the probability of adjudication. Factors associated with adjudication in the model, including the correction for the problem, were detention, offense circumstances, referrals from sources other than the main police departments, no parent and/or attorney at the court hearing, and nonsuburban jurisdictions. The direction of their effect reversed for the latter three factors, and the absence of a race effect remained in the corrected model.

For the original model, B/SE ratios provoke confidence that residential placement is more likely for white youths and influenced by detention at an earlier stage, prior record, a drug-related offense, youth problems, multiple offenses, and poor family. For the corrected model, race is not a factor, but otherwise the criteria remain significant in distinguishing cases with residential placement outcomes, and the direction of lambda suggests that unobserved factors that influence adjudication may similarly effect disposition.

Race-Specific Models

Those *B/SEs* identified as statistically significant in each of the race-specific models are identified in Table 5.2.[14] The three factors consistently associated with intake were multiple offenses, prior records, and suburban locations. Additionally important for formal processing of white youths were family problems, person-related offenses, poverty, and school problems. For black youths, other factors were main police department referrals, drug-related offenses, age, and higher referral rates. For Latinos, intake also was associated with school and/or personal problems, drug-related offenses, and main police department referrals.

Only multiple offenses consistently generated satisfactory *t* values in the original race-specific models of petition. For whites, petitions appear influenced by prior record, multiple offenses, suburban and urban courts, offenses against persons, poor families, and recorded school problems. Petitions also are apt to be filed more simply based on suburban jurisdictions, referrals from the main police department of the county, and multiple offenses for blacks; and referrals from the main police department of the county, multiple offenses, and youth problems for Latinos.

Models including the correction for potential bias showed that the unobserved factors that lead to intake have an inverse effect on the probability that petitions are filed for cases involving white youths (lambda = −.816, *B/SE* = 2.557). Given the consideration of other factors at intake, family problems added to the likelihood of petitions for white youths. Sample selection bias was not problematic for petition outcomes of cases involving minorities. In the corrected model for blacks, smaller referral rates, urban courts, circumstances of the offense, and referrals from the main police department assisted in cases having formal petitions. The model showed that occurrences of petitions for Latino youths were no better than chance.

In the original models, independent tests of adjudication by race showed that the fewest factors "explained" adjudication among Latino youths. These factors were detention, prior record, and school and personal problems. Slightly more factors entered the model of adjudication for black youths. In that model, detention,

TABLE 5.2 Summary of Significant Factors Affecting Juvenile Justice Outcomes by Race: Original Models and Models Corrected for Sample Selection Bias

	Intake Outcome	Petition Outcome		Adjudication Outcome		Placement Outcome	
	Original	*Original*	*Corrected*[a]	*Original*	*Corrected*[b]	*Original*	*Corrected*[c]
Factors affecting white youths							
	No. of offenses	No. of offenses	Family problem	Detained	Lambda	Detained	Detained
	Prior record	Prior record	Lambda	Prior record		Prior record	No. of offenses
	Suburban area	Suburban area		No. of offenses		No. of offenses	Family problem
	Family problem	Urban area		Youth problem			Prior record
	Person offense	Person offense		Drug offense			
	Poor family	Poor family		Urban area			
	School problem	School problem		School problem			
				Suburban area			
				Referral rate			
Chi-square	254.47	181.97	30.41	182.27	81.46	174.27	120.69
p	.00	.00	.00	.00	.00	.00	.00
Log likelihood	−249.67	−312.07	−19.47	−342.38	−218.49	−148.37	−116.73
n	630	630	447	627	414	627	295
Factors affecting black youths							
	Suburban area	Suburban area	Referral rate	Detained	Detained	Detained	Detained
	No. of offenses	Main police	Urban area	Circumstances	Circumstances	Prior record	Poor family
	Prior record	No. of offenses	Circumstances	Suburban area	Prior record	Poor family	
	Main police		Main police	Prior record			
	Drug offense			Youth problem			
	Age			Age			
	Referral rate						

114

	Intake Outcome	Petition Outcome		Adjudication Outcome		Placement Outcome	
	Original	Original	Corrected[a]	Original	Corrected[b]	Original	Corrected[c]

Factors affecting black youths (continued)

	Intake Outcome	Petition Outcome		Adjudication Outcome		Placement Outcome	
Chi-square	141.56	105.08	32.94	138.18	83.34	181.23	113.64
p	.00	.00	.00	.00	.00	.00	.00
Log likelihood	-185.08	-289.95	-104.60	-374.25	-279.88	-185.57	-160.31
n	650	650	557	643	501	643	349

Factors affecting Latino youths

	Intake Outcome	Petition Outcome		Adjudication Outcome		Placement Outcome	
Factors	No. of offenses School problem Youth problem Suburban area Drug offense Prior record Main police	Main police No. of offenses Youth problem		Detained Prior record School problem Youth problem	Person offense	Prior record Detained Drug offense	
Chi-square	131.55	53.18	12.16	68.90	65.62	122.76	104.72
p	.00	.00	.66	.00	.00	.00	.00
Log likelihood	-125.22	-222.31	-70.24	-286.34	-191.20	-190.23	-133.88
n	472	472	402	468	364	468	263

a. The selectivity bias term (lambda) was estimated using intake as the first-stage equation.
b. Lambda was estimated using petition as the first-stage equation.
c. Lambda was estimated using adjudication as the first-stage equation.

circumstances of the event, suburban courts, prior record, youth problems, and age had greater weight on substantiated delinquency. The largest number of factors affected adjudication of white youths. These factors were detention, prior record, multiple offenses, youth problems, drug-related offenses, urban courts, school trouble, suburban courts, and county rate of referral. In the corrected model for whites, the effects shown for adjudication are absent when the control for petition is added. In addition, the unobserved factors that lead to formal petitions for white youths have the reverse effect on the probability of adjudication. Significant effects remained for detention, offense circumstances, and prior records for blacks and for person-related crime among Latinos.

The original model for only the white youths identified detention, prior record, and multiple offenses as those factors that contribute to placement outcomes. The model for black youths also identified detention and prior record, but found poor families important instead of multiple offenses. Prior record and detention also influenced residential placement of Latino youths, as did drug-related offenses, but no multiple charges or poverty. In the corrected models, no factors helped distinguish the placement of Latino youths; detention and prior records made the outcome more likely for black youths; and detention, multiple offenses, family problems, and prior records affected the outcome for white youths.

For the second assessment of the logit results, the proportion of cases accurately predicted by the models is tested according to the true distribution of each outcome. Formal processing beyond intake screening occurred for 81% of the total sample, including 71% of the whites, 87% of the blacks, and 86% of the Latinos. The probability that the models accurately predicted these distributions was assessed (tables not shown). The models each err in classification about 20% of the time, but seem equally successful at predicting which cases moved forward and which were dismissed or handled informally. An additional 127 cases in the sample (33 whites, 56 blacks, and 38 Latinos) left the system at the petition stage. Petitions were filed for 74% of the total sample, including 66% of the whites, 78% of the blacks, and 78% of the Latinos. Classification error occurred in between 23% and 29% of the cases. The model for blacks was better able to classify petitioned cases (86%) than those that were dismissed or handled informally (48%). Both petitions and absence of petitions were approximately equally well classified in each of the other models.

Delinquency was substantiated by the court for 52% of the total sample, including 47% of the whites, 54% of the blacks, and 56% of the Latinos. The model fared better for white youths (73% correctly classified) and less well for Latino youths (66% correct). The better fit for white youths was the result of greater success by the model with classifying the absence of adjudication, rather than cases adjudicated. This difference in accurate classification was not as great among other models. Out-of-home placement within either public or private facilities was experienced by 16% of the total sample, including 12% of the white youths, 15% of the black youths, and 23% of the Latino youths.[15] The models correctly classified between 73% and 82% of the cases.

Models of Detention

The prominence achieved by detention in nearly all models of adjudication and out-of-home placement suggests specific concern for this decision stage. Detention could occur immediately on referral to court or subsequently until adjudication. Detention was primarily within secure confinement facilities, less often in shelters, and readily accessible to every court.[16] Among the sample cases, 37% were detained, including 23% of the white, 41% of the black, and 51% of the Latino youths. Correct classification by the models did not differ much by race. Among the total sample, the risk of detention was greater for black and Latino youths with a prior record who had a drug-related offense;[17] an offense against a person; multiple offenses; had personal, family, and/or school problems; were in a suburban court;[18] were referred from the main police department of the county; and who were older. Results from the total model indicate that, given similar other factors, detention was more common for Latino youths, followed by black youths (Table 5.3).

Detention models within each race group showed different factors with satisfactory *t* values. Prior record and multiple offenses

TABLE 5.3 Factors Affecting Detention

Factors	Total B	B/SE	White B	B/SE	Black B	B/SE	Latino B	B/SE
Constant	−5.27	−7.33	−4.85	−2.98	−3.60	−2.58	−9.04	−6.27
Number of offenses	.16	5.29	.24	3.89	.13	2.75	.19	2.94
Drug offense	.85	5.59	−.10	−.33	1.57	5.83	1.11	3.91
Person offense	.43	3.21	.06	.22	.54	2.37	.89	3.43
Circumstances	.07	1.35	−.05	−.50	.08	.05	.22	2.07
Prior record	.49	9.12	.44	4.16	.69	7.40	.29	2.97
Youth problem	.25	3.43	.27	2.16	.01	.08	.50	3.46
School problem	.24	2.13	.24	1.18	−.02	−.10	.42	2.11
Family problem	.30	4.52	.41	3.15	.47	4.23	−.01	−.04
Absent father	.09	.69	.09	.37	.17	.77	−.20	−.75
Poor family	.03	.22	.37	1.14	−.40	−1.79	.18	.75
Black	.73	4.68						
Latino	1.01	5.97						
Sex	.06	.34	.17	.56	−.25	−.87	.29	.67
Age	.10	2.49	.06	.80	−.02	−.29	.27	3.52
Main police	.36	2.64	.34	1.28	.27	1.26	.37	1.30
Referral rate	.26	2.00	.24	.90	.05	.24	.66	2.54
Urban area	.02	.06	−.31	−.42	.84	1.40	−1.10	−1.38
Suburban area	.66	3.89	.75	2.54	.79	2.93	−.17	−.38
English second language							−.08	−.33
Chi-square		149.87		124.82		205.27		149.87
p		.00		.00		.00		.00
Log likelihood		−901.46		−276.67		−333.08		−249.42
n		1,738		627		643		468

a. Significant factors appear in bold print.

were consistently related to detention. Among white youths, fewer factors affected detention. They included prior record, multiple offenses, and family and personal problems. Detention was a greater risk for black youths with prior records, drug- and/or person-related offenses, multiple charges, family problems, and in suburban courts. Detention among Latino youths was influenced by drug-related offenses, person-related offenses, circumstances suggesting probable involvement or victim injury, prior record, multiple charges, age, youth problems, school attendance problems, and county referral rate.

DISCUSSION OF THE RESULTS

The issue of differential treatment in juvenile justice is complicated, and, as our findings indicate, empirical tests of the situation also are not straightforward. Of course, research can provide valuable assistance in determining whether race is statistically related to outcome when other associated criteria are controlled. Conditional relationships also can be clarified by statistical analysis. Race-specific models can help identify whether the other factors associated with outcome relate differently depending on race. Thus race effects that occur only under certain conditions of other variables can be identified. In this study, disparities between white, black, and Latino youths and different criteria associated with their juvenile justice outcomes were shown in the results of both types of analyses. Even when multiple methods compare favorably, however, explanations for racial disparity in juvenile justice outcome are not so clear.

Minority youths were overrepresented among referrals to juvenile court in 1989. Descriptive findings of this study suggested that this initial overrepresentation did not increase at stages of greater penetration in the system. This does not mitigate the fact that blacks constituted the majority of those detained and in out-of-home placements. As the doctrine of *parens patriae* dictates and as many juvenile justice experts agree, juvenile justice intervention may serve the best interest of youths. It follows, therefore, that some may argue minority overrepresentation indicates that the interests of minority children differ from those of whites and that the state may be better suited for the role of parent to minorities. They argue, in essence, that greater rates of detention and placement of minorities may actually benefit the nonwhite youths. The mandate from OJJDP to study the situation and growing concern that juvenile justice has adopted a more punitive orientation suggest otherwise. To resolve this issue, it is necessary to compare the experiences of white and minority youths who have similar cases.

Results for the total sample show that both black and Latino youths were more likely than whites with similar offenses, prior records, and school problems to have their cases formally processed, especially in nonrural court settings. It also is clear that detention of

Latino and black youths was more common than detention of similarly situation whites. Minority status seemed to be accorded more
importance at detention than even person-related offenses; any
personal, family, or school problem; location; referral source; or
court caseload. The race effect with detention and the subsequent
importance of detention suggest that an indirect race effect also may
result in adjudication and placement more often for minorities, and
especially for blacks. Based on initial findings that Latinos are more
often sent to public facilities, Latinos and blacks are more often sent
to private residential care, and whites are more often recipients of
privately run group homes and drug and alcohol treatment, concern is underscored that perhaps de facto racial segregation occurs
at placement.

In addition, the results show that offense-related, system-
related, and social history factors are accorded different weight depending on race. For example, the main police agency of the county
and court caseload have a significant influence on formal processing
of cases involving minorities. Suburban and, to a lesser extent,
urban courts more often formally process white and black youths.
Circumstances of the offense and poverty also merit greater attention for blacks than other youths. White youths are more apt than
minorities to proceed in the system when they have family problems. These results are fairly direct. It is among their findings at
subsequent stages within juvenile justice that the interpretation of
race bias becomes muddied.

Similar results between the original logit models and those
including the Heckman correction for sample selection bias lend
support for their veracity. It is when the findings depart from one
another that the interpretation becomes more difficult. For example,
if the original model is true, then black youths seem more apt to
have petitions filed than other youths from similar courts with
comparable number of offenses, prior records, and school problems.
If the model adjusted for factors at intake and the cases that exited
the system is preferable, however, then filing of petitions seems
merely the result of smaller caseloads in some counties. Another
example is residential placement. The original model suggests that
white youths more than similar minorities are removed from their
homes, whereas the corrected model implies no difference by race.

We cannot resolve this methodological dilemma based on the results of this study alone. Rather, these findings can contribute to the debate on what strategy is best for measuring the cumulative process of any justice system. Although we consider it theoretically meaningful to distinguish between outcomes for cases available at the decision stage and cases that have already exited the system, the Heckman procedure for doing this is not without its problems. For example, the cumulative effects between all decision stages cannot be examined because the method is designed only for two stages. In addition, even discussion about econometric aspects associated with the technique by those engaged in labor force participation research, the topic for which this procedure was ideally aimed, suggests that rather than solve the selection problem, this method trades one assumption for another (Manski, 1989). Other techniques may be found that are better able to control for the sample selection problem. Alternately, judgments may conclude that each stage merits its own assessment, regardless of preceding decisions or factors affecting them. We consider it imperative that debate of this issue become more active within criminology.

RECOMMENDATIONS FOR JUVENILE JUSTICE

In addition to stimulating discussion within the research community, the knowledge gained from this study can inform and provide foundation for policy debate. Of course, the limitations of both data and estimation techniques should be recognized. Many factors known by administrators were not reflected in case files and, therefore, were not available as variables in the study. Many obstacles encountered in other research were overcome, but other difficulties existed for the analyses and interpretation of statistical findings. The results of this study, therefore, offer no absolute solution to the problem of racial disparity in Pennsylvania, but should serve as source for discussion about the countless possibilities that exist for the future. Several suggestions for modification of juvenile justice policy are offered for consideration.

Early stages of juvenile justice should be targeted for additional examination. The greater effect of police referrals on the restrictive outcomes of minorities suggests that the police effect penetration in the system. The rate at which youths are referred to court may provide insight to this process. Are higher rates of referral among minorities the result of behavioral differences among youths, police reactions to more calls for service, or patrolling targeted disproportionately at neighborhoods with greater number of minority residents? The power wielded by police from departments responsible for referrals at a higher rate than other sources, and presumably those in closest proximity to the court, also should be investigated. Police concerns for public safety via detention may be shared more often by intake officers when police officers are familiar. The alternative strategies for preventing absconding and maintaining public safety in other police jurisdictions should be compared. Departmental referral policies should be identified to determine whether large departments tend to refer all cases, whereas smaller departments informally divert less serious cases. Evidence of the latter policy should be examined for criteria associated with race. Professionalism in presentation on police reports also should be compared.

Appropriate use of secure confinement, shelter release, home confinement, and outright release should be specified in policy. Use of detention as punishment before adjudication must not occur. The more appropriate use of detention and alternatives to secure confinement would free up space and create opportunities for treatment for youths most in need at this early stage. Greater opportunities for use of diversion and informal adjustment for minorities also should be considered in light of the findings of formal outcomes related to race at early stages. The number of shelter care facilities, foster care homes, and diversion programs also should increase statewide. The doctrine of *parens patriae* is undermined and problems created for criminal justice when suitable community-based solutions are not found for minority youths but do exist for white youths.

Criteria used by individual intake officers should be evaluated to determine whether factors that may more often negatively affect minorities are accorded importance. Racially neutral criteria in detention decisions should be established, especially in view of the findings that both Latino and black youths are differentially detained when the same is not true of white youths. Cultural bias, including value judgments not based on fact (such as notions that minority parents may not provide adequate supervision for their children or that certain neighborhoods are not conducive to growing up well), must not influence detention. If criteria may affect minorities indirectly, their use should be abandoned.

Policy standards should designate situations in appropriate outcomes for formal processing, informal supervision, diversion, and outright dismissal. Structured guidelines ensure greater consistency in outcome and are capable of reducing racial disparity. More equitable outcomes in juvenile justice will lead to greater public confidence in the system. Individual discretion is reduced, as is accountability (or blame) attributed to individual judges or probation officers. When standards for intake and detention are considered racially, and sexually, bias free, efforts should be undertaken to ensure their statewide use. This may be achieved through education of their importance, followed by voluntary implementation, or by administrative mandate. Guidelines need not be mandatory, as commonly feared, but can allow for individual consideration of unique situations. Standards also can be modified with great frequency and ease to accommodate the evolution of juvenile justice.

It also may be wise to promote the hiring of personnel with training and life experiences from other countries, of diverse races, religions, and languages. The hiring of more minorities will not in itself ensure diversity in experience or sensitivity to race differences, although their value as positive role models serves to recommend employment policies to encourage greater representation of minorities in juvenile court positions working with youths and families. It is important that personnel with knowledge and experience in cultural diversity be employed not only as intake and probation officers but also in positions of administration and policy making.

Periodic training workshops should be conducted for all juvenile justice personnel. Participation should be mandatory and supported by administration. Greater motivation must be provided to juvenile court judges to increase their interest in juvenile justice. Judges must be called on to assume the leadership role in educating juvenile court personnel to sensitivity in race differences. Decision makers must be trained to distinguish poverty from parental neglect, and to recognize the family values and structures that may differ from their own. Desensitization of stereotypes based on race and sex is critical for equity in juvenile justice.

Provisions should be made for systemic feedback of case outcomes. This is very important because early stage outcomes affect later stage outcomes, and persons involved at early stages are not necessarily those present at later stages. It is beneficial for representatives at each stage to recognize their role in juvenile justice and be familiar throughout with outcomes by race, sex, and court. The absence of routinely available feedback mechanisms also precludes professional growth and is a shortcoming in any organization.

Finally, policies must exist to promote equity and ensure personnel and youths who encounter juvenile justice intervention, as well as their families, that discrimination is not tolerated. A mechanism should be in place to ensure a system response to complaints of individual racial and sexual bias. The policy may allow for self-monitoring, periodic surveys of personnel and referred youths, or an official procedure for investigation and response to complaints. The administration of juvenile justice must be assured of an investigation and a response when personnel make inappropriate comments or actions directed at minorities. These policies will increase awareness and sensitivity about cultural bias, as well as affect professionalism and individual accountability within the system.

As many realize, policy changes tend not to happen quickly, and the evolution of juvenile justice is no exception. Obviously, some initiatives are suited to more rapid implementation than others. It would be valuable for leaders in juvenile justice to recognize that the problem of racial bias is not straightforward and attempt, first, to accomplish small and more immediate change. The success of an initial effort should allow support from more broadly based constituencies to be obtained more easily. It is important to institutionalize the objective of juvenile justice free from racial and sexual bias as a long-term goal and pursue a policy agenda explicitly aimed at reaching that goal.

NOTES

1. Urban counties are Philadelphia and Allegheny; suburban counties are Chester, Delaware, and Montgomery; more rural counties are Beaver, Berks, Dauphin, Erie, Lancaster, Lehigh, Mercer, Northampton, and York. The suburban courts are contiguous to Philadelphia, including primarily more affluent bedroom communities. The more rural courts also included counties with cities smaller than Philadelphia and Pittsburgh.

2. Handling missing data in this way may "avoid loss of statistical power from fewer cases if data are missing randomly and capitalize on the information inherent in the traits present (coded 1) in the variable of interest and on information available on other variables" (Cohen & Cohen, 1983, p. 284).

3. Lambda is inversely related to the probability of being included in the sample; if the probability of being in the sample is one then there is no sample selection and lambda is zero.

4. The 1,797 study cases were weighted to approximate the distribution of a representative sample of the population rather than the actual sample with some categories of race, court, and offense type oversampled. The procedure involved assignment of weights to the sample cases in each cell relative to the number of cases that might have been observed had a representative sample been chosen [(cell population × cell sample)/total population]. Weighting resulted in 1,982 cases estimating a representative sample, which was 34 fewer than expected and due to rounding of decimals in the computation.

5. A summary index of youth problems was computed with each case receiving 1 point each for alcohol-related, drug-related, or mental health/retardation problem (excluding learning disabilities) noted in the case file. It was possible for a youth to have between zero and three problems. Each trait is accorded equal weight in the index because there is no reason to believe that each decision maker adopts the same relative consideration of traits.

6. Suspensions/expulsions and school dropouts were given 1 point each for a range of zero to two school problems.

7. Four pieces of information were considered best able to characterize prior juvenile record. In a cumulative index, 1 point was given for a (one or more) prior adjudication. Adjudication, rather than prior referrals, restricted prior record to previously substantiated delinquency cases. This restriction was lessened somewhat with the addition of another point for youths whose first delinquency referral had occurred before age 13. This age cutoff was based on the distribution of cases and identified one fifth of the prior delinquents as those youths with the earliest onset of court referral, a concept noted in the literature as important in juvenile justice outcomes. Recent prior court involvement, especially in the form of cases currently pending in court or youths presently under court supervision is important; consequently, each of these traits received 1 point. Thus the prior juvenile record index had a range of 0 to 4.

8. Data on the following five family-related problems were available: parental substance abuse; a parent with known criminal record; a deceased parent; siblings with court records; and a current dependency, abuse, or neglect file on the referred youth. Only one Latino youth experienced all five problems.

9. A poor family is one with known annual wages of less than $8,000 or no income (coded 1) and distinguished from families with higher wages or unknown family income (0). The categories of income are crude, but considered fairly accurate, especially for distinguishing welfare recipients from families with income because of state policies for acquisition of child care and medicaid dollars for indigent youths under court-ordered supervision. Information on family income was known for 65% to 86% of the youths, and race was not related to the missing cases.

10. This classification identifies any such charge among the three most serious charges of the current referral or the single most serious prior referral. The stratified sampling by offense category contributed to the representation of offenses against persons and property and those that are drug related at the referral stage, but not to specific statutes. Statute violations involving drug sales and cocaine possession were more common among minorities, and marijuana possession was more common among whites.

11. An index of circumstances was computed to reflect all available factors that might enhance the likelihood that the referred youth had committed the offense or escalated the severity of the crime. These traits, accorded 1 point each, were as follows: admissions by the youth of his or her involvement, evidence of the crime in the possession of the youth at the time of referral, a witness to the offense, involvement of at least one co-offender, and a victim required medical attention or worse (sample cases involved 4 deaths). Scores for the event circumstances index range from 0 to 5, with higher scores representing more likelihood of the youth's involvement and gravity of offense.

12. Offenses at referral, petition, and adjudication stages were recorded in case files according to Pennsylvania statute number. It was not common practice in 1989 for case files to distinguish felony and misdemeanor violations, although this information may well have been available to probation officers and judges. Several statute numbers in Pennsylvania may be classified as either felony or misdemeanor offenses. These ambiguous statutes represent the most serious charge at referral for roughly one third of the sample cases. Thus felony/misdemeanor distinctions would be misspecified for so many cases as to be problematic.

13. Forty-five cases for which age was unknown were deleted from the analyses.

14. Analyses for these models included all the variables shown in Table 5.1, as well as English as the first language for Latino youths, but are summarized here for ease of presentation.

15. Public facilities were the more common experience for Latino youths who received placement, shared with black youths for private residential facilities; however, white youths were more often than minorities sent to group homes and drug treatment programs. When the type of facility was compared among the placed youths, the distribution was the following: public facilities—17% of white, 19% of black, and 29% of Latino youths; private residential—24% of white, 31% of black, and 36% of Latino youths; privately run group homes or foster care facilities—25% of white, 16% of black, and 8% of Latino youths; and drug and alcohol treatment centers—16% of white, 4% of black, and 11% of Latino youths.

16. Thirteen counties had local court-operated detention facilities; one county used a nearby facility in an adjacent county. Among those detained, the most common experience was detention for only 1 day by youths in each racial group. The average length of detention was 18 days for white youths, 21 days for black youths,

and 20 days for Latino youths. The range in length of their detention was 1 to 87 days for white, 98 days for black, and 140 days for Latino youths.

17. Bivariate comparisons of detention by race independently for certain drug-related offense statutes showed that minorities always were more often detained than whites, even for marijuana possession, which more often involved white youths.

18. Concern that detention in suburban courts involves many youths from Philadelphia is not supported. Of the 87 nonresidents with referrals to suburban courts, only 25 were detained.

6

Racial Disparities in the Confinement of Juveniles
Effects of Crime and Community Social Structure on Punishment

GEORGE S. BRIDGES

DARLENE J. CONLEY

RODNEY L. ENGEN

TOWNSAND PRICE-SPRATLEN

Despite extensive writing and research on the administration of juvenile justice, the relationships between race, criminal behavior, and racial and ethnic disparities in the confinement of juveniles are poorly understood. Although studies generally agree that minority youths are punished for crimes at disproportionately high rates given their number in the general population (Bishop & Frazier, 1992; Bridges, Conley, Beretta, & Engen, 1993; Kempf et al., 1990), studies disagree about the precise causes of disproportionality. A

AUTHORS' NOTE: The research reported in this chapter was supported with a grant from the Governor's Juvenile Justice Advisory Committee of Washington State. We would like to acknowledge the assistance of Charis Kubrin in completing the manuscript.

officials to manage effectively the heavy flow of cases through the legal process.

These rules have the effect of minimizing the discretionary decision making of justice officials. Prosecutors and judges must handle cases and make decisions according to established guidelines and rules rather than by personal rules of thumb, feelings about defendants or victims, or their perceptions of community crime problems. Accordingly, capricious decision making against youths of color accused of crimes is less likely in urban than rural courts. In rural courts, the status characteristics of youths such as their race or ethnic origin are more likely to influence the outcomes of criminal cases adjudicated in juvenile courts (Feld, 1991; Pope & Feyerherm, 1990a, 1990b).

Other sociologists argue, however, that urbanization may have a different effect. In many urban areas, minority populations are segregated into ghettos and slums. As minority populations increase in these core urban areas, officials' perceptions of threat may also increase. As perceived threat increases, law enforcement officials may adopt informal policies or practices of evaluating criminal cases to assist in controlling the crime problem and increased minority threat (Bridges et al., 1987). These policies may produce racial disparities in the handling of criminal cases if they screen or target cases using factors that are related, even remotely, to race. Thus the concentration of minority populations in urban areas may actually exacerbate racial and ethnic disparities in the punishment and confinement of youths. By escalating fear among law enforcement and court officials, increased urbanization may actually increase the likelihood that prosecutors target minority youths for surveillance and control.

In sum, the role of community social structure in racial and ethnic disparities in the punishment of juveniles is unclear. Few studies have examined the effects of the characteristics of areas and their impacts on the differential processing of youths through the administration of juvenile justice. At least four aspects of community social structure are hypothesized to influence confinement disparities. The first is the rate of serious and violent crime. Confinement rates for youths of color will be higher in counties and jurisdictions where those youths have higher involvement in crime.

Furthermore, minority confinement rates may also be higher in those counties where violent and serious crime rates are generally high, regardless of racial or ethnic differences in rates of arrest. The second is the degree of minority concentration in the population—that is, the percentage of persons of color. Although the direction of the relationship is uncertain, disparities in confinement between white and minority youths will be strongly related to the percentage of minorities in the population. Third, the degree of economic inequality between whites and minorities in areas will influence white and minority rates of confinement. Disparities in confinement will be greatest in those communities where levels of economic inequality between whites and nonwhites are greatest. Thus youths of color will be confined at significantly higher rates than will white youths in communities where they are most heavily represented among the very poor. Finally, the degree of urbanization of communities will influence confinement disparities. If urbanization actually increases bureaucratization of the juvenile court, then disparities in confinement between whites and minorities will be lower than in rural areas. Conversely, if urbanization results in the concentration of minority populations in core urban areas, disparities in confinement between whites and minorities will be higher than in rural areas.

METHOD

Data and Measures

The study collected data on crime patterns, the administration of juvenile justice, the social standing of racial and ethnic groups, the minority concentration of the population, and other aspects of the demographic composition of all counties in Washington State for 1990, in addition to data on the race and ethnicity of juveniles confined in state juvenile correctional facilities for 1990 and 1991.[1] The measures constructed from these data—aggregated to the county level—provided indicators of (a) white and nonwhite rates of confinement; (b) aspects of county social structure; and (c) county crime, referral, and court workload levels.[2] For each county, the white and minority confinement rates were calculated by initially dividing the number of white and minority youths confined in the state's juvenile correctional facilities by the total number of white or minority youths (i.e., under age 18) in the county population, and then multiplying by 1,000. These confinement rates therefore represent the number of white and minority youths per 1,000 in the county population that were confined to the Washington State Division of Juvenile Rehabilitation, and the rates allow us to make comparisons between districts whose populations vary greatly in size (see Bridges & Crutchfield, 1988; Bridges et al., 1987; Duncan, 1966; Liska & Chamlin, 1984).[3]

Three measures of county social structure were included in the analysis. The first, percentage nonwhite, reflects the degree of minority concentration in the county population. Second, a measure of urbanization was included—the percentage of the county population residing in a central city. Third, the ratio of the percentage of minorities on public assistance to the percentage of whites on public assistance was included as a measure of the economic deprivation of whites relative to minorities.

The analysis also incorporated data on county crime rates, juvenile referral rates, and court workloads. Violent crime (i.e., homicide, rape, robbery, and assault) rates for each county were included in the analysis to ascertain whether juvenile confinement disparities are associated with county levels of violent crime. White and minority referral rates were also included in the analysis to examine the relationships between race-specific referral and confinement rates. This latter measure was included because many writers have argued that racial differences in imprisonment and confinement are almost solely attributable to racial disparities in offending (Blumstein, 1982; Hindelang, 1978; Langan, 1985). Finally, a measure of workload for the juvenile courts in each county was included in the analysis. The workload of each county's juvenile court was measured as the ratio of annual juvenile referrals to the number of juvenile judges. Levels of workload typically influence the degree of bureaucratization of courts and court administration. Courts with particularly heavy workloads are more bureaucratized than are courts with less heavy workloads (Blumberg, 1967; Farrell & Swigert, 1978). As a result, courts with heavy workloads rely more on formal rules of procedure and allocate scarce resources to cases defined by established priorities or guidelines. Because judges in these courts typically are afforded less discretion, their decisions are less likely to be influenced by a defendant's social status or other extralegal characteristics of cases.

Counties were chosen as the unit of analysis primarily because they correspond to the legal jurisdiction of the juvenile court in Washington State. Counties typically have their own sets of juvenile justice officials, including a juvenile court, juvenile probation officers, prosecutors specializing in juvenile cases, and judges who handle only juvenile crimes. Furthermore, each county has its own rules of criminal procedure pertaining to the handling of juvenile cases, above and beyond the rules specified by state laws of criminal procedure.

Another reason for using counties as the unit of analysis is that aggregate rates of juvenile confinement are most likely to be sensitive to minority concentration and levels of crime and arrest at the county level. The county court is the center of the legal response to juvenile crime. Criminal cases involving juveniles flow from different municipalities to the county juvenile court, with the prosecutors and judges—in some counties a single prosecutor and a single judge—administering punishments for crimes by juveniles across the entire county. Because prosecutors and judges are elected officials, they are particularly sensitive to the pressures of county problems and community social pressures (Bridges et al., 1987; Eisenstein & Jacob, 1977; Myers & Talarico, 1987).

Interviews and qualitative data were also collected in conjunction with the study. Juvenile judges, prosecutors, probation officers, and law enforcement officers were interviewed in 6 of the state's 39 counties with the largest minority populations. The interviews focused on problems of youths, crime, and juvenile justice in their communities. Furthermore, project staff completed approximately 100 hours of observation of police-citizen interaction, participating in patrol shifts with police officers in each of the six districts.

Model

There is little evidence in prior research on the relationships between crime, social structure, and disparities in the confinement of juvenile offenders. Few previous studies have examined the relationship between community characteristics and white and minority rates of confinement. Thus it is unclear whether aspects of community social structure are actually related to disparities in the confinement of youths and, if they are related, whether they have differential effects on the confinement of white and minority youths. Of concern here is whether each aspect of social structure increases or decreases minorities' chances of confinement, increases or decreases whites' chances of confinement, or has no influence on either group's chances of confinement.

Figure 6.1 exhibits the model used in the analysis. The figure orders the hypothesized causal relationships between aggregate confinement rates for juveniles, juvenile referral rates, juvenile court caseload, rates of serious and violent crime, urbanization, and the concentration of the minority population. To assess the effects of county social structure, crime rates, and race-specific referral rates on disparities in confinement, separate regression analyses were performed on white and minority confinement rates and on the ratio of minority to white confinement rates. By comparing the unstandardized regression weights across separate models for whites and minorities, it is possible to ascertain whether the structural correlates of confinement have differential effects on white and minority rates of confinement (see Myers & Talarico, 1987).

The analysis employed logarithmic transformations of all of the variables specified in Figure 6.1. The logarithmic transformations were used for two reasons. First, by converting the variables with logarithms, the effects of "outlier" cases in the analysis are reduced. The transformation has the effect of reducing the amount of variation in any variable attributable to extreme values associated with individual counties. Second, the transformation has the effect of shifting the analysis from a simple additive model to a multiplicative model. This shift transforms the analysis from one based on a model wherein the estimated confinement rate in any county may be greater than zero when the arrest or referral rate in that county is a zero (i.e., due to the intercept term) to a model in which the confinement rate will be zero when the arrest rate is zero. Previous studies have found that the multiplicative model typically adds explanatory power to analyses of areal characteristics and rates of

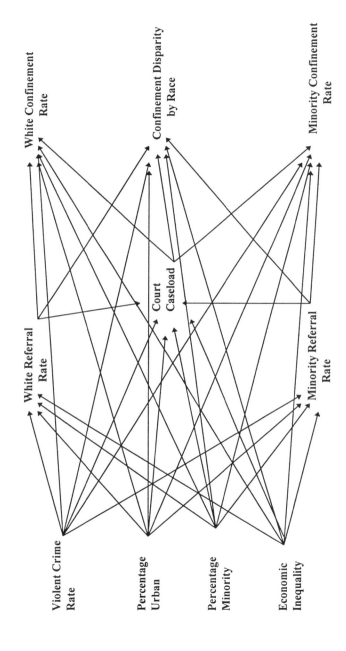

Figure 6.1. Factors Influencing Juvenile Referral, Confinement, and Racial Disparity: Theoretical Model

imprisonment or confinement (see Bridges & Crutchfield, 1988; Bridges et al., 1987).

FINDINGS

Table 6.1 shows the rates of confinement of white and minority youths and the ratio of minority to white confinement rates across Washington counties. There is considerable variation in confinement rates between counties and also between the white and minority confinement rates within counties. White confinement rates range from 0 to 2.16 per 1,000 in the population and average .96, whereas minority confinement rates range from 0 to 4.62 per 1,000, averaging 1.46. The ratio in confinement rates ranges from 0:1 in counties where no minority youths were committed to juvenile institutions, to a ratio of 5.7:1. On average, minority youths are confined at a rate 1.6 times that of white youths.

As would be expected given the wide variation in the confinement rates and ratios, white and minority confinement rates are not strongly correlated ($r = .25$, $p = .17$). This suggests that separate analyses of the rates are necessary—factors influencing the confinement rate of minority youths may not necessarily be related to the confinement of white youths and vice versa. Furthermore, the disparity between white and minority confinement rates, as reflected in the confinement ratio, is strongly and positively related to the minority confinement rate ($r = .91$, $p = .00$) but is not significantly related with the white confinement rate ($r = -.14$, $p = .47$). This suggests that the variation in racial disparity may be due primarily to differences between counties in the confinement of minority youths.

Figure 6.2 summarizes the findings in the form of a trimmed path model. Tables 6.2 and 6.3 present the results (unstandardized and standardized, respectively) of regressions predicting the white and minority referral rates, juvenile court caseload, white and minority confinement rates, and the ratio of minority to white confinement rates. The discussion below describes the most noteworthy findings.

TABLE 6.1 District Rates of Confinement and Disparity by Race:
Washington State

County	White Confinement Rate	Minority Confinement Rate	Disparity Ratio
Adams	1.90	.00	.95
Asotin/Garfield	.78	2.93	3.75
Benton/Franklin	.66	1.73	2.64
Chelan	.86	.00	.00
Clallam	.50	.00	.00
Clark	1.06	1.37	1.29
Cowlitz	1.31	1.11	.84
Douglas	1.11	.00	.00
Ferry	.67	.00	.00
Grant	1.12	.65	.58
Grays Harbor	.84	1.59	1.89
Island	.83	.91	1.09
Jefferson	1.93	2.40	1.24
King	.55	3.11	5.70
Kitsap	.80	1.45	1.81
Kittitas	.94	.00	.00
Klickitat	2.16	1.45	.67
Lewis	1.14	3.59	3.13
Mason	1.17	.90	.77
Okanogan	2.15	4.62	2.15
Pacif/Wahkiakum	1.72	.00	.00
Pierce	.64	2.45	3.79
Skagit	.89	1.04	1.17
Snohomish	.81	1.02	1.26
Spokane	.90	2.29	2.54
Stevens	.00	.00	
Thurston	1.31	2.10	1.60
Walla Walla	.61	.45	.73
Whatcom	1.39	3.02	2.17
Whitman	.00	1.60	
Yakima	.81	2.56	3.16

NOTE: Confinement rates are per 1,000 juveniles in the county, by race (1990 census). The disparity ratio equals the ratio of the minority confinement rate to the white confinement rate.

Juvenile Referral Rates

The results of the regression analyses provide only partial support for the argument that racial disparities in confinement are a reflection of disparities in rates of arrest and court referral. Whereas the rate at which youths are referred to the court predicts the county

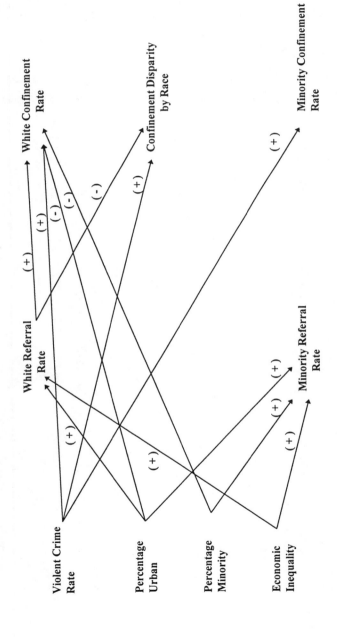

Figure 6.2. Factors Influencing Juvenile Referral, Confinement, and Racial Disparity: Significant Predictors
NOTE: Significant factors only, $p < .10$.

TABLE 6.2 Unstandardized Regression Coefficients Predicting Juvenile Referral Rates, Confinement Rates, Court Caseload, and Racial Disparity in Confinement

County Characteristics	White Referral Rate	Minority Referral Rate	Court Caseload	White Confinement Rate	Minority Confinement Rate	Disparity Ratio
White referral rate	—	—	-14.483 (48.871)	.229 (.082)	—	-.562 (.279)
Minority referral rate	—	—	65.729 (48.540)	—	.140 (.159)	.344 (.245)
Court caseload	—	—	—	.002 (.112)	.193 (.218)	.205 (.260)
Violent crime rate	-.288 (.333)	-.097 (.335)	-63.438 (55.720)	.250 (.141)	.796 (.265)	.678 (.279)
Percentage minority	.317 (.254)	.747 (.255)	23.706 (49.460)	-.285 (.111)	-.366 (.229)	-.316 (.243)
Economic inequality	2.883 (.732)	3.843 (.737)	-11.694 (171.896)	.135 (.385)	.183 (.814)	.612 (.830)
Percentage urban	.420 (.128)	.433 (.129)	27.050 (25.638)	-.182 (.069)	-.039 (.129)	.186 (.135)
Constant	-2.045 (1.100)	-4.378 (1.107)	57.223 (236.233)	.813 (.599)	-.997 (1.370)	-1.237 (1.439)
Adjusted R^2	.452	.591	.173	.340	.294	.401

NOTE: Standard errors are in parentheses.

TABLE 6.3 Standardized Regression Coefficients Predicting Juvenile Referral Rates, Confinement Rates, Court Caseload, and Racial Disparity in Confinement

County Characteristics	White Referral Rate	Minority Referral Rate	Court Caseload	White Confinement Rate	Minority Confinement Rate	Disparity Ratio
White referral rate	—	—	-.108	.614	—	-.646
Minority referral rate	—	—	.573	—	.238	.497
Court caseload	—	—	—	.004	.183	.193
Violent crime rate	-.144	-.041	-.237	.333	.580	.471
Percentage minority	.205	.414	.115	-.492	-.345	-.268
Economic inequality	.541	.619	-.016	.068	.050	.155
Percentage urban	.489	.433	.236	-.568	-.066	.307
Adjusted R^2	.452	.591	.173	.340	.294	.401

rate of confinement for white youths (B = .23, p = .01), it does not significantly predict the rate of confinement for minority youths (B = .14, p = .39) once other characteristics of counties are controlled. Consistent with the separate regressions of white and minority confinement rates, the referral rates of white youths are negatively related to county-level racial disparity (B = −.56, p = .06), and the referral rates for minority youths are positively related (B = .34, p = .18). The effects of the white and minority referral rates on racial disparity in confinement are in the expected directions, but the latter is clearly not significant. Based on these results, it would be erroneous to conclude that racial disparities in confinement are primarily or solely the result of differential rates of arrest and referral of minority youths. Clearly, minority rates of referral are poor predictors of minorities in confinement across Washington counties.

Violent Crime

Juvenile confinement rates, and the disparity between minority and white confinement, also are related to overall rates of violent crime in the counties. For minority youths, the relationship between the overall violent crime rate and the rate of juvenile confinement is quite strong (B = .80, p = .01), but for white youths the relationship is much weaker and not significant at conventional levels of probability (B = .25, p = .09). Therefore, net of the rates of court referrals for juveniles, both the white and the minority confinement rates are generally higher in counties with higher rates of violent crime. It appears, though, that the minority confinement rate is most strongly influenced by violent crime. Consistent with these findings, the violent crime rate is positively related to racial disparity in the confinement of youths (B = .68, p = .02), indicating that the differences between minority and white confinement rates are greatest in counties with higher rates of violent crime, net of the influence of white and minority referral rates. These findings, and the finding that the violent crime rate does not predict youth referral rates (see Table 6.2), suggest that the higher rates of confinement found in those counties with high violent crime rates are due to factors other than simply crimes committed by youths.

Minority Concentration

In the present study, minority concentration is inversely related to the rates of confinement for both whites ($B = -.28$, $p = .02$) and minorities ($B = -.37$, $p = .12$), although this effect is statistically significant only in predicting white confinement rates. Furthermore, minority concentration does not significantly predict the racial disparity in confinement net of other factors. These findings thus offer no support for the hypothesis that youths of color are confined at higher rates in communities with large minority populations, once differences in crime and referral are controlled, but do indicate that white youths are confined at lower rates in those counties.

Although minority concentration does not appear to be important as a direct cause of racial disparity in youth confinement, regressions predicting white and minority juvenile referral rates (see Figure 6.2) indicate an indirect effect through rates of referral for minority youths. The percentage of racial or ethnic minorities in counties does not predict the rate of court referrals for white youths ($B = .32$, $p = .22$), but is significantly and positively related to the referral rate for minority youths ($B = .75$, $p = .01$).

Economic Inequality

The analyses yielded surprising findings on the effects of economic inequality between whites and minorities on disparities in confinement. County levels of economic inequality have only limited influence on disparities in confinement—inequality has no significant direct effect on the confinement of either white ($B = .13$, $p = .73$) or minority ($B = .18$, $p = .82$) youths. However, inequality is associated with racial disparities in confinement indirectly through rates of referral. Racial economic inequality is positively related to the referral rate for white ($B = 2.88$, $p = .00$) and minority ($B = 3.84$, $p = .00$) youths, but because the referral rate for whites is significantly and negatively related to confinement disparity, and the minority referral rate is not, inequality is associated—indirectly— with lower levels of disparity in confinement. In other words, counties with relatively high rates of racial economic inequality often experience high rates of referral for both white and minority youths, but the former is more strongly related to disparity in confinement. To the extent that higher white referral rates are related to lower levels of disparity, greater economic inequality between minorities and whites may be related to lower levels of disparity.

Urban Concentration

Similar to the effects of minority concentration, the degree of county urbanization is directly associated with the confinement of white youths, but not with that of minority youths. Heightened urbanization actually diminishes white confinement rates ($B = -.18$, $p = .01$) but has no effect on minority confinement rates ($B = -.04$, $p = .76$). Although this results in a positive relationship between urbanization and confinement disparity, it is nonsignificant ($B = .19$, $p = .18$).

Even though urbanization may not directly predict racial disparity in the confinement of youths, it is an important factor influencing referral rates (Table 6.2). Like economic inequality, higher levels of urbanization are associated with high referral rates for white ($B = .42$, $p = .00$) and minority ($B = .43$, $p = .00$) youths. This suggests a possible indirect effect of urbanization, decreasing racial disparity by increasing the white referral rate, which is negatively related to confinement disparity.

Court Workload

At the bivariate level, court workload is positively related to disparity in confinement ($r = .35$, $p = .07$) and to the rate of confinement for minority youths ($r = .33$, $p = .07$), but not to the confinement rate for white youths ($r = .09$, $p = .63$). Contrary to our predictions, the county court workload does not significantly predict rates of confinement for either white or minority youths once other county characteristics are controlled and does not predict racial disparity in confinement.

In sum, disparities in county rates of confinement of juvenile offenders are not due simply to differential rates of referral or offending. The most important factors contributing to racial and ethnic disparities in confinement across counties are the rates at which white youths are referred to the court and the overall violent crime rate. Both the white and minority rates of confinement increase significantly with increases in violent crime, but the effect is much stronger for minority youths. Most important, this pattern persists even after controlling for white and minority differences in rates of referral to the juvenile court. Although other aspects of county social structure (urbanicity, minority concentration) influence rates of confinement of white youths, they do not directly and significantly predict either minority confinement rates or racial disparity in confinement.

There is evidence that the presence of urbanized cities and city governments—and the attendant bureaucratization of the legal system—differentially influences the outcomes of cases adjudicated in juvenile courts. Urban counties may be somewhat more differentiating in their handling of juvenile offenders than are less urbanized counties, increasing racial disparities in confinement by simultaneously referring all youths to the juvenile court at higher rates, but confining white youths in correctional facilities at slightly lower rates than less urban counties. Economic inequality appears to have a similar effect by producing higher rates of referral for youths in counties where economic inequality is high. Minority concentration, like urbanization, produces lower levels of confinement for whites in counties where the concentration of minorities is high.

DISCUSSION

Differential treatment of minority youths in the juvenile justice system may cause disparities in the confinement of white and minority youths. In terms of the structural effects of community characteristics on levels of disparity, this differential treatment is reflected in the differential influence of the referral rate and violent crime rate on confinement. Most important, minority youths were much more likely to be confined than white youths in communities where the violent crime rate was high, regardless of racial differences in rates of referral in those communities.

There exist alternative explanations of this finding. For example, the violent crime rate might have the observed differential influence on confinement rates, even if the actions of juvenile justice officials were not influenced by the race or ethnicity of youths accused of crimes. High violent crime rates may often be associated with a small number of youths who have extensive histories of criminal behavior (Tracy, Wolfgang, & Figlio, 1990; Wolfgang et al., 1972). Furthermore, as is the case in Washington State, courts typically impose more severe penalties on these types of offenders than those with no prior criminal involvement. If youths of color are more likely than white youths to have prior involvements in crime, they are much more likely than whites to be confined for crimes. Disproportionately high minority rates of confinement in counties with high violent crime rates would, therefore, stem from a disproportionate number of minority youths with prior criminal histories.

Although empirical examination of this hypothesis is beyond the scope of the present analysis, the findings of at least two previous studies support its rejection. First, there exists no significant evidence of racial or ethnic differences in levels of prior criminal conduct that contribute to disparities in sentencing (Bridges et al., 1993; Crutchfield & Bridges, 1986). Second, the imposition of more severe penalties for "chronic" or "habitual" offenders has no differential influence on racial or ethnic disparities in rates of confinement (Bridges & Crutchfield, 1988).

Officials' perceptions of threats to public order may assist in explaining the relationship between the violent crime rate and racial and ethnic disparities in confinement. Tittle (1994) suggests that the emotion of fear is pivotal in understanding aspects of inequality in the legal process:

> Other individuals, groups of individuals, or events may pose an imminent danger to anybody's property or life, and when they do, fear is stimulated. . . . Fear lie[s] behind generalized prejudicial or stereotypical judgments about individuals and categories of individuals, and they energize tendencies toward social control. . . . To understand and predict patterns of formal social control, therefore, one must be able to pinpoint the main foci of identity and fear among court personnel. (p. 42)

To examine this issue, formal interviews of justice officials and community leaders were conducted as part of a larger project on the correlates of racial disproportionality in the administration of juvenile justice. These interviews offer support for the perspective that racial disproportionality in the confinement of youths may be related to officials' concerns about crime, fears of minority youths, and perceptions of minorities grounded in racial stereotypes.

Many officials viewed disparities in confinement as an unfortunate consequence of disproportionate minority involvement in serious and violent crimes. Although empirical evidence presented in this chapter does not support the view that disparities in confinement are caused by differential minority involvement in crime, many officials felt that their communities had experienced a recent increase in crime rates among youths and that much of the increase in violent crimes had occurred among youths of color. Many felt that this escalated level of violence contributed to increased likelihood of racial differences in arrest, adjudication, and confinement to correctional facilities.

Some officials viewed disproportionality as a direct result of significant and, in their opinion, substantial ethnic and racial differences in criminal behavior (see Sampson & Laub, 1993). Typically, their concern was the serious threat to the community created by high rates of violent crime. Many felt that youths of color were more likely than white youths to represent a significant threat of violence to the community and that a firmer response by the legal system to that threat was needed. A commissioner in one county stated:

> My impression is that the blacks not only represent 8% of our criminals in juvenile [out of a total black population of one half of one percent] but that they represent some of the more so-called hard-core juvenile criminals and the ones committing the more serious crimes.

Others expressed concerns about threats to prevailing moral values. In a small, rural community that had recently experienced a relatively rapid influx of Latinos and increased crime, a municipal official perceived his community's problems in terms of demographic and social changes linked to the Latino population:

There's a distrust among us, because there are so many burglaries, there's so many assaults, there's so much weapons, . . . and our officers, you talk to some of the officers who have almost finished their 20 years, and they'll say, "I'm getting out of here as soon as I can." That the level of violence is going up, they can see more and more weapons, more and more violence, and most of that beating on each other, because of either women or money, or drugs, or all in combination, or machoism or "my pride" or "you looked at me the wrong way." There is a real gap in cultures here. . . . These people formed this as a Christian community and then [Latinos] say, "Well, it's about time for you to change. We want the downtown to be a Mexican adobe village."

In many instances, however, juvenile court officials were more likely to express concerns about the welfare of minority youths than any fear or perceived threat to community moral order. Most viewed the juvenile court as a juvenile welfare agency of last resort and that disproportionality in confinement actually reflected the court's attempt to provide minority youths with social services that they might otherwise not receive. One judge's views on the sentencing of minority youths were as follows:

I don't see sending them away [to confinement] as always a negative. Detention and commitment gets them away from trouble, it also gets them away from their families. And in many cases the families are terrible influences. I've had children say to me, "No, I don't want to leave detention. I don't want to go home. If I go home, I don't get my own room. . . ." Sending these kids homes is sentencing them to misery. . . . Would you want to send them back to a house where there are 10 children and two adults for a two-room apartment?

Similarly, the director of the juvenile court in one county attributed disproportionality to the response of the court to the criminal histories of black juveniles. The emphasis reflected the same social-welfare orientation:

It seems like by the time we get black kids, . . . I don't know what the reason for this is, but it seems like they have real horrendous criminal histories and they have real serious crimes and that I'm thinking that the judicial officers, the judges, might see, might have a tendency to commit them due to what they see as a lack of resources, a lack of family or community support.

Although these qualitative data do not establish any causal relationships between community crime rates, perceptions of minority youths either as symbolic threats or youths in need of services, and racial and ethnic disparities in confinement, they underscore the importance of integrating structural and social-psychological explanations of the administration of juvenile justice. Quite clearly, the interviews suggest that the empirical relationship observed between the violent crime rate and racial disparities in confinement may have more to do with officials' orientation on the social welfare needs in their community than with any perceived threat of crime by minority youths. Although law enforcement and political officials interviewed in the study typically perceived crime as a threat to community order, juvenile court officials were more likely to perceive it as a reflection of unmet welfare needs of the poor and disadvantaged. At least in the case of juveniles, court officials seemed to retain an interest in "child saving." This orientation typically translated into policies of differential rates of detention and confinement for children of color.

Scholars concerned about racial disproportionality in juvenile justice must pursue explanations that identify the separate effects of structural and social-psychological explanations of court processes. Structural explanations stress the importance of community social structure on the actions of law enforcement agencies and the courts. Often, however, these explanations overlook the important social-psychological mechanisms by which aspects of community social structure actually influence the decisions of law enforcement personnel, judges, and other court officials. Subsequent research must explain the circumstances under which changes in the crime rate, particularly the rate of violent crime, influence officials' concerns and fears about their community. Furthermore, research must ascertain how increased officials' concerns, coupled with traditional stereotypes of racial and ethnic minorities, translate into law enforcement, prosecution, and judicial policies that place minority youths at a significant disadvantage in the legal process.

NOTES

1. In Washington State, most judicial districts correspond to counties. However, because some counties have relatively small populations, and thus too few cases to warrant the existence of a county juvenile court, they share the use of a juvenile court with an adjacent county. For the purposes of the present analysis, data on these "merged" counties have been adjusted accordingly. County demographic characteristics reflect the combined populations of the merged counties.

2. Because no single source contains all of the information required for the necessary analyses, our data were drawn from four sources: (a) 1991 admissions to the Washington State Division of Juvenile Rehabilitation, (b) county crime rates from the FBI's 1990 *Uniform Crime Reports*, (c) 1990 census data for the state of Washington, and (d) 1991 juvenile court records for all counties in Washington State.

3. Race-specific analyses are impossible due to the small numbers of minority youths in many Washington counties. Therefore, black, Latino, Asian, and Native Americans are combined in these analyses.

7

The Overrepresentation of Minority Youths in the California Juvenile Justice System
Perceptions and Realities

JAMES AUSTIN

There has been growing concern in California about the use of incarceration for youths, in general, and the overrepresentation of minority youths in secure juvenile facilities. For many years, California has had the nation's highest rate of youth incarceration. Its 1989 youth incarceration rate, based on a 1-day count of juveniles housed in public facilities for delinquency offenses, was 463 per 100,000 juveniles. This is not only the highest figure for any state, but it is also more than twice the national average of 207 (Table 7.1).

The ethnic pattern of distribution for these incarcerated juveniles is somewhat different in California than for the nation as a whole. California incarcerates a much lower share of Anglo American youths, a slightly lower share of African American youths, but

AUTHOR'S NOTE: The preparation of this chapter was assisted financially through Grant JE 90011079-00 from the California Office of Criminal Justice Planning (OCJP). The opinions, findings, and conclusions presented are those of the author and not necessarily those of OCJP. This chapter is based on an earlier report prepared by the National Council on Crime and Delinquency for the OCJP. That report was co-authored by Juanita Dimas, David Steinhart, and myself and can be obtained by contacting NCCD.

TABLE 7.1 Custody Rates for Juveniles in Public Facilities by Three
Major Offense Groups: California and United States, 1989
(per 100,000 juveniles)

Offense Group	United States	California
Criminal offenders	207	463
Status offenders	9	2
Nonoffenders	3	1

SOURCE: From Office of Juvenile Justice and Delinquency Prevention (1991), Juveniles in Public
Facilities (secure and nonsecure).

TABLE 7.2 Juveniles in Public Facilities: California and United States,
1-Day Counts, 1989

Ethnicity	United States N	United States %	California N	California %
Anglo American	22,201	40	4,193	26
African American	23,836	42	5,862	37
Latino	8,671	16	· 5,205	33
American Indian	637	1	77	1
Asian/Pacific Islander	778	1	532	1
Total	56,123	100	15,869	100

SOURCE: From Office of Juvenile Justice and Delinquency Prevention (1991), 1-day counts of
juveniles in public facilities (secure and nonsecure).

a much larger share of Latino youths compared to national figures
(Table 7.2). The higher proportion of Hispanic/Latino youths is
primarily due to California's large Latino youth population, which
exceeds that of most states.

More significantly, the incarceration of minority youths has
increased over the past few years. Between 1985 and 1989, the
absolute number of white youths in custody actually declined by
10% (Table 7.3), whereas the number of black and Hispanic youths
increased by 48% and 38%, respectively. The largest growing population was Asian/Pacific Islander, although their numbers are relatively small compared to the other groups.

A number of studies have been conducted during the past
decade attempting to explain these trends and the extent to which

TABLE 7.3 California Children in Custody Ages 10 to 17, Public Juvenile Facilities, 1985-1989

Ethnicity	1985		1987		1989		% Change
	N	%	N	%	N	%	
Anglo American	4,597	66.7	4,556	31.2	4,140	26.5	−9.9
African American	3,879	31.2	5,096	34.9	5,737	36.8	+47.9
Latino	3,706	29.8	4,458	30.6	5,125	32.9	+38.3
American Indian	87	0.7	166	1.1	76	0.5	−12.6
Asian/Pacific Islander	178	1.4	307	2.1	521	3.3	+192.7
Total	12,447	100.0	14,583	100.0	15,599	100.0	

SOURCE: From Bureau of Justice Statistics (1989); Office of Juvenile Justice and Delinquency Prevention (1991).

race or ethnicity independently may influence juvenile court decisions to place youths in secure facilities. There is broad agreement in the literature that minority adolescents are overrepresented at all stages of the juvenile justice system as compared to their numbers in the general population (Pope, 1979; Pope & McNeely, 1981; Velde, 1977). McCarthy and Smith (1986) examined the effect of race, sex, and social class on juvenile court dispositions.

Their findings suggested that, although initial screening decisions were not discriminatory, later ones were. Thus there seemed to be an "amplification effect" as minority youths were processed through the juvenile justice system. Amplification effects were also reported by Fenwick (1982) and Fagan et al. (1987).

However, many of these studies are largely descriptive and are unable to reach definitive conclusions simply because the data used for analysis do not permit the researchers to isolate the direct effects of ethnicity on juvenile justice decision making. Although there is little doubt that various ethnic groups are arrested, detained, and sentenced to secure facilities at higher rates than other ethnic groups, it is not always clear whether ethnicity alone is the basis for the disproportions noted.

Researchers tend to disagree as to the most appropriate explanation for the high rates of confinement of minority youths. One view is that minority incarceration rates can be explained by the disproportionate involvement of minority juveniles in serious and violent youth crime. For example, Hindelang (1982) reported that black youths have higher rates of arrest for offenses such as robberies, rapes, aggravated assaults, and simple assaults. These more serious FBI Index crimes would seem more likely to result in decisions to detain and, ultimately, to institutionalize offenders.

There is some support for this view in the research findings of Krisberg et al. (1987). Their examination of FBI data on juvenile arrests by race for Part I offenses (including murder, rape, robbery, aggravated assault, burglary, larceny, auto theft, and arson) revealed that Anglo American youths accounted for approximately two thirds of all Part I juvenile arrests in 1977-1982. During this same period, African American youths accounted for about one third of all Part I arrests, and Native American and Asian American youths each accounted for 1%. These arrest ratios do not explain the disparities in youth incarceration rates as shown above. However, if only the most violent crimes (murder, forcible rape, robbery, and aggravated assault) are examined, blacks account for about half of these offenses, which approximates their proportions of confined youths.

A comprehensive review of the literature since 1970 conducted by Pope and Feyerherm (1990a, 1990b) found that most, but not all, studies reveal ethnicity as a significant variable in juvenile justice outcome decisions. However, there is considerable debate on whether the ethnicity effect is direct (i.e., causal), indirect, or spurious. For example, in a study using Florida case records over a 2-year period, Frazier and Cochran (1986) examined the effects of social and legal characteristics on detention, intake, disposition, and severity of disposition. They found that race influenced initial detention decisions in that black youths were more likely to be detained than white youths. Furthermore, whether or not a youth was detained influenced all subsequent decisions because detained youths received the most severe dispositions.

In the only study of national trends in 1977, 1979, and 1982, Krisberg et al. (1987) found that minority youths were incarcerated at a rate three to four times that of Anglo Americans, and that minority youths tend to be confined in secure facilities, whereas Anglo American youths represent the majority of those confined in private facilities. The rates of overrepresentation were most pronounced for African American males. The data also show differential treatment across time periods. From 1977 to 1979, when rates of youth incarcerations were declining, minority rates did not decrease as sharply as did Anglo American rates. Anglo American rates accounted for 75% of the entire decline. From 1979 to 1982, when rates of youth incarceration were increasing, minority youths bore the brunt of the increase, representing 93% of the entire increase. Thus, over time, the disproportionate rate of incarceration has become more pronounced when examined on a national level (Krisberg et al., 1987).

A unique feature of the above national study is a state-by-state calculation of Anglo American and minority arrest rates in 1979. These data reveal large disparities between some states and few differences among others. The researchers conclude that

> there are a number of states where minority youth incarceration rates are close to those for Whites. In other jurisdictions, however, rates of minority incarceration are four to five times greater than rates of White incarceration. These interstate differences are intriguing and suggest the need for a much more localized analysis of differential incarceration patterns. (Krisberg et al., 1987, p. 190)

These studies expose the need for a more thorough research approach to the problem of overrepresentation of minority youths in the juvenile justice system. Aggregate data on state and local populations of juveniles in custody are clearly inadequate as a sole source of information. Individual records offer the researcher the capability of isolating the effects of race and ethnicity on secure confinement decisions by controlling statistically for nonethnic factors. Even with this analytical refinement of the analysis, statistical methods cannot by themselves be expected to illuminate all factors that contribute to ethnic disproportionality in the incarcerated youth population. Quantitative analysis must be supplemented by qualitative research into the effects of human judgment and discretion on juvenile confinement decisions.

The issues raised above led the U.S. Congress in 1988 to amend the federal Juvenile Justice and Delinquency Prevention Act (JJDPA) to require participating states to evaluate and address the overrepresentation of minorities in their incarcerated juvenile populations. The federal goal, according to the federal Office of Juvenile Justice and Delinquency Prevention (OJJDP), is that states should

> develop and implement policies and practices which are racially and ethnically neutral and which produce unbiased, neutral results. . . . The ultimate goal is for each state to improve the juvenile justice and youth services system by creating a comprehensive community-based service system that provides services for all youth equally . . . regardless of race or ethnic background. (JJDPA of 1974, Public Law 93-415, as amended)

This chapter summarizes research that addresses this federally mandated objective by examining the extent to which California, the nation's most populous state, incarcerates minority youths on the basis of race. The study also provides examples of how quantitative and qualitative evaluation methods can be used to reach definitive conclusions regarding the extent and causes of minority overrepresentation. Finally, the recommendations of local juvenile justice officials to reduce the effects of race on juvenile justice decision making are presented.

DATA SOURCES AND RESEARCH METHOD

This study relied on quantitative data that consisted of aggregate-count data as well as case-based juvenile court referral and disposition data. Once these data had been collected and analyzed, a series of "town meetings" were held with juvenile justice officials, private not-for-profit service providers, and youth advocacy groups. As described later, the purpose of these meetings was to have these officials respond to the quantitative analysis and findings and offer their own interpretations and recommendations for reforms that might address the observed overrepresentation of minority youths.

The following were the primary sources of data for the study:[1]

Children in Custody (CIC) Surveys of Youths Confined in Local and State Facilities. The U.S. Department of Justice has been conducting national surveys of public and private juvenile facilities for nearly two decades. This CIC survey provides biannual, 1-day aggregate census data on the number and ethnicity of youths confined in most of the nation's public and private juvenile facilities.

Aggregate Arrest and Juvenile Court Case Disposition Data. Since 1980, California's Bureau of Criminal Statistics (BCS) has published annual *Criminal Justice Profiles* containing summary data on juvenile arrests, probation status, and court dispositions. These profiles, both for state and county populations, provided aggregate information on state and county juvenile justice populations, including relevant measures of ethnicity.

Individual Juvenile Court Referral, Detention, and Court Disposition Case Data. Individual cases from the point of arrest through court disposition also were obtained from the California BCS, which maintains a case base in its juvenile court disposition data system. The individual case files included processing decisions (arrest, petition filing, disposition) and information on the detention and commitment of youths to local or state facilities. The individual case files permitted the National Council on Crime and Delinquency (NCCD) to determine whether disparities in the treatment of ethnic groups remained after controlling for various factors, such as severity of offense.

Youth Population Census Data. A key source of population data used to calculate indexes of minority representation in this report was the *Report of Enrollment and Drop-Out Figures, 1989* (California Department of Education, 1991). Population estimates of the California Department of Finance proved less useful because they did not contain all requisite data elements (age, county, and ethnicity).

DEFINITIONS OF
JUVENILE AND MINORITY GROUPS

For purposes of this study, a *juvenile* was defined as a person under the age of 18 who is subject to (or under) the jurisdiction of the California juvenile court in a delinquency proceeding. Excluded from the scope of the study were persons under 18 years of age who had been waived or transferred to the jurisdiction of the adult criminal court for prosecution on a serious crime listed in California's adult court transfer statute. Almost without exception, the juveniles covered by this study were minors aged 10 through 17 who had not been waived to adult court.

A concern raised early in the study was how minority groups should be defined. Terms commonly used in minority-related research efforts include *white, Hispanic, black,* and *Asian and other.* Various groups, from academics to lay persons, express their own preferences in terminology. As an example, *African American* has gained increasing acceptance as a substitute for black; however, even within the African American/black community there are disagreements about the correct terminology. Such lack of consensus makes it difficult for well-intended researchers to be precise or even agreeable to those who read their work. This concern has been addressed by choosing to use, for most applications, the following ethnic group terms: Anglo American (traditionally referred to as white), Latino (traditionally referred to as Hispanic), African American (traditionally referred to as black), and Asian American (traditionally referred to as Asian).

STATISTICAL
MEASURES OF OVERREPRESENTATION

In assessing the extent of overrepresentation, the following two statistical measures of over- or underrepresentation of minority youth groups were applied to the data.

The Minority Proportion Index. A minority proportion "index" has been suggested by OJJDP to assess the extent of ethnic representation. This index compares the percentage of youths from a minority group at a single processing point to the percentage of the total youth population occupied by that minority group. For example, if African Americans represented 40% of juveniles incarcerated in the Youth Authority but constituted 10% of the state youth population, their minority proportion index of representation in the Youth Authority would be 4.0 (.40/.10 = 4.0). An index value greater than 1.00 indicates overrepresentation, and a score below 1.00 reflects underrepresentation.

Minority Incarceration Rates. Obviously, the proportionality index measure is not a complete nor wholly valid measure of overrepresentation. Jurisdictions that "fail" the index measure may also have very low incarceration rates, which in some instances is a far more accurate measure of minority overrepresentation. To correct for this situation, minority-specific youth incarceration rates also are used. This rate is expressed as the number of minority youths incarcerated in one type of facility per 100,000 members of that minority youth group in the state population.[2]

THE EXTENT OF OVERREPRESENTATION OF MINORITY YOUTHS IN CALIFORNIA

Similar to most states, African Americans (and particularly African American males) are heavily overrepresented in California's juvenile facilities.[3] Of the 13,767 youths incarcerated in California, 5,093 (37%) were African American as compared to their 8.7% representation in the total youth population (Table 7.4). Not surprisingly, African Americans have the highest custody rates (1,950 per 100,000; 4.25 index score) followed by Latinos (430 per 100,000; .94 index score). In sharp contrast, Anglo American and Asian American juveniles are underrepresented in California secure public facilities (index scores of .58 and .36, respectively).

It also should be noted that female juvenile offenders have consistently lower rates and indexes of incarceration than males, both in total and for each ethnic group. In fact, an often-neglected fact is that an index for sex overrepresentation would produce high levels of overrepresentation. For example, although males constitute approximately 51% of the youth population, they represent 92% of the secure-facility population (or an index of 1.80). Conversely, the female index score is .16. This trend of extremely low indexes of females persists for the various minority groups. However, as among the males, female African Americans have the highest rates and Asian American females have the lowest rates of incarceration.

TABLE 7.4 California Juveniles in Custody by Ethnicity and Sex, Secure Public Facilities Only, 1989

Ethnicity	State Population[a]		Juveniles in Custody[b]		Rate[c]	Index Score[d]
	N	%	N	%		
Anglo American	1,405,369	46.6	3,701	26.8	263	0.58
Male	719,840	23.8	3,231	23.5	449	0.99
Female	685,529	22.8	470	3.4	69	0.15
African American	261,118	8.7	5,093	37.0	1,950	4.25
Male	130,922	4.5	4,739	34.4	3,620	7.64
Female	130,196	4.5	354	2.6	272	0.58
Latino	1,036,403	34.4	4,458	32.4	430	0.94
Male	525,677	17.4	4,188	30.4	797	1.75
Female	510,726	17.0	270	2.0	53	0.12
Asian American/other	309,985	10.3	515	3.7	166	0.36
Male	158,022	5.2	466	3.4	295	0.65
Female	151,963	5.0	49	0.4	32	0.08
Total	3,012,875	100.0	13,767	100.0	457	N/A
Male	1,534,461	50.9	12,624	91.7	823	1.80
Female	1,478,414	49.1	1,143	8.3	77	0.17

a. SOURCE: California Department of Finance population estimates, 1989, ages 10-17.
b. SOURCE: 1989 Children in Custody census of public juvenile detention, correctional, and shelter facilities.
c. Rates per 100,000 juveniles were computed by dividing the number in custody by the number of youth population for each gender and racial/ethnic group, and multiplying by 100,000.
d. Index score is percentage in custody divided by percentage of state population.

These data show that only African American males are being overrepresented in the juvenile justice system. Anglos and Asian Americans have rates below their proportions as represented in the state youth population, whereas Latinos are represented at a level consistent with their representation in the youth population.

The remainder of the research sought to identify those juvenile justice and offender factors that produce these results. The first step was to see if overrepresentation occurs at the various decision points of the juvenile justice system (from arrest through disposition). For example, it may be that the decision to arrest is more important than subsequent decision points in explaining ethnic bias. Table 7.5 shows the ethnic distribution of juveniles in the state population, as well as the distribution (number, percentage, and rate) by ethnic group of juveniles at five stages of processing, from arrest through

TABLE 7.5 California Juvenile Population, Arrests, and Admissions to Secure Detention, Private Facilities, Secure County Facilities, and CYA, 1989

	N	%	Rate[c]	Index[e]
Population[a]				
Anglo American	1,405,369	46.65	—	—
African American	261,118	8.67	—	—
Latino	1,036,403	34.40	—	—
Asian American/other	309,985	10.29	—	—
Total	3,012,875	100.00	—	—
Arrest[b]				
Anglo American	94,782	39.78	6,744.28	0.85
African American	45,960	19.29	17,601.24	2.22
Latino	81,639	34.27	7,877.15	1.00
Asian American/other	15,860	6.66	5,116.38	0.65
Total	238,241	100.00	7,907.43	—
Secure detention[b]				
Anglo American	17,759	34.07	1,263.65	0.73
African American	13,660	26.20	5,231.35	3.02
Latino	17,006	32.62	1,640.87	0.95
Asian American/other	3,706	7.11	1,195.54	0.69
Total[d]	52,131	100.00	1,730.27	—
Private facility[b]				
Anglo American	2,148	43.79	152.84	0.94
African American	1,219	24.85	466.84	2.87
Latino	1,325	27.01	20.55	0.79
Asian American/other	213	4.34	427.44	0.42
Total[d]	4,905	100.00	162.80	—
Secure county facility[b]				
Anglo American	4,128	30.14	293.73	0.65
African American	2,908	21.23	1,113.67	2.45
Latino	5,885	42.97	567.83	1.25
Asian American/other	774	5.65	249.69	0.55
Total[d]	13,695	100.00	454.55	—
CYA[b]				
Anglo American	660	19.20	46.96	0.41
African American	1,380	40.17	528.50	4.63
Latino	1,210	35.23	116.75	1.02
Asian American/other	185	5.38	59.68	0.52
Total[d]	3,435	100.00	114.01	—

NOTE: CYA = California Youth Authority.
a. SOURCE: California Department of Finance population estimates, 1989, ages 10-17.
b. SOURCE: California Bureau of Criminal Statistics, 1989, ages 10-17.
c. Rates per 100,000 juveniles computed by dividing the number in custody by the number of youth population for each ethnic group, and multiplying by 100,000.
d. Youths of unknown ethnicity were omitted from these totals.
e. Indexes are based on the racial/ethnic groups' proportions in the general populations. Calculations are made by dividing the ethnic group's percentage representation at the legal point of interest by the ethnic group's percentage of the total youth population. An index value over 1.00 indicates overrepresentation; an index value under 1.00 indicates that the group is underrepresented.

detention, placement, and secure commitment using aggregate data (Table 7.4).

African American youths are overrepresented at arrest (2.2 times their share of the youth population), but their index continues to rise at each decision point until, at the deep end of the system—commitment to the California Youth Authority (CYA)—they are overrepresented by a factor of 4.6. By contrast, Anglo American youths are proportionately filtered out of the juvenile justice system as the severity of the sanction increases; their rate of representation at arrest is .85, dropping to .65 among those juveniles committed to secure county facilities and to .41 among those committed to the CYA. Latino youths show little variation in their rates of representation in the state youth population, and Asian American youths maintain their low rates of representation.

The next issue is whether these ethnic disparities at each of the major decision points persist after statistical controls are applied. Table 7.6 shows the percentage of juveniles in each ethnic group who were detained, cross-referenced to other factors such as offense, age, sex, probation status, and prior offense history. Here one can see that African Americans have higher detention rates even when controlling for relevant background attributes. For example, within the class of juveniles referred for violent felony offenses in 1989, 64.7% of African Americans with violent felony referral offenses were detained versus 47.1% of Anglo youths in this offense class and 60.7% of Latino youths in this offense class.

The same results emerge when one examines commitments to the CYA (Table 7.7). For example, among juveniles with violent felony offenses, 11.4% of African American youths with violent felonies were committed to the CYA in 1989 versus 3.4% of Anglos, 9.4% of Latinos, and 8.6% of Asian/other youths with these offenses. For every offense class except "misdemeanor drug," African American youths had the highest percentage of CYA commitments.[4]

In broad terms, this analysis unveils a picture of persistent, differential treatment for some minority groups after having accounted for prereferral factors such as offense and prior record. This leads one to the observation that some ethnic disparities in detention and sentencing outcomes are limited to African Americans and cannot be fully explained by the juvenile justice attributes

TABLE 7.6 California Juveniles With Court Dispositions: Percentage Detained by Ethnicity, Controlling for Other Factors

			Ethnicity			
Characteristic	*Anglo American*	*Latino*	*African American*	*Native American*	*Asian American/ Other*	*Total*
Number of youths	60,539	47,564	26,982	906	8,591	144,582
Overall % detained	30.6	35.9	48.5	43.0	38.8	36.3
Referral offense						
Felony violent	47.1	60.7	64.7	59.6	58.0	11,629
Felony property	38.8	38.4	49.5	47.4	49.4	35,880
Felony drug	43.1	59.9	71.9	37.5	61.8	7,704
Felony sex	37.2	44.4	50.3	—[a]	39.1	1,716
Felony weapons	32.7	36.5	56.7	55.6	46.8	2,081
Misdemeanor assault and battery	33.6	31.0	35.8	37.5	35.5	11,517
Misdemeanor property	15.9	18.9	22.8	27.1	15.1	18,626
Misdemeanor drug	20.8	28.1	29.4	36.7	23.2	3,660
Misdemeanor sex	30.8	17.1	31.4	75.0	20.0	654
Misdemeanor alcohol	14.1	24.2	24.4	39.2	12.1	6,838
Misdemeanor weapons	20.4	28.4	47.2	—[a]	39.6	1,733
Status offense	35.1	35.1	40.5	32.9	42.6	10,044
Probation violation	65.3	57.6	62.9	69.7	52.8	7,997
Probation/CYA status						
On probation or CYA	59.5	58.4	67.2	62.4	61.4	29,950
Not probation or CYA	24.9	29.9	40.9	36.2	34.1	115,032
Sex						
Male	30.3	36.7	50.3	42.5	40.4	115,551
Female	31.6	31.6	39.9	44.5	29.6	28,031
Age						
Ages 10-15	28.4	31.8	44.3	39.6	36.9	73,581
Ages 16-17	31.5	38.3	52.8	46.9	40.8	74,718
Number of offenses						
One only	24.6	30.4	40.5	38.8	32.9	81,960
More than one	39.5	43.0	56.3	47.5	47.5	62,622

NOTE: CYA = California Youth Authority.
a. Indicates where the number of cases available for statistical analysis is less than 30. Consequently, there are insufficient cases to compute reliable percentages.

TABLE 7.7 California Juveniles With Court Dispositions: CYA
Dispositions by Ethnicity, Controlling for Other Factors

| | | | | | Asian | |
Characteristic	Anglo American	Latino	African American	Native American	American/ Other	Total
Number of youths	64,300	49,800	28,401	926	8,760	152,187
Overall % to CYA	0.9	2.1	4.0	1.1	1.6	1.9
Referral offense						
Felonies						
Felony violent	3.4	9.4	11.4	3.7	8.6	12,555
Felony property	1.6	2.0	3.0	2.0	1.3	37,506
Felony drug	1.0	4.1	7.2	—a	5.0	7,886
Felony sex	1.7	2.8	3.4	—a	0.0	1,798
Felony weapons	0.6	1.8	5.6	—a	0.6	2,214
Misdemeanor assault and battery	0.4	1.0	1.1	0.0	1.1	11,695
Misdemeanor property	0.1	0.1	0.1	0.0	0.1	20,388
Misdemeanor drug	0.8	2.1	1.2	0.0	0.0	4,764
Misdemeanor sex	1.0	0.0	2.7	—a	0.0	677
Misdemeanor alcohol	0.0	0.2	0.7	0.0	0.0	6,897
Misdemeanor weapons	0.4	1.7	2.3	—a	0.0	1,836
Status offense	0.1	0.0	0.2	0.0	0.0	10,548
Probation violation	1.9	2.1	3.9	0.0	1.5	8,320
Probation/CYA status						
On probation or CYA	4.2	7.2	9.4	3.8	5.4	30,180
Not probation or CYA	0.2	0.8	1.9	0.2	0.8	122,007
Sex						
Male	1.0	2.4	4.7	1.5	1.7	122,480
Female	0.3	0.3	1.1	0.0	0.8	29,707
Age						
Ages 10-15	0.4	1.0	2.2	0.4	0.7	74,179
Ages 16-17	1.3	3.1	5.9	1.3	1.9	78,008
Number of offenses						
One only	0.6	1.3	2.8	0.8	1.1	87,495
More than one	1.3	3.2	5.2	1.3	2.4	64,692

NOTE: CYA = California Youth Authority.
a. Indicates where the number of cases available for statistical analysis is less than 30. Consequently, there are insufficient cases to compute reliable percentages.

of that ethnic group. If the federal goal of racial and ethnic neutrality for the incarcerated youth population is ever to be achieved, these planners and policymakers must address not only ways to prevent criminal behavior but also ways to eliminate system-based bias or disparity, which independently may affect decisions to incarcerate juveniles.

COUNTY-LEVEL ANALYSIS

Research Approach

The same form of quantitative analysis was developed for the four target communities. Table 7.8 summarizes the major trends for each county, reflecting some levels of diversity among these counties. For example, in San Francisco, Latino rates of overrepresentation for both arrest and confinement are low, whereas in the other three counties they reflect state rates. But despite these differences, the overall patterns observed at the state level persist, namely, that African Americans have extremely high rates of arrests and confinement, Latino rates are roughly equivalent to their proportions in the youth population, and Anglos and Asians have low or extremely low rates.

The next task was to ascertain the reactions of local officials and advocacy groups to these statistical trends. To accomplish this objective, a standard format for collecting subjective information from the target counties was developed. The format was centered around half-day discussion groups convened in each target county. The discussion or "focus group" format was chosen, in lieu of personal interviews, because it would be most productive to draw information from a dialogue and exchange of views between representatives of diverse interest groups within each target community.

In the invitation process, the researchers sought to balance the attendance evenly between representatives of public juvenile justice agencies and representatives of private, community-based youth advocacy and service organizations. At least one representative from each type of key public agency involved with the administration of juvenile justice (selected from law enforcement agencies,

TABLE 7.8 Trends in Arrest and Confinement for the Target Counties

	Anglo American	African American	Latino	Asian American/ Other
San Francisco				
Rate of arrest	Even	Very high	Low	Low
Rate of secure confinement	Low	Very high	Low	Low
Los Angeles County				
Rate of arrest	Low	Very high	Nearly even	Low
Rate of secure confinement	Low	Very high	Nearly even	Very low
Merced County				
Rate of arrest	Low	Very high	Even	Very low
Rate of secure confinement	Low	Very high	Even	Very low
Sacramento County				
Rate of arrest with a referral to probation	Low	Very high	Nearly even	Very low
Rate of secure confinement	Low	Very high	Even	Very low

probation departments, juvenile court, district attorney, public defender, schools, and some other public agencies) was invited. It was not possible to gain perfectly balanced representation of every target county organization with a potential interest in the topic matter. Rather, the intent was to invite the agencies and individuals who seemed best positioned to provide valuable insight into the nature of racial bias in juvenile justice.

Prior to the meetings, each participant was sent a briefing package, which consisted of a four-page questionnaire and a set of data charts and tables. The questionnaire served to focus the attention of participants along common lines in advance of the meeting and to provide a supplemental record of responses. Each meeting began with a half-hour briefing on the project, including a presentation of aggregate county juvenile justice data. Participants were then asked for comments on the accuracy of the data. In fact, some dissatisfaction with the available data was reported at each county meeting, as referenced in the individual county reports that follow.

The remaining discussion time was divided between discussion on the causes of local patterns of minority over- and underrepresentation in the justice system and discussion of solutions for the imbalance or disproportionality that had been observed. The discussion was facilitated by NCCD project staff to ensure uniform coverage from county to county and to produce, to the extent possible, specific and concrete responses.

Perceived Causes of Overrepresentation

During these meetings, the causes and remedies to overrepresentation were listed and ranked. Although there was some variation among the counties, the same themes were cited in each meeting. After the meeting was held, a written report was sent to each participant listing those major points that seemed to reflect the consensus of each group.

What follows is a summary of the primary causes of the overrepresentation and their solutions.

Institutional racism within the juvenile justice system is a primary cause for the overrepresentation of minorities.

The thrust of this observation is that racism, in the form of negative stereotypes, is historically embedded in American culture and is reflected in the institutions of the justice system. One such stereotype is that African Americans are expected to act violently; when this stereotype is held by law enforcement officers and other juvenile justice officials, it leads to selective overarrest and overincarceration of minority youths, especially black youths. One judge admitted that when he adjudicates a black youth he views that youth very differently than other youths even though he is charged with a similar offense. Specifically, black males are seen as less controllable with limited family support if returned to the community. In the same vein, it was suggested that many black and Hispanic youths are labeled as gang members in Los Angeles simply because of their race and residential location. Conversely, Anglo, and even more so Asian, youths were viewed by decision makers as having more family and institutional resources, which reduces their risk for further involvement in the justice system.

Staffing within law enforcement agencies, probation departments, and juvenile courts is largely Anglo American and does not reflect the ethnic distribution in the society as a whole.

Lack of ethnic balance and Anglo American dominance of high-level juvenile justice jobs contribute to the overrepresentation of certain minority groups in secure juvenile justice facilities. The assumption is that by increasing the numbers of minority staff at the executive levels, law enforcement and the juvenile justice system would become more attuned to the special needs and problems of lower class ethnic youths and their communities.

Poverty and joblessness affecting minority youths are largely to blame for high offense and incarceration rates for these individuals.

All discussion groups expressed concern about the social and economic conditions that precede and contribute to delinquent conduct. In particular, African American youths have poor job prospects and economic opportunities and thus turn to nonlegal economic pursuits, such as selling drugs. Poor social and economic circumstances also lower self-esteem, which also contributes to misconduct. It was viewed as no coincidence by the participants that neighborhoods with high crime and arrest rates also have the highest rates of poverty.

Different family and cultural values explain both over- and under-representation of certain ethnic groups in the juvenile justice system.

In each discussion group, participants spoke about the relationship between family and cultural values and involvement with the juvenile justice system. Some participants believed that Asian American families were best equipped to handle youth conduct problems within the structures of home and community; however, some Merced County participants qualified this observation by suggesting that "old-line" Asian families were better at controlling youth misconduct than newer, immigrant Asian families, especially Southeast Asians. San Francisco participants noted that Latino families, as well as Asian, tended to be two-parent families with relatively strong disciplinary values. Participants in all groups singled out African American families as more often dysfunctional than those of other ethnic groups, with a greater proportion of single-parent/absent-father families and with a less consistent ability to resolve youth behavior problems when they first arose.

Minority youths being processed in the juvenile justice system,
as well as their parents, do not always understand how the system
works. This problem is intensified when language barriers are present.

The suggestion here is that many youths lack familiarity with the legal process and do not understand the "mumbo jumbo" that goes on between attorneys, judges, and probation officers, especially in court proceedings. Juvenile justice personnel may, in turn, not be able to communicate effectively with parents and children from different cultural backgrounds. Latinos and some Asians—especially new immigrant youths and their parents—may have an inadequate command of English as well as insufficient translator support in official proceedings. This lack of communication and understanding may have a negative effect on sentencing decisions and may foreclose options that are open to youths and parents who are more conversant with the system.

The juvenile justice system lacks the resources needed to respond
effectively to delinquency in general and to minority youth problems
in particular. Diversion and alternative disposition programs that used
to be available have disappeared, leaving juvenile justice decision makers
with fewer options, and this contributes to higher incarceration rates for
some minority groups.

Frustration and disappointment were expressed in all focus groups over the declining base of resources for juvenile justice programs and services. The reduction in service level has had a disproportionately strong effect on minority groups, contributing in turn to disproportionately high arrest and incarceration rates for some minority youths. Los Angeles participants expressed concern that no resources were available for efforts to discourage first-time offenders from re-entering the criminal justice system; many youths on probation supervision, for example, were "banked" with little or no attention or service. When sanctions are ineffective, kids learn that they can ignore the justice system until it comes down hard on them. When services are absent, situations that contribute to delinquency get worse. All county groups underscored the need for more youth services, including family counseling, community recreation centers, and basic support (including food and shelter) for poor families.

Schools have failed to provide minority youths with the educational and personal development needed to overcome adverse social and economic conditions.

Some participants singled out schools for failing to rescue minority youths, already suffering difficult circumstances, from educational failure and eventual delinquency. Some suggested that Anglo American youths had preferred access to good schools, and that Latino or Asian youths with language problems failed to receive adequate attention to special needs. African American youths, some suggested, were likely to be classified early as behavior problems and to be forced out of the classroom or otherwise discouraged from succeeding in school. Schools (and other public agencies) were blamed for failing to experiment sufficiently with school-based, coordinated service models that could deliver help where needed directly to children attending school.

Drug involvement often leads quickly to arrest and prosecution, especially for African American youths. The lack of substance abuse prevention and treatment programs at the local level means that little can be done to stop the growth of minority arrests for drug-related crimes.

Some participants, particularly in Sacramento County, noted that African American youths were often apprehended for drug-related offenses, both selling and using. Where local programs for drug-involved youths are lacking, as they are in Sacramento County, judges may order commitments to the CYA because the CYA has drug treatment slots.

Proposed Solutions

*Increase the ethnic balance in law enforcement, probation,
and court agencies that administer the juvenile justice system.*

Anglo American dominance or other ethnic imbalance within
juvenile justice agencies should be addressed by recruitment of more
minority staff, at the line, management, and policymaker levels. The
need pertains to law enforcement officers, probation personnel,
judges, and state corrections officials. The effort to improve ethnic
balance might be facilitated by establishing local, multicultural
committees to examine staffing patterns at justice agencies and to
assist in the implementation of necessary changes.

*Institute and require cultural sensitivity training for
police officers, beginning at the recruit stage.*

Police need training in cultural awareness and sensitivity so
they can communicate with minority youths and families in local
neighborhoods. They need to understand cultural values, to avoid
stereotyping members of other ethnic groups, and to work more
closely with minority communities. Police need better understanding of the differences between good and bad gangs. Cultural
sensitivity training should begin early in law enforcement officers'
careers, starting at the training academies.

*Address the root causes of crime with programs designed
to improve social and economic conditions that contribute to
delinquent behavior.*

High minority crime and incarceration rates, especially among
African American youths, are unlikely to abate unless we create new
economic opportunities for minority youths. Vocational training
and employment programs must be offered as alternatives to street
gangs and crime. Low self-esteem among African American youths
will continue to create trouble without new economic incentives to
deter youths from criminal pursuits. In particular, local business
communities should become involved with minority communities

and with schools to discuss youth work prospects and skill development. Governments should offer economic incentives (e.g., tax credits) to businesses that train and hire minority youths.

Implement programs to help African American
youths develop self-esteem.

Black youths need training and positive programs to develop self-esteem; this is linked to the need to improve social and economic conditions that erode self-esteem.

Increase the involvement of minority communities
and citizens in the making of juvenile justice policy.

Minority individuals and organizations—including neighbors, citizen groups, churches, and service organizations—are in the best position to understand the values and problems of minority youths, but are generally excluded from the juvenile justice policy-making process. Important community decisions about who gets arrested, who gets detained, and who gets incarcerated should be made with input from local minority communities. Better mechanisms for community involvement must be devised.

Establish new family support services in minority communities.

In all target counties, the need for family preservation and support services was identified. Some families need counseling and intervention services to prevent the breakup of the family. Others need economic or child-rearing support—for example, child care that can help single parents maintain employment, or tangible support (money, food, shelter) for families that are extremely poor. Sacramento County participants said the demand for these services far exceeded the supply; Merced County participants noted that there was not one family outreach/in-home service program in the county.

Change school policies toward minority youths who are at
high risk of dropping out. Implement coordinated, school-based
service plans creating a multiagency service capability at school sites.

Every discussion group mentioned the need for improved school services. Some urged that the basic school curricula should be more compatible with minority cultural values, which would improve educational performance by minority youths. Others suggested that schools offered a natural solution to the problem of fragmentation in youth service delivery. In particular, Los Angeles County participants noted that the county's gridlocked public transportation system made it difficult to deliver services to the individuals and families that need them, and that schools were the logical sites for coordinated delivery of necessary services. Promising state and national models of coordinated school-based services should be tested and implemented in California districts.

Establish drug treatment programs where needed.

Because it appears that minority youths, especially black youths, are disproportionately involved in drug offenses, greater treatment capability is needed at the local level. In particular, this need was urged by Sacramento County participants, who want a residential drug treatment program to serve as an alternative to the commitment of juvenile drug offenders to the CYA.

Institute objective risk-screening criteria and objective
needs assessments in juvenile justice systems to reduce
system bias where it may exist.

One suggestion for the reduction or elimination of bias in juvenile justice decision making was to adopt objective risk criteria and objective needs assessment instruments, especially at probation agencies. Well-designed screening systems can safely reduce incarceration levels and can objectify the juvenile justice decision-making process. Good models of objective juvenile-screening instruments already exist.

Expend local funds addressing the disproportionate representation
of minorities in the juvenile justice system in the following ways:

- Cultural sensitivity training for police, probation officers, and judges
- Community-based agencies providing family counseling and support services to minority clients
- Voucher service systems allowing youths and families to redeem vouchers for needed services with public or private providers
- Social workers and case advocates to help minority youths and families navigate the juvenile justice system and to develop alternative-to-institution dispositions
- Drug treatment programs, including residential treatment
- Mentoring programs to link positive role models to high-risk youths and to build self-esteem and responsibility among these youths
- Job training and placement programs for minority youths
- Police diversion and other preadjudication diversion programs; fund them in proportion to local minority representation in the justice system
- Dedicate assets captured in the war on drugs to minority programs in proportion to rates of minority representation in the juvenile justice system

Change state law and policy as follows:

- Reduce massive expenditures for incarceration in youth training schools and invest resultant savings in community corrections programs at the local level

Three of the four focus groups produced strong statements in favor of shifting state correctional dollars to the local level, where innovative treatment and prevention programs could be established and could be targeted for minority communities.

- Reexamine the punitive emphasis of state juvenile justice policy and refocus priorities to make rehabilitation work

Criticism was aimed at the grandstanding of politicians trying to appear tough on crime rather than focusing on the needs of minority youths with heavy involvement in the justice system. Those needs should be addressed by investing in programs that prevent minority youths from entering and staying in the criminal justice system. In particular, the present state allocation of $200,000 for delinquency prevention programs was called "absurd for a state of this size."

- Restore AB 90 (County Justice System Subvention) funds cut in previous budget cycles.
- Provide counties with "flexible" human service dollars so that local spending priorities, rather than state mandates, can be met. This would pave the way for the establishment of innovative programs serving the interests and needs of minority communities.

SUMMARY

In summary, several observations are worth noting. First, both the qualitative and quantitative data showed that race does play at least an indirect role in juvenile court decision making, which in turn affects the rates of confinement for various ethnic groups. Second, among minority groups, African American males are being overrepresented at extremely high rates from the point of detention through CYA commitments. Although a significant proportion of this overrepresentation can be attributed to a high rate of arrest, African American males continue to receive more severe dispositions than their counterparts, even when this and other relevant factors are controlled for. Similar to the results reported by Huizinga and Elliott (1987) on a national level, differences in incarceration rates among racial groups cannot be explained by differences in offense behavior among these groups. Third, local juvenile justice officials concur with these findings. They believed that institutional racism, and all of its attending consequences, is the primary cause of overrepresentation. Thus, although some important reforms can be made within the juvenile justice system itself, addressing the preconditions and social framework for such overrepresentation is far more important than attempting to reform juvenile justice.

Any comprehensive strategy to reduce the incarceration of minorities must address factors external to the justice system that impinge on differential delinquency rates and thus on differential incarceration rates. As long as African American youths have higher rates of poverty, single-parent families, high school drop-outs, and higher unemployment rates, these same factors should be counted in the calculus of possible causes for minority youths' overrepresentation in crime and thus incarceration. Reducing minority overrepresentation requires fundamental changes in the larger social environment that forms the basis for these disparities.

NOTES

1. Most of the data cited in the study were 1989 data. This was the base year for the Children in Custody survey results and for the California Bureau of Criminal Statistics' aggregate and individual case file data cited in the report. The data base year may seem stale to some readers, because this study was completed in September 1991, some 21 months after the close of calendar year 1989. In fact, when NCCD conducted this research, 1989 was the most recent year for which all pertinent data were available. Moreover, 1989 may stand for quite some time as the benchmark year for California state and county statistics on minority youth incarceration. After 1989, the California Bureau of Criminal Statistics will no longer collect probation and court data on the commitments of minors to county facilities; this function was abandoned in 1990 as a cost-saving measure. At the time of this writing, the data tapes from the next U.S. Children in Custody survey based on 1990 admission and 1991 counting day figures were not available.

2. Much of the data presented in the text of the report is aggregate data based on total admissions or counts of youths in a particular facility type. It is impossible, using gross facility counts, to conduct an analysis that controls for factors besides ethnicity, such as severity of offense. To move beyond this limitation into a more refined and revealing zone of analysis, NCCD analyzed BCS case transaction data files on juveniles in California facilities to control for the influence of nonethnic factors that may affect the differential commitment rates for minority youths.

3. The definition of *secure facility* used in this table and the associated text is the federal (OJJDP) definition. The California definition or understanding of secure facility is not necessarily the same as the federal. Juvenile camps and ranches, for example, may be either secure or nonsecure by federal standards, but are most often counted as secure county facilities by county agencies reporting to California's BCS. Depending on the number of facilities that fall within secure facility definition, counts of California juveniles in secure confinement may vary by as many as 2,000 youths.

4. A logistic analysis was also completed and showed that a residual ethnic effect persisted even after statistical controls are applied. However, the effects of race were clearly diminished.

8

Juvenile Justice Processing of American Indian Youths
Disparity in One Rural County

LISA M. POUPART

The American public is increasingly becoming aware of the disproportionate overrepresentation of minorities in the criminal justice system. In 1990, the *Milwaukee Journal* reported that, nationally, 23% of all Black males and 10.4% of all Latino males were either on probation, on parole, or in prison in 1990. These numbers are especially alarming when one considers the substantially lower percentage of these minorities in the general population. According to the most recent census figures, Blacks comprise about 12% and Latinos comprise about 9% of the total U.S. population ("23% of Young Black Males," 1990).

These numbers remain staggering when one examines the juvenile justice system, where minority youths are also disproportionately overrepresented at all stages of the system. However, a body of literature exists to suggest that those youths are not involved in crime at the same rates at which they are overrepresented in the system. Rather, the literature indicates that minority youths, when compared to white youths, are more likely to receive more severe dispositions throughout the juvenile justice decision-making process (Arnold, 1971; Bishop & Frazier, 1988; Kempf et al., 1990; McCarthy, 1987; Pope & Feyerherm, 1990a, 1990b; Thornberry, 1973).

179

Although a sizable amount of research exists regarding Black minorities in both the adult and juvenile systems, there is a tremendous lack of information regarding the processing of American Indians. The purpose of the present study is twofold. The first is to explore the existing literature that is concerned with American Indian criminality. The second purpose is also exploratory in nature in that it will examine one rural Wisconsin county to explore the possibility that American Indian youths are processed differentially in that county's juvenile justice system.

LITERATURE REVIEW

As indicated, there is a tremendous lack of information regarding American Indians in the adult and juvenile justice systems. This lack of information may be accounted for in two ways. First is the problem of size. Because American Indians comprise such a small percentage of the total population, it is difficult for researchers to gain a sample size that is large enough to conduct a study that will yield meaningful results.

A second reason for this lack of information is the problem of multiple jurisdictions. Today, many American Indian tribes retain the legal right to support a tribal police department and a tribal court. Furthermore, although both tribal police and courts may be in existence, the American Indians residing on those reservations may also be subject to federal and/or state policing and prosecution, depending on the circumstances of the offense. Thus it is difficult to conduct a study when many jurisdictions could be involved in a single case.

The literature that does exist can be examined in two parts. The first body of literature is concerned with establishing the extent to which American Indians are officially represented in the system. The second body of literature seeks to explain why the overrepresentation of American Indians at all stages in the adult and juvenile justice systems exists. This chapter will examine each of these parts separately, beginning with those articles that establish the degree to which American Indians are represented in the system.

AMERICAN INDIAN ADULTS
IN THE CRIMINAL JUSTICE SYSTEM:
THE EXTENT OF THE PROBLEM

Two of the earliest studies that addressed the extent of American Indian adult criminality are those by Stewart (1964) and Reasons (1972). Each study examined American Indian arrest rates using Uniform Crime Report (UCR) data. Stewart examined UCR data for 1960. The author found for that year that the arrest rate for American Indians was three times higher than for Blacks and eight times higher than for whites. When the author examined the arrest rates by type of crime, he found that 71% of all American Indian arrests were for alcohol-related offenses. Stewart (1964) further found that for non-alcohol-related offenses, the American Indian was arrested at a rate higher than the national rate and slightly less than the rate for Blacks.

Reasons (1972) criticized Stewart's (1964) study because he failed to examine data beyond a 1-year period. Thus Reasons replicated Stewart's findings for off-reservation crimes, using longitudinal UCR data for the period 1950 to 1969. Like Stewart, Reasons found that American Indians were consistently more likely to be arrested when compared to Blacks and whites. However, Reasons (1972, p. 320) found that for alcohol-related offenses, American Indians are 8 times more likely to be arrested than Blacks and 20 times more likely than whites. When comparing non-alcohol-related crimes, the author found American Indian arrest rates to be similar to the arrest rate for Blacks, but less than the arrest rate for whites.

In another study examining the extent of the official rates of American Indian adult criminality, Levy, Kunitz, and Everett (1969) explored the rate of homicide among the Navajo. Using the model employed in Wolfgang's (1966) study of criminal homicide in Philadelphia, the authors examined the Navajo police files dated between 1956 and 1965. The authors found that the homicide rate among the Navajo was relatively stable and comparable to the national rate (Levy et al., 1969). Furthermore, the authors found that the use of alcohol did not increase the rate of homicide nor was it associated with violent homicides among the Navajo when compared to Wolfgang's findings.

A 1977 study by Jensen, Strauss, and Harris further supports Stewart's (1964) and Reasons's (1972) findings. Jensen et al. examined census and UCR data for 1970. The authors found the arrest rate of American Indians to be from 7 to 22 times that of Blacks and whites for alcohol-related offenses. In urban areas, the authors found the non-alcohol-related arrest rate for American Indians to be four times greater than for whites and only somewhat higher than for Blacks. Furthermore, in rural areas, the authors found American Indians were arrested one and one half times more often than whites and twice as often as Blacks for non-alcohol-related offenses.

The use of UCR data in determining the extent of American Indian arrests is misleading. Not only does the use of these official reports grossly underestimate the total amount of crimes committed, but Harring (1982) noted that UCR data did not include crimes committed on reservations. Furthermore, Harring stated that UCR data for rural areas was only 80% complete; this is especially problematic given the fact that 50% of all American Indians were living in rural areas (p. 95). Harring examined the Bureau of Indian Affairs' records of crimes reported to reservation police and found that on-reservation arrests were as high or higher than those reported in the UCR data, thus suggesting that American Indians are arrested at high rates.

More recently, Flowers (1988) also examined the extent to which American Indians are arrested. Using 1980 census data and 1985 UCR data, the study showed that the disparity in American Indian arrests is not as great as shown in previous studies (Jensen et al., 1977; Reasons, 1972; Stewart, 1964). Flowers found that for violent crimes, the American Indians' arrest rate was three times lower than that of Blacks. The author also stated that Blacks had the highest arrest rate for all offenses, followed by American Indians and Latinos. Furthermore, Flowers noted that only when alcohol-related offenses are considered is the Indian arrest rate higher than that of all other groups. This disparity, the author suggested, is not as great as indicated in prior studies.

The extent to which American Indian adults are represented in official rates within the criminal justice system has been examined not only by comparing arrest rates but also through the comparison of incarceration rates. It is not surprising that like arrest rates, the incarceration rate of the American Indian adult is disproportionately higher than the distribution of American Indians in the general population.

In citing prison statistics, Reasons (1974) stated that in 1950, American Indians made up 1% of all prisoners in state and federal institutions. The author further stated the percentage of American Indians in prison compared to their numbers in the U.S. general population is 3.4, compared to .6 for whites, 1.8 for Latinos, and 3.7 for Blacks.

Similarly, Flowers (1988, pp. 111-112) noted that in 1984, American Indians comprised approximately 2% of federal prisoners and 1% of state prisoners, even though they account for .6% of the general population. Flowers further stated that American Indians have the second highest incarceration rate for all institutions in the United States, following Blacks, who have the highest rate, and that the rate for American Indians is two times that of whites and only slightly higher than Latinos.

By region, American Indians comprise less than 3% of the entire state population for North Dakota, but make up between 25% and 35% of the state's prison population (North Dakota Advisory Committee to the U.S. Commission on Civil Rights, 1978). In Montana, American Indians account for 3.9% of the state population and 33.3% of all prisoners in the state prisons (Native American Rights Fund in the Inequality of Justice, 1978). Similarly, in Minnesota, American Indians in prisons are estimated to be 25 times their proportion in the general state population. That is, they comprise .6% of Minnesota's state population and 12.5% of the prison population (Native American Rights Fund in the Inequality of Justice, 1982).

Thus an overview of the literature describing American Indian arrest and incarceration rates describes the extent to which American Indian adults, like Black and Latino adults, are disproportionately overrepresented in the criminal justice system. The next section suggests that this is also true for American Indian juveniles in the juvenile justice system in the United States.

AMERICAN INDIAN JUVENILES
IN THE JUVENILE JUSTICE SYSTEM:
THE EXTENT OF THE PROBLEM

Although we know that American Indian youths, like other racial minorities, are disproportionately overrepresented at all stages of the juvenile justice process, very few studies have examined the issue. In examining the UCR arrest data for 1985, Flowers (1988) found that American Indian juveniles had relatively high rates of arrest. The study shows that although American Indian youths comprised .6% of the general juvenile population, they made up .9% of all arrests and 1.0% of all index crimes. Furthermore, they made up 1.5% of all alcohol-related offenses. Flowers (1988) added that the disproportionate amount of arrests for American Indian youths are often overlooked because of their low number of total arrests.

Other studies have examined the official levels of involvement of American Indian youths within the juvenile justice systems of particular jurisdictions. Minnis (1963) examined adult and juvenile delinquency on the Shoshone-Bannock Indian Reservation in Fort Hall, Idaho. In an analysis of the Tribal Law and Order Office Records from 1934 to 1960, Minnis found the arrest rate of Fort Hall was 161 per 1,000 compared to 46.4 for 1,789 cities in the United States. The author noted a gradual rise in delinquency rates between 1955 and 1960. However, Minnis (1963, p. 335) added that a large proportion of all the arrests in Fort Hall were for nonserious offenses such as those involving "personal demoralization" (drunkenness, vagrancy, disorderly conduct, etc.).

In 1974, Forslund and Meyers examined officially recorded juvenile delinquency rates on the Wind River Reservation in Wyoming. The authors found high levels of delinquency—American Indian youths were five times more likely to appear in court than the general population. Forslund and Meyers further suggested that the majority of those cases overwhelmingly involved minor offenses such as status and alcohol-related offenses. In addition, through the use of a cohort analysis, Forslund and Meyers found that recidivism among the American Indian youths added to the delinquency rates in Wind River.

In a similar study, O'Brien (1977) compared Forslund and Meyers's (1974) findings with delinquency rates at the Warm Springs Reservation in central Oregon. O'Brien stated that in 1973, American Indian juveniles comprised .64% of Oregon's general population, but accounted for 7% of all referred juvenile offenses. O'Brien (1977) stated that in Oregon, "Indian juveniles were statistically overrepresented by a factor of 11" (p. 357). The author further added that although the delinquency rate at Warm Springs is 5 to 6 times higher than the national average, this can mainly be accounted for through status offenses and victimless crimes, as was found in Forslund and Meyers's study of Wind River.

More recently, Parry (1987) examined delinquency rates among Alaskan youths. The author noted that in 1985, the arrest rate for Alaskan youths appeared to be higher than the national average; however, for serious offenses the Alaskan rate was considerably lower. When examining delinquency rates, Parry found that native youths (Eskimo/American Indian) comprised fewer referrals (over 1,000) compared to whites (over 4,000). Furthermore, the author found that 30% of all native referrals were for liquor violations, whereas referrals for property offenses were low.

Although there have been very few studies examining the official rates of delinquency among American Indian youths, even fewer have documented the extent of their incarceration. One of the very few studies that has explored this issue is that conducted by Krisberg et al. (1987). The authors examined the incarceration rates of minority youths using statistics gathered from the U.S. Bureau of the Census, Children in Custody series. The study found that American Indian males had the second highest incarceration rate (second only to Blacks) in all public juvenile correction facilities in 1979. American Indian males were incarcerated at a rate of 362.8 per 100,000 (Krisberg et al., 1987, pp. 184-185). In addition, the study found that American Indian females were incarcerated at a rate of

73.3 per 100,000, which is close to that of Black females, who had the highest rate at 76.9 (pp. 185-186).

In summation, the existing research literature examining the rates at which American Indian juveniles are represented in the juvenile justice system is scant at best. However, those articles reviewed in this portion of the chapter tend to support the notion that American Indian juveniles, like adults, are disproportionately overrepresented in official rates within the American justice system.

EXPLAINING DISPROPORTIONATE OVERREPRESENTATION

Two main perspectives have been brought forth that seek to explain the disparate representation of minorities in official statistics. One perspective suggests that minorities are involved in criminal activity at a much higher rate than nonminorities. Thus minorities are represented at disparate rates in the system because they commit a disproportionate amount of crime. The second major perspective suggests that criminal and juvenile justice decision makers are biased in their decisions regarding minorities. As one may expect, very few studies applying either of these theories have been conducted with respect to American Indian minorities.

Higher Involvement

Those studies that have been conducted to determine whether American Indians are involved in criminal activity at higher rates have primarily focused on the self-reported behavior of American Indian youths. In a comparison of white and Indian delinquency, Forslund and Cranston (1975) administered self-report questionnaires to high school students on the Wind River Reservation in Wyoming. The authors found higher reported rates of delinquency for both male and female American Indians when compared to whites. However, this self-reporting tended to be for minor property and status offenses. Furthermore, when controlling for socioeconomic status, Forslund and Cranston (1975) found a reduction in the number of offenses for which there was a significant difference between racial groups, suggesting that both white and American Indian youths have similar rates of delinquency.

To determine if attachments to peers and family acted as behavior controls, Robbins (1985) conducted a study of Indian youths on three reservations in Florida. The author examined self-reported delinquency rates and self-reported levels of attachment to family and peers. Robbins found that although the Indian juveniles reported higher rates of delinquency than whites, they also reported high levels of attachment. In 1985, Robbins conducted a similar study to determine if commitment to goals and belief in societal rules controlled behavior. Again, the author found the Indian youths reporting high rates of delinquency and high rates of commitment to Indian norms and beliefs.

Thus it is clear that few studies exist that directly seek to assess the level of involvement of American Indians in crime. Many writers have been concerned with the disproportionate overrepresentation of Indians in the criminal and juvenile justice systems and have thus set forth an array of perspectives to explain higher involvement. May (1982) has categorized these theories to include social disorganization (Jensen et al., 1977; Levy et al., 1969; Minnis, 1963; O'Brien, 1977); acculturation/culture conflict (Jensen et al., 1977; May, 1982); and economic conflict (Hayner's 1942 study as cited in Flowers, 1988; French, 1982; Stewart, 1964). It appears, however, that those writers may have taken a great conceptual leap of faith in setting forth their theories when, in actuality, little research exists to suggest whether American Indians are in fact involved in crime at higher rates. The next section will explore those studies that have examined the possibility that American Indians are treated differentially when compared to whites.

Differential Treatment

Several other research studies seeking to explain the disparate number of American Indians in the criminal and juvenile justice systems have focused their attention on the decision-making patterns of officials.

The research literature in this area has tended to focus solely on the sentencing of American Indians compared to whites. One of the first quantitative studies examining this stage of the criminal justice process is that by Hall and Simkus (1975). In the first portion of a two-part study, the authors analyzed records from a western state's board of pardons. The study examined the records of American Indians and whites sentenced to probation from July 1966 to March 1972. Hall and Simkus (1975) found that American Indians were less likely to receive deferred sentences and more likely to receive partially suspended sentences involving incarceration in the state prison. This relationship remained when the authors controlled for offense type, prior record, and other factors. In the second portion of this study, Hall and Simkus analyzed data from a 1-year cohort of offenders sentenced for felonies from July 1966 to July 1967. The authors found the same results in the first part of their study, with the exception that prior record and previous detentions tended to decrease the relationship slightly (Hall & Simkus, 1975).

Pommersheim and Wise (1989) also studied sentencing, this time using the data from entrance records of male inmates in the South Dakota prison system. Here, however, the authors found American Indians were not more likely to receive harsher sentences when seriousness of the offense, prior record, and conviction variables were considered (Pommersheim & Wise, 1989).

In a similar study, Hutton, Pommersheim, and Feimer (1989) examined the effect of race on sentence severity for females in the South Dakota Correctional Facility. The authors found that American Indian females were serving an equal percentage of the maximum penalty when compared to whites. In other words, the authors did not find that race had a significant relationship between punishment and severity.

Winfree and Griffiths (1975) also examined the parole decision. The authors explored the parole failure rate of both American Indian and non-Indian offenders. The study found that American Indians were more likely to fail on parole than non-American Indian offenders. In addition, Winfree and Griffiths suggested that factors such as systematic bias may be influencing American Indians' failure at parole and that further research must focus on this issue.

In 1984, Bynum and Paternoster examined the impact of race on the decision to grant parole. Using data from an Upper Plains state, the authors found that race was a major determinant of parole and that American Indians were less likely to receive release (Bynum & Paternoster, 1984). The authors stated that although American Indians received shorter sentences overall, this did not influence the fact that they did not receive parole. Furthermore, the authors argued that American Indians are likely to receive racially biased outcomes at those decision-making points, such as parole, where officials are allowed wide discretion and are not guided by formal criteria (Bynum & Paternoster, 1984).

One of the few studies existing that examined the effects of racial disparity and American Indian youths in the juvenile justice system was by Schwartz, Harris, and Levi (1988). The authors examined the jail and lock-up populations for Minnesota juveniles. Schwartz et al. found that American Indian juveniles were the largest minority group held in the county jails and lock-ups. Furthermore, the authors found that American Indians were held significantly longer than whites on all types of charges (Schwartz et al., 1988). This suggests that American Indian juveniles were treated more punitively than whites.

The delinquency of Ponca Indian youths in Kay County, Nebraska, was the subject of a study by Heerman (1975). In examining juvenile case records between 1968 and 1972, Heerman found a statistically significant difference between the dispositions of whites and American Indians. In the study, American Indian youths were carried through adjudicatory stages and received convictions 94% of the time compared to 85% for whites. In addition, when Heerman (1975) examined the types of crimes committed, the author found that both races were equally likely to commit similar delinquent acts.

The effects of racial bias on police referrals to the juvenile court were examined by Fisher and Doyle-Martin (1981). The study found that American Indian, Black, and Latino youths were more likely to be referred to the juvenile court than white youths. The authors found that factors such as prior record, severity of offense, and gang affiliation did not account for the disparate number of minority youths referred to court.

Thus the literature concerned with the effects of race on the processing of American Indians in the system is sparse. The findings that do exist tend to be conflicting. That is, although some studies have found evidence of differential treatment, others have not. There is a need for further inquiry into this area to add to our understanding of the problem.

STATEMENT OF PURPOSE

As described in the preceding section, several studies exist that have described the overrepresentation of American Indians in the adult and juvenile justice systems. Those studies have indicated that American Indians, like Black and Latino minorities, are disproportionately overrepresented at many points in the systems. Many authors have assumed that because American Indians are represented in the system at higher rates, they must be committing crime at increased rates as well. Those authors have examined a wide array of causal theories in an effort to explain disproportionate involvement.

Thus there is a particular need for those studies that seek to explore the potential causes of the disparate representation of American Indians in the adult and juvenile justice systems. Such studies may address why so many American Indians are present in the system.

The purpose of the present study is to examine the processing of American Indian youths in one Wisconsin county to determine whether these youths appear to receive disadvantageous outcomes when compared with white youths at various decision-making points in the juvenile process.

American Indian youths, rather than adults, are the subject of this inquiry for two major reasons. First, the juvenile justice processing research tends to suggest the presence of differential treatment in the system. For example, in an analysis of 46 previously existing research articles examining the processing of minority youths, Pope and Feyerherm (1990a, 1990b) found that two thirds of those studies indicated that minority youths were treated disparately. Second, unlike in the adult system, decision makers in the juvenile justice system are allowed a large amount of discretionary authority. The underlying premise of granting such latitude is to enable officials to decide cases on an individual basis to accomplish a treatment-oriented goal. However, it is possible that such discretionary power may be used to disadvantage certain youths. Thus it appears that the disparate treatment of minorities may be more evident within the juvenile system where official decision makers are allowed discretionary authority and where some previous literature does, in fact, establish the presence of differential treatment.

METHODOLOGY

Existing research examining the impact of discriminatory decision making has identified the need to focus on multiple decision points as a process rather than a series of individual decision-making points (Liska & Tausig, 1979; Zatz, 1987). Through an examination of multiple decision points, it is possible to identify whether the system as a whole works to disadvantage certain groups of youths.

In an effort to examine a series of decision points, the research model used in the present study is one designed and implemented by Pope and Feyerherm (1991). In one portion of a three-stage study, the authors examined the processing of white and minority youths in the juvenile courts of California and Florida for 1985. The authors examined the juvenile justice system as a dynamic process, whereby decisions and events that occur early on in the system have a direct effect on the likelihood of sanctioning and conviction decisions that occur later on. Thus the authors designed an analytic model that focused on multiple decision points as a process, allowing them to determine the impact and interrelationships of those decision points as they affect the movement of white and minority youths through the system.

Sample Selection

The data for the current study were derived from the juvenile court records from one rural Wisconsin county. This county's American Indian population is 7.14% and is substantially higher than the state and national averages of .63% (U.S. Bureau of the Census, 1989). It was necessary to focus on a county that had a large American Indian population to allow a basis for the comparison to white youths.

Because the county examined in the study is rural, the juvenile court processes a relatively low number of cases per year. Thus all delinquency cases formally and informally closed after December 31, 1985, and prior to January 1, 1991, were included in the analysis ($N = 543$).

Design and Measurement

The four decision points examined in this study are the decision at intake, the detention decision, whether a delinquency petition was filed, and the final disposition of the case (see Figure 8.1). The model used in the study expresses the relational process of those decision points and can be represented as a "branching network" or "decision-tree model" whereby those decision points that occur earlier affect those that occur later in the system (Pope & Feyerherm, 1991).

A cross-tabulation of each of the decision points by race while controlling for any prior decision points in the model allows us to establish the proportion of youths at each point in the system. An examination of those proportions allows us to (a) determine the probability of youths moving from one point to the next and (b) determine those probabilities separately for white and American Indian youths (Pope & Feyerherm, 1991). Thus the model allows us to identify particular combinations of decisions that are particularly likely to disadvantage minority youths (Pope & Feyerherm, 1991).

Using the bold-faced path in Figure 8.1 as an example, the model enables us to determine the race of those youths who (a) are referred to prosecutor at intake, (b) are not detained, (c) have a delinquency petition filed, and (d) receive in-home supervision as a final disposition.

The method employed in this study is limited in the degree to which it can determine whether racial bias is actually present within juvenile court decision making (Pope & Feyerherm, 1991). Although the findings may suggest the presence of disparity in treatment, the model employed has not considered other legal factors that may

REFERRAL   DETAINED   PETITION   DISPOSITION

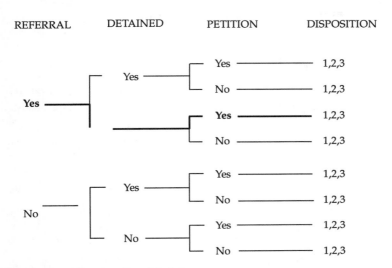

Figure 8.1. Decision-Tree Model
SOURCE: Adapted from Pope and Feyerherm (1991).
NOTE: Disposition codes are 1 = in-home supervision/probation, 2 = out-of-home supervision/probation, 3 = placement in correctional facility or transfer to adult court.

influence outcome. Thus the findings cannot prove the existence of racial bias; they merely suggest whether further examination into the decision-making process is required.

In addition, by employing Pope and Feyerherm's (1991) decision-tree model, the choices available to juvenile court decision makers have been summarized into dichotomous outcomes. This means that in coding the data, cases fell into one of two possible categories at each decision point prior to disposition. The authors warn that although this simplification is necessary to construct the general operation of the system, it overlooks specific differences within each of the categories (Pope & Feyerherm, 1991). Such simplification restricts us from identifying additional differences that may occur. In this analysis, for example, no distinction is made between those cases that are closed or those that are resolved informally at intake. Those two outcomes, however, are not equal, and one may be viewed as less favorable than the other. However, both outcomes have been viewed synonymously in this study.

RESULTS

The total number of youths that fell into each category is presented in Appendix A. It is necessary to report the total number of youths in each cell because in those cases where few youths are represented, the percentages alone may be misleading. The results of the cross-tabulation, then, are presented in Appendix B. In both appendixes, values are reported at each decision point for both white and American Indian youths.

Intake

At the intake decision point, a youth may receive one of two possible outcomes. The case may be (a) closed or handled informally by the intake worker or (b) referred to a prosecutor for further processing.

At this decision point, a total of 190 white and 87 American Indian youths had their cases closed or informally handled (Appendix A). The results of the cross-tabulation of the decision at intake by race shows that 61.3% of the whites had their cases closed or handled informally, whereas only 37.3% of the American Indians received this outcome (Appendix B).

Those 277 cases that were resolved at intake were not referred further and thus have dropped out of the system entirely. Therefore, they are not represented in numbers beyond intake in the decision-tree models in Appendixes A and B. At the other decision (to refer to prosecutor), 38.7% of the white and 62.7% of American Indian youths were referred. This is a difference of 24.0%.

These results show that significantly fewer American Indian youths had their cases closed or resolved at intake. Rather, they were more likely than white youths to have their cases referred to a prosecutor. Thus American Indians were more likely to receive the more punitive outcome at the intake stage.

Detention

The detention decision refers to whether a youth was released or placed in either nonsecure or secure detention prior to the filing of the delinquency petition. The findings show that none of those children who had their cases closed or resolved at intake were detained. Of those children who had their cases referred to a prosecutor, few were detained prior to the filing of the delinquency petition. A total of 9 whites and 21 American Indians were placed in detention at this stage. Although both groups were detained at low levels in absolute numbers, the rate at which American Indian youths were detained is still more than twice that of their white counterparts.

The results of the cross-tabulation of the detention decision by race show that 7.5% of the whites and 14.6% of the American Indians were detained—a difference of 7.6%. Thus, although two times as many American Indian youths were detained, few were placed in detention prior to the filing of a delinquency petition, regardless of their race.

Petition

There are two possible outcomes for those cases that reached the petition stage. The outcome determines whether a prosecutor elected to file a delinquency petition. For all youths who had delinquency petitions filed, 119 were white and 143 were American Indian. Thus all but one were referred to a prosecutor and had delinquency petitions filed in their cases.

The cross-tabulation of the decision to file a delinquency petition by race while controlling for the prior decisions yielded the following: For those youths who were not detained, 99.2% of the American Indians and 100% of the whites had petitions filed. For those detained, all had delinquency petitions filed. This indicates, then, that there are no differences between the two groups at this decision point. Thus the results show that regardless of race, delinquency petitions were filed in almost all cases that reached this stage.

Disposition

The disposition stage determines the final outcome that a youth received, either in the form of a consent decree or by appearing before a juvenile court judge. Wisconsin statutory law provides for

13 possible dispositions for a child adjudged delinquent (Wis. Stat. 49.34). Of those 13 dispositions, the juvenile court imposed a restitution and/or a community service order in nearly all cases reaching this final stage. In addition to restitution and/or community service, the juvenile court imposed one of the following three dispositions on all cases:

1. Probation—juvenile living in own home or home of friend, relative, and so on
2. Probation—juvenile placed out of home in a residential facility (county, private, or mental health)
3. Incarceration or waiver—juvenile transferred to the state juvenile correctional facility or waived into adult court

Appendix A shows that of all delinquent youths who received in-home probation, 107 were white and 111 were American Indian. For the most severe disposition, two whites and nine American Indians were sentenced to a correctional facility, and one Indian youth's case was waived to adult court. Thus American Indian youths received the more punitive outcomes.

The results of the cross-tabulation show that of those youths who were detained and had delinquency petitions filed, 55.6% of the whites and 23.8% of the American Indians were placed on in-home supervision. In addition, 33.3% of the whites and 52.4% of the American Indians were placed on out-of-home supervision. Finally, 11.1% of the whites and 23.8% of the American Indians were transferred to a juvenile facility or waived into adult court. For those youths who were not detained and had delinquency petitions filed, 92.7% of the white and 86.9% of the American Indian youths received in-home supervision. Of those who received out-of-home supervision, 6.4% were white and 10.7% were American Indian. Of those who received the more punitive outcome, .9% were white and 2.5% were American Indian.

The one American Indian youth who was not detained and did not have a delinquency petition filed in his or her case was waived into adult court. Thus 100% represents the one youth who fell on that branch of the decision-tree model.

The results of this analysis show that although the actual number of youths differing at disposition is low, whites are more likely to receive the least severe disposition more often than American Indians. Thus American Indian youths were slightly more likely to receive the more punitive outcome.

DISCUSSION

The results of this analysis show that in the juvenile justice system from 1986 to 1990 in the county examined, American Indian youths were more likely to receive the more severe outcome at more than one decision point. In addition, at no single decision point were white youths found to be at a disadvantage when compared to American Indians. The greatest disparity occurred at the intake decision. White juveniles were significantly more likely to have their cases closed or resolved informally, whereas American Indian juveniles were more likely to have their cases referred to a prosecutor for additional handling. This indicates that further efforts to reduce disparity in this county's juvenile system must focus on the intake decision point.

At the decision to detain, the detention rate was nearly two times greater for American Indian youths; however, both groups were found to be detained at very low levels. The cross-tabulation found only a 7% difference between the races. This difference is not great and can be attributed to random chance. However, the higher detention rate of American Indian youths does suggest a disadvantage to that group. That disadvantage is consistent with the overall trend of the data.

At the petition-filing stage the county prosecutors filed delinquency petitions in nearly all cases. The decision to file a petition may be a rubber stamp of the intake worker's decision to refer a case on for filing. If youths are not filtered out at intake, they are processed on through the system and have delinquency petitions filed in all cases regardless of race.

At the disposition stage, American Indian youths were less likely to receive the least severe outcome—in-home probation. Although the absolute numbers of American Indian youths who received more punitive dispositions are low, the finding that they are disadvantaged at this stage is consistent with the finding that in-home supervision is ordered for them less often than for white youths.

Thus the overall trend of this analysis suggests that American Indians are at a disadvantage in the juvenile justice system in the county examined. Pope and Feyerherm's (1991) model would indicate that such findings do not prove the existence of discrimination because the analysis did not take into consideration those legal variables that may affect a youth's outcome in the system. Pope and Feyerherm (1991) noted, however, that the central purpose of their model is to identify those points in the system that require further inquiry in an effort to prevent racial bias in processing.

This analysis suggests, then, that further research in the county in question ought to examine those legal variables, such as seriousness of the offense and prior record, as they affect a youth's outcome. In addition, this study suggests that any efforts to prevent further differential treatment of American Indian youths in the county in question ought to focus on the intake stage, where the greatest disparity occurred.

APPENDIX 8-A Total Number of Youths at Each Decision Point

INTAKE	DETENTION	PETITION	DISPOSITION
W I	W I	W I	W I

Refer 120 <u>146</u>

Yes 9 <u>21</u>

Yes 9 <u>21</u>
- 1) 5 / <u>5</u>
- 2) 3 / <u>11</u>
- 3) 1 / <u>5</u>

No 0 <u>0</u>
- 1) 0 / <u>0</u>
- 2) 0 / <u>0</u>
- 3) 0 / <u>0</u>

No 110 <u>123</u>

Yes 110 <u>122</u>
- 1) 102 / <u>106</u>
- 2) 7 / <u>13</u>
- 3) 1 / <u>3</u>

No 0 <u>1</u>
- 1) 0 / <u>0</u>
- 2) 0 / <u>0</u>
- 3) 0 / <u>1</u>

SOURCE: Adapted from Pope and Feyerherm (1991).
NOTE: The first figure is n for white youths, the second is for American Indian youths. Total n of cases closed or handled informally = 190 for white youths, 87 for American Indian youths. Disposition codes are 1 = in-home supervision/probation, 2 = out-of-home supervision/probation, 3 = placement in correctional facility or transfer to adult court.

APPENDIX 8-B Percentage of Youths at Each Decision Point

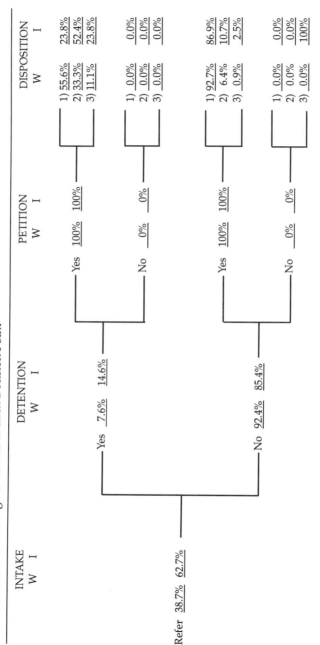

SOURCE: Adapted from Pope and Feyerherm (1991).
NOTE: The first figure is percentage for white youths, the second is for American Indian youths. Total percentage of cases closed or handled informally = 61.3 for white youths, 37.3 for American Indian youths. Disposition codes are 1 = in-home supervision/probation, 2 = out-of-home supervision/probation, 3 = placement in correctional facility or transfer to adult court.

9

Equity Within the Juvenile Justice System
Directions for the Future

CARL E. POPE

Five years ago, Pope and Feyerherm (1990a, 1990b) examined more than two decades of research that focused on race and the processing of juvenile offenders. The results of that examination underscored the fact that racial differences were apparent in many jurisdictions and across various decision points. Minority youths were often found to be at greater risk of receiving the most severe outcomes compared to white youths. Moreover, this analysis demonstrated that approximately two thirds of the research findings showed that minority youths (principally youths of color) were disadvantaged within those juvenile justice systems examined. To date, approximately 13 states have completed (in one form or another) Phase 2 research efforts focusing on juvenile processing, and all have found either direct or indirect race effects.

More recently, a special edition of the *Journal of Research in Crime and Delinquency* (Pope & Clear, 1994) focusing on race and punishment contained four articles examining race effects in both the adult and juvenile justice systems. Again, all of these articles underscored the fact that race was not an insignificant factor with regard to the administration of justice. For example, Wordes et al. (1994) examined detention differences in juvenile processing between minority and white youths across five Michigan counties. Their findings suggested that "across all analysis, youth who were African American or Latino were consistently more likely to be placed in secure detention. This was observed in the detention practices of both the police and the courts" (Wordes et al., 1994, p. 162).

Their analysis revealed that minority youths were more at risk of being detained even when relevant legal variables were introduced. As they note, and the literature suggests (Pope & Feyerherm, 1992), this has implications for later decisions, especially those pertaining to secure confinement.

This book reports findings regarding the disproportionate processing of minority youths in jurisdictions located within the states of California, Florida, Michigan, Minnesota, Pennsylvania, Wisconsin, and Washington. Consistent with the research noted above, these studies again suggest that minority youths are often at greater risk of receiving the more severe outcomes compared to white youths. For example, as Frazier and Bishop note in Chapter 2:

> Our quantitative analyses indicate that nonwhite juveniles referred for delinquency offenses in Florida receive more severe (i.e., more formal and/or more restrictive) dispositions than their white counterparts at each of the four stages in processing. Specifically, after controls are introduced for age, gender, seriousness of referral offense, and seriousness of their prior records, we find significant race effects. (p. 27)

Taken together, the research reported in this book and elsewhere strongly suggests that concerns regarding fairness within juvenile justice systems are not unwarranted. Indeed, much of the data underscore the point that minority youths, especially those of color, are often disadvantaged compared to majority youths. Thus it is not surprising that local, state, and national efforts are increasingly focusing on this problem and that further action should be taken to address and alleviate racial disparities.

POLICY AND PROGRAM DIRECTIONS

In 1990, the National Council of Juvenile and Family Court Judges produced a volume devoted to minority youths in the juvenile justice system. This journal examined the effect of race at various stages of the juvenile system, including arrest, detention, intake, transfer, adjudication, and disposition. It was noted that minority youths encountered numerous problems at each of these stages that were often quite different than those experienced by white youths. As a judicial response to these problems, a series of policy recommendations were presented. These recommendations included cultural diversity training, system monitoring, continued research, and a variety of other approaches that are too detailed to recount here. The reader is referred to that volume for a more complete listing and discussion.

Based on analyses of data, a number of policy recommendations are also presented by the authors in this book. For example, Austin in Chapter 7 presents what are perceived to be the causes of minority overrepresentation and then proposes specific solutions within each area. These recommendations are broad based and cover not only juvenile justice systems but also include schools, the family, service providers, and the legislature. Similarly, Frazier and Bishop in Chapter 2 provide four recommendations to help ensure equality and fairness in the processing of both white and minority youths. One of their major recommendations is the development of a racial, ethnic, and cultural diversity curriculum that juvenile justice personnel be required to complete. This was also noted by Austin in Chapter 7 and by the National Council of Juvenile and Family Court Judges (1990). In their qualitative analysis, Frazier and Bishop found that minority families are frequently perceived as being deficient by personnel within the juvenile justice system. As they note in Chapter 2, "Taken individually or together in various combinations, these views about minority families indicate racial bias, attitudes that feed on and support racial bias, and they ultimately operate to justify the system's bent toward treating youths from minority families more formally and more harshly" (p. 35). Thus it would seem that some degree of cultural and racial sensitivity would be in order.

In general, strategies designed to reduce the overrepresentation of minority youths in secure facilities can be conceived of across two separate dimensions. First, there are those designed to affect the juvenile justice system directly, such as the cultural diversity training noted above. Second, there are those designed to affect the environment within which the juvenile justice system operates. I begin this discussion with the former—programs geared specifically to the operation of the juvenile justice system.

RECOMMENDATIONS
REGARDING JUVENILE PROCESSING

Policy recommendations designed to affect the juvenile justice system follow two separate tracks. The first deals with measures to identify the nature of the problem if it does exist and the second with steps to alleviate disproportionate representation. With regard to the former, the following recommendations are made.

Development of a systematic monitoring procedure to determine
the percentage of minority/majority youths being processed through
each stage of the juvenile justice system at regular intervals

The literature and the analysis of the California and Florida data conducted by Pope and Feyerherm (1992) clearly demonstrate that differential processing can occur at any stage of the juvenile justice system. This analysis also suggests that racial/ethnic differences are more pronounced at the earlier processing stages (i.e., intake and detention). Therefore, those jurisdictions concerned with this problem will need to implement a system to identify those stages where disproportion occurs and the extent to which it exists. Furthermore, such monitoring will need to be undertaken at regular intervals to determine the nature of any changes in the system.

One model that could be used to accomplish this was a branching network analysis developed by Pope and Feyerherm (1992) and applied to juvenile justice data from California and Florida. Basically, the decision points for both the California and Florida data were presented as a branching network, thus identifying those points where differences between minority/majority youths were greatest. In addition, by examining the end states (dispositions) one could determine the probabilities of receiving lesser and more severe dispositions for different racial/ethnic youths. Although this model was illustrated with statewide data, it also could be applied to various jurisdictional levels (e.g., county and local agencies). As an example, see Chapter 8 in this book.

Furthermore, this model can be used to assess the extent to which local jurisdictions vary from the statewide average. For both California and Florida, it was demonstrated that some counties departed markedly with regard to severity of disposition when compared to the state as a whole. In other words, there were some counties in which minority youths received much more severe dispositions compared to majority youths and others in which they did not. Although this analysis demonstrates that there are differences, it did not examine the nature of these differences—whether they are accounted for by "selection bias" or other factors. Nonetheless, it does target those counties that may need further analysis. Although the focus here was on the end states or disposition, the same technique could be applied to any decision point.

To use this model, data must be provided in a transactional framework. In other words, the data must be present in the form of computerized records with the ability to link one stage of the system to the next. Although many states have this capability, some do not. In some states, juvenile justice information is only available in the form of summary tallies. In these instances, a disproportionality index can be used to monitor disparate outcomes. This index was developed to assist the states in meeting the 1989 formula funding requirements under the Juvenile Justice and Delinquency Prevention Act.

Under this requirement, states are mandated to demonstrate whether minority youths are disproportionately overrepresented at various stages of juvenile processing compared to their population base. Information pertaining to the total number of youths processed at a stage would be entered along with the number of minority youths. Comparisons would then be made between the percentage of minority youths processed and their representation in the total population, thus producing an index of disproportional treatment. This technique could be applied to specific minority groups (e.g., blacks, Latinos) and to various stages of processing. It could also be used on a state, county, or local level. Thus both the transactional and summary models could be used to monitor the juvenile justice system.

An intensive examination of those stages in the juvenile justice
system with the widest gaps between minority and majority youths

Once those stages of juvenile processing with the largest gaps between minority and majority youths have been identified, they need to be targeted for further evaluation. For example, if it is found that minority youths are substantially more likely to be detained in secure facilities, then the criteria used in reaching that decision must be examined. In some jurisdictions, there are little or no criteria for making a detention decision. It may, for example, be based on the subjective impression of the intake worker. Thus different intake workers may be using vastly different criteria, which may in turn lead to an overrepresentation of minorities. Even in those jurisdictions that are more legalistic with articulated criteria, intake workers may not be applying them across the board, or the criteria may have subtle racial biases built into them. In any event, the nature of decision making must be examined.

One strategy for accomplishing this would be to systematically review all existing criteria and guidelines. This would be followed by an evaluation to determine whether the criteria were justified under existing juvenile statutes or whether there might be subtle racial differences operating. For example, if "idleness" (whether the youth is in school or employed or doing nothing) is important in reaching a detention decision, then one needs to examine racial differences by this characteristic. If black youths are more likely to be "idle," and therefore more likely to be detained, this may in part account for larger percentages of blacks in secure facilities. A determination then needs to be made whether or how this criterion should be used. If nothing else, this procedure can be used to determine how existing criteria may or may not account for minority overrepresentation.

Following this review (or in the absence of any written criteria), a representative sample of decision makers (e.g., intake workers) could be surveyed. The goal here would be to identify (either through questionnaires, structured interviews, or focus groups) the manner in which decisions are reached. In other words, intake workers would be asked to self-report the characteristics they consider to be most important to them in reaching a decision to detain in a secure facility. Responses could then be cross-referenced against actual cases. Decisions could then be made regarding the process—whether it is working sufficiently well, requires some alterations, or needs to be completely reworked. The point to all this is not to assess blame but merely to aid in understanding the dynamics of decision making.

Implementation of a research
plan to test the racial bias hypothesis

There are various analytic strategies that could be employed to determine whether a race effect exists. Depending on the type of data available (if they exist in computerized records or have to be compiled from case files), one could examine the relationship between any decision point and an array of social and legal factors. For example, if previous monitoring reveals that minority over-representation exists at the point of detention, then both direct and indirect race effects could be examined. There are a number of statistical procedures that would support such an analysis (e.g., multivariate contingency tables, path analytic techniques, logistic regression, log linear and discriminate function analysis, and the like) as well as various qualitative strategies. The decision to detain could be analyzed for minority and majority youths, with possible controls for gender, age, income, family status, instant offense, prior commitments, current status, or other factors, depending on their availability.

The results of this analysis would indicate in a statistical sense whether race makes a difference and, if it does, the manner in which it operates. For example, it may be the case that racial status is linked to family stability, which in turn affects the probability of being detained. In other words, youths coming from single-parent households may face a higher probability of detention than those coming from a two-parent household. In many major metropolitan areas, evidence suggests that minority youths are less likely to reside with both parents compared to majority youths. Therefore, family status may be the mechanism linking race to detention. Or it may be the case that income level makes a difference. Family stability may only be predictive for those residing in low-income areas. Or it may be a factor only for those youths charged with less serious offenses or those with no previous juvenile court commitments. On the other hand, for certain jurisdictions racial status may play no role as evidenced by the analysis. In this situation, overrepresentation of minority youths could not be attributed to the operation of the juvenile justice system. Solutions to the problem then would have to focus elsewhere.

The above scenario underscores the fact that the analysis and conclusions drawn from it can be relatively straightforward or extremely complex. Nonetheless, it does provide a foundation from which informed decisions could be made and policy generated. The basic point is that it is too often the case that we do not know what is going on within specific juvenile justice systems. Although we may know that minorities are disproportionately represented, we have no knowledge of why this is the case or any concrete information to guide us. If nothing more, an analytic strategy as outlined here would provide that basic information needed to make informed decisions. Various examples of such strategies are provided in this book.

Given the procedures outlined above, if race is found to be a factor in accounting for minority overrepresentation, then a strategy for reducing its influence must be developed. The following recommendations are offered to help accomplish this goal.

Implementation of training workshops
focusing on race and juvenile processing

As noted earlier, the goal here would be to sensitize and train principal actors (e.g., probation officers, judges) in the juvenile justice system with regard to race-related issues. Such training programs have proven successful in other criminal justice areas, and there is no reason to suspect that they could not make an impact here. For example, sentencing institutes have proven somewhat successful in articulating sentencing philosophy and reducing disparity. Under this model, judges from various jurisdictions attend workshops at a central site over a period of a few days. During this time, differences in sentencing philosophies are discussed and evaluated. Often, training exercises are prescribed using mock trials.

Sentencing councils have a similar objective although they involve judges from a single court. Actual cases are discussed among judges and recommended sentences are given. Through the use of both institutes and councils, it is hoped that some degree of unanimity will be achieved in sentencing, thus reducing disparate outcomes. There are a variety of training models that could be used that, in turn, could be adapted to the needs of specific jurisdictions. Among the topics to be discussed could be all or some of the following:

- Overview and summary of the history of race relations in this country
- Race relations as they pertain to the adult and juvenile justice systems (e.g., within incarcerated populations)
- Structural and economic conditions as they pertain to the ghetto underclass and the implications for the justice system
- Review and discussion of the existing research literature as it pertains to minorities and the juvenile justice system (what we know and what we don't know)

The topics suggested above are exemplary of the type of issues that could be used to sensitize juvenile justice actors generally to race-related problems. More specific programs geared toward achieving racial equity could include the following:

- Workshops with various actors (probation officers, judges, etc.) focusing on the nature of decision making in their respective areas (i.e., how decisions are made and what influence race might play)
- Discussion of various alternative strategies for decision making (e.g., use of guidelines as noted below)
- Training sessions geared toward implementing different decision-making models

The objectives of the strategies discussed above are, first, to sensitize juvenile court personnel to minority issues and, second, to develop techniques to reduce disparity, if it does exist, and to ensure equity in processing. The specific nature of the training programs can be developed depending on the needs of the particular jurisdiction and the specific objectives desired.

Establish a "checks-and-balances" system
with regard to juvenile processing decisions

In some jurisdictions, decisions are made by individuals without any provision for review. For example, it is not uncommon for probation officers to decide whether the case should be closed/dismissed or processed further (intake) or whether the juvenile should be held in detention and in what type of facility. Typically, such decisions are within the sole discretion of the intake worker (whether following stipulated guidelines or not) and are not subject to review. In other jurisdictions, there are provisions for further review. Intake workers make a recommendation of whether to file a petition of delinquency, which is subsequently reviewed by the District Attorney's office, which then makes the final determination.

In those instances where intake and detention decisions are reached independently, it may be feasible to consider a restructuring of the decision-making process. One way of doing this would be to involve multiple decision makers. In other words, it would be the responsibility of more than one intake worker to review a particular case and concur with the decision to process through intake or place a youth in detention. This would provide for a system with shared responsibility and accountability (a checks-and-balances system).

Another possibility would be to develop some type of review procedure of individual decisions. Typically, this could take the form of a review panel. This panel (composed of any number of probation officers, district attorneys, etc.) would have responsibility for reviewing all intake and detention decisions to ensure that they meet acceptable standards (e.g., established guidelines, statutory criteria).

Using either of these models, it would then be possible to establish a procedure for routine audit and review to ensure that processing decisions are racially neutral. Introducing a checks-and-balances system will necessarily increase staff workload and introduce additional steps in the decision-making process. However, if the primary goal is to ensure that processing decisions are made in a fair and racially neutral manner, then such steps are certainly worth consideration.

Development of guidelines to aid
decision makers in reaching outcome decisions

Guideline-based decision making has been used effectively in a variety of areas, including parole, sentencing, and pretrial release. The overall goal is to delineate the criteria on which decisions should be based and to simplify the decision-making process. One assumption underlying a guideline-based approach is that discretion will be reduced, thus decreasing disparity in outcome. One of the earliest uses of this approach was in the development of parole guidelines in the federal correctional system. Although the technique used to construct parole guidelines can be quite complex, the conceptual basis is relatively straightforward. First, the criteria generally used in reaching parole decisions are examined and quantified. Those criteria that are the best predictors of parole outcome (e.g., prior convictions, prior commitments, age at current offense) are cross-classified with the severity of the current offense. The result is a salient-factor score that specifies a range of time during which an inmate should be considered for parole. These guidelines were in use in the federal system until abolished in 1987 when parole was eliminated.

Many states and the federal system currently use a guideline approach to determine appropriate sentences for adult offenders. Federal sentencing guidelines went into effect in 1987 and are conceptually similar to the former parole guidelines. Again, a grid is constructed on the basis of two scores (seriousness of the offense and offender characteristics that are predictive of recidivism). Based on these characteristics, judges determine the appropriate sentences. Sentencing guidelines were designed, in part, to constrain judicial discretion and thereby reduce sentence disparity. Following the same logic, pretrial release guidelines establishing criteria by which to release defendants prior to trial are now being implemented in some jurisdictions.

A guideline-based approach could be implemented at a number of stages in juvenile processing (e.g., intake, detention, and disposition). If properly constructed, guidelines could reduce discretion in reaching outcome decisions and help to ensure equity in processing. It should be noted, however, that there are some potential problems that need to be addressed when instituting such an approach. For example, the starting point in establishing guidelines is to examine the previous patterns of decision making to identify those criteria that are most appropriate. If previous decisions were not racially neutral, one merely builds the past into the present and the end result will be the same. Similarly, if any factor built into the guidelines is not racially neutral, then a guidelines approach may be more subtle with regard to racial disproportionality but no less real. Given these attendant problems, it is still possible to develop a guideline-based approach that will help to ensure fairness in juvenile processing. The overall emphasis should be the development of guidelines leading to the "least restrictive" alternative. For example, detention guidelines should focus on keeping youths out of confinement rather than bringing them into confinement.

THE SOCIAL CONTEXT
OF YOUTH CRIME AND JUSTICE

Although improvements within the juvenile justice system are worthy endeavors, they are not likely to be successful without attending to the myriad social problems affecting cities and their residents throughout the country. Through the use of focus groups, Austin reported that the impact of racism is paramount for many juvenile justice practitioners. But as he notes in Chapter 7,

> They believed that institutional racism, and all of its attending consequences, is the primary cause of overrepresentation. Thus, although some important reforms can be made within the juvenile justice system itself, addressing the preconditions and social framework for such overrepresentation is far more important than attempting to reform juvenile justice. (p. 177)

We now turn our attention to one of the most important preconditions that affects the lives of all Americans but especially those residing in inner cities.

In *The Declining Significance of Race*, Wilson (1978) examined the relationship of blacks to the economic structure of society from both a historical and contemporary perspective. In doing so, he identified three stages of American race relations: The first encompassed the period of antebellum slavery; the second extended from the last quarter of the 19th century to the New Deal era; and the third, the post-World War II, modern industrial era. Essentially, what Wilson argued was that during the first two eras, blacks were systematically excluded from any meaningful participation in the economy because of their race. Labor markets, up to the end of the New Deal era, were characterized by a system of institutionalized racism. However, the advent of World War II opened up expanded job opportunities for blacks, which ushered in a period of progressive transition from race inequalities to class inequalities. In sum, the gist of Wilson's argument was that race has become intermixed with class in determining the life chances of black Americans within the labor market. Unfortunately, opportunities for many black Americans have become greatly diminished as both their class position and their race have excluded many of them from any meaningful economic participation.

What began to occur in the 1960s and continues into the 1990s is the creation of a permanently entrenched black underclass (Wilson, 1978). The changing nature of the economy (e.g., the decline in industrial and manufacturing jobs and the rise of a service economy) has created a separate class composed mostly of blacks (but also including other minority groups, as well as poor whites) who have little chance of successful competition in a largely advanced technological society. A major characteristic of the underclass is "their poverty and the social decay in which they are forced to survive" (Pinkney, 1984, p. 170). Often unable to subsist within the legal economy, many of the underclass youths take refuge in the illegal subeconomy such as prostitution, gambling, and drugs (Fagan, Piper, & Moore, 1986; Miller, 1986). Frequently, they express their frustration in acts of expressive and instrumental violence, as witnessed in the resurgence of youth gang activity (Hagedorn, 1988). As a result, members of the underclass comprise the bulk of juvenile and adult institutionalized populations and represent the most frequent clients of the criminal justice system.

Expanding on Wilson's thesis, Leman (1986) examined the origin of the underclass by focusing on the city of Chicago and a series of migratory patterns that began in the early 1800s. These migrations involved the large-scale movement of blacks from rural southern plantations to the industrialized north. They came principally to improve their economic position by obtaining jobs in the industries of northern cities such as Chicago, Milwaukee, Detroit, and other rust-belt cities. The second migration, occurring during the 1960s, involved the departure of a large number of middle- and working-class blacks from the inner cities. Seeking a better quality of life, those leaving the inner cities relocated in more affluent neighborhoods, with improved housing, schools, and other services. As Silberman (1978) noted, an indirect effect of this second migration was the removal of black leadership, economic power, and role models. Anderson's (1990) recent ethnographic study of poor, urban communities illustrates the point. Older generation blacks (the "old heads") have become less effective as role models and guides for the younger generation of black males. The streets and the peer group have replaced them as tutors. Thus the gangs and other problem youths have become the focal point of youthful attention, increasing the chances of delinquent behavior. In one sense, then, inner cities were left to stagnate and perpetuate a vicious cycle of pathology, disorganization, poverty, and crime.

Wilson (1987) again brought attention to the plight of the underclass with the publication of *The Truly Disadvantaged*, which identified numerous pathologies, the social processes leading to such destruction, and a future agenda to ameliorate such ills. Recently, the *Annals of the American Academy of Political and Social Science* published a special edition (Wilson, 1989) devoted to the problems of the ghetto underclass. The 13 articles in that volume dealt with such topics as race and class exclusion, urban industrial transition, single-parent families, the urban homeless, the logic of workfare, and related topics. The object of the volume was to provide a forum for scholarly discussion of the issues surrounding the evolution of the underclass as identified by Wilson (1978, 1987) and Leman (1986). Wacquant and Wilson (1989), for example, note that problems associated with both joblessness and economic exclusion have triggered a process that they term *hyperghettoization*. Under this process, stabilizing forces of the inner city have deteriorated, and as they note,

Social ills that have long been associated with segregated poverty—violent crime, drugs, housing deterioration, family disruption, commercial blight, and educational failure—have reached
qualitatively different proportions and have become articulated
into a new configuration that endows each with a more deadly
impact than before. (Wacquant & Wilson, 1989, p. 15)

The decline of business and industry, the reduction in entry-level
service positions, and the like have created stagnant pockets of the
city that breed despair and hopelessness. Although such conditions
affect all members of the underclass, they are more pronounced and
have more serious implications for black adolescents (Hawkins &
Jones, 1989).

In their examination of recreational programming as a deterrent
to gang involvement, Lovell and Pope (1993) note:

Conditions in America are such that the gates to undesirable
consequences are wide open. Nothing short of changes in national
priorities to address inner city conditions, unemployment, and the
effects of social and political tension will suffice. Moreover, little
will change unless and until we end political and individual denial
of the extent and nature of the conditions prevalent in our inner
cities, until we come to the firm realization that too many citizens
are living desperate and hopeless lives in conditions not of their
own choosing—especially children. (p. 332)

CONCLUSION

This discussion has highlighted some steps that can be undertaken to ensure that the juvenile justice system is indeed just and
has underscored the destitute conditions under which a sizable
portion of America's urban poor now exist. If a large segment of
people are made to survive under conditions so vastly different than
those encountered by the mainstream of U.S. citizens, it would not
be unreasonable to expect differences in behavior and outcome. One
could argue that the structural and economic realities of the urban
ghettos are driving forces for entry into both the adult and juvenile
justice systems. Thus policy initiatives must not only address prob-

lems in the case processing of juvenile offenders, as noted earlier, but also preexisting social conditions. Only by such a two-pronged attack can we have any chance of reducing crime among our youths and the disproportionate overrepresentation of minorities within the juvenile justice system.

References

Aday, D. (1986). Court structure, defense attorney use, and juvenile court decisions. *Sociological Quarterly, 27,* 107-119.

Akers, R. L. (1992). *Drugs, alcohol and society: Social structure, process, and policy.* Belmont, CA: Wadsworth.

Aldrich, J., & Nelson, F. (1984). *Linear probability, logit, and probit models.* Beverly Hills, CA: Sage.

Anderson, E. (1990). *Streetwise: Race, class and change in an urban community.* Chicago: University of Chicago Press.

Arnold, W. R. (1971). Race and ethnicity relative to other factors in juvenile court dispositions. *American Journal of Sociology, 77,* 211-227.

Bailey, W. C. (1981). Preadjudicatory detention in a large metropolitan juvenile court. *Law and Human Behavior, 5,* 19-43.

Bailey, W., & Peterson, R. (1981). Legal versus extra-legal determinants of juvenile court dispositions. *Juvenile and Family Court Journal, 32,* 41-59.

Barth, E. A. T., & Noel, D. L. (1972). Conceptual frameworks for the analysis of race relations. *Social Forces, 50,* 333-348.

Barton, W. H. (1976). Discretionary decision-making in juvenile justice. *Crime & Delinquency, 22,* 470-480.

Bell, D., Jr., & Lang, K. (1985). The intake dispositions of juvenile offenders. *Journal of Research in Crime and Delinquency, 22,* 309-328.

Bishop, D. M., & Frazier, C. S. (1988). The influence of race in juvenile justice processing. *Journal of Research in Crime and Delinquency, 25,* 242-263.

Bishop, D. M., & Frazier, C. (1990). *A study of race and juvenile justice processing in Florida.* Report submitted to the Florida Supreme Court Racial-Ethnic Bias Study Commission, University of Florida, Gainesville.

Bishop, D. M., & Frazier, C. (1992). Gender bias in juvenile justice processing: The implications of the JJDP Act. *Journal of Criminal Law and Criminology, 82,* 1162-1186.

Bishop, D. M., & Frazier, C. E. (1994). *Race effects in juvenile justice decision making: Findings from a statewide analysis.* Unpublished manuscript.

217

Bittner, E. (1976). Policing juveniles: The social context of common practice. In M. K. Rosenheim (Ed.), *Pursuing justice for the child* (pp. 69-93). Chicago: University of Chicago Press.

Black, D. J., & Reiss, A. J., Jr. (1970). Police control of juveniles. *American Sociological Review, 35,* 63-77.

Blalock, H. M. (1957). Percent nonwhite and racial discrimination in the South. *American Sociological Review, 42,* 743-755.

Blalock, H. M. (1967). *Toward a theory of minority group relations.* New York: John Wiley.

Blau, J. R., & Blau, P. M. (1982). Costs of inequality: Metropolitan structure and violent crime. *American Sociological Review, 47,* 114-129.

Blumberg, A. S. (1967). The practice of law as a confidence game: Organizational co-optation of a profession. *Law and Society Review, 1,* 15-39.

Blumstein, A. (1982). On the racial disproportionality of United States' prison populations. *Journal of Criminal Law and Criminology, 73,* 1259-1268.

Bogan, W. (1988, February 18). *Testimony before the House Subcommittee on Human Resources.*

Bookin-Weiner, H. (1984). Assuming responsibility: Legalizing preadjudicatory juvenile detention. *Crime & Delinquency, 38,* 39-67.

Bortner, M. A. (1982). *Inside a juvenile court: The tarnished ideal of individualized justice.* New York: New York University Press.

Bortner, M. A., & Reed, W. L. (1985). The preeminence of process: An example of refocused justice research. *Social Science Quarterly, 66,* 413-425.

Bortner, M., Sunderland, M., & Winn, R. (1985). Race and the impact of juvenile deinstitutionalization. *Crime & Delinquency, 31,* 35-46.

Bridges, G. S., Conley, D., Beretta, G., & Engen, R. L. (1993). *Racial disproportionality in the juvenile justice system: Final report.* Olympia: State of Washington, Department of Social and Health Services.

Bridges, G. S., & Crutchfield, R. D. (1988). Law, social standing and racial disparities in imprisonment. *Social Forces, 66,* 699-724.

Bridges, G. S., Crutchfield, R. D., & Simpson, E. E. (1987). Crime, social structure and criminal punishment: White and nonwhite rates of imprisonment. *Social Problems, 34,* 345-361.

Bridges, G. S., DeBurle, L., & Dutton, T. (1991). *Treatment of minority youth in the juvenile justice system.* Unpublished manuscript, University of Washington, Department of Sociology.

Bureau of Justice Statistics. (1989). *Children in custody, 1975-85: Census of public and private juvenile detention, correctional, and shelter facilities* (NCJ-114065). Washington, DC: Government Printing Office.

Buriel, R., Loya, P., Gonda, T., & Klessen, K. (1979). Child abuse and neglect referral patterns of Anglo- and Mexican Americans. *Journal of Behavioral Sciences, 1*(3), 215-227.

Bynum, T., & Paternoster, R. (1984). Discrimination revisited: An exploration of frontstage and backstage criminal justice decision-making. *Social Research, 69,* 90-108.

Bynum, T. S., Wordes, M., & Corley, E. (1993). *Disproportionate representation in juvenile justice in Michigan: Examining the influence of race and gender* (Tech. Rep. No. 33839-3J91 to the Michigan Committee on Juvenile Justice).

Byrne, J., & Sampson, R. (Eds.). (1986). *The social ecology of crime.* New York: Springer-Verlag.

California Department of Education. (1991). *Report of enrollment and drop-out figures, 1989*. Sacramento, CA: Author.

Carter, T. J. (1979). Juvenile court dispositions: A comparison of status and nonstatus offenders. *Criminology, 17,* 341-359.

Carter, T. J., & Clelland, D. (1979). A new-Marxian critique, formulation and test of juvenile dispositions as a function of social class. *Social Problems, 27,* 96-108.

Chambliss, W. J., & Seidman, R. (1971). *Law, order and power.* Reading, MA: Addison-Wesley.

Chused, R. (1973). The juvenile court process: A study of three New Jersey counties. *Rutgers Law Review, 26,* 488-615.

Cicourel, A. V. (1968). *The social organization of juvenile justice.* New York: John Wiley.

Clarke, S. H., & Koch, G. G. (1980). Juvenile court: Therapy or crime control, and do lawyers make a difference? *Law and Society Review, 14,* 263-308.

Coffee, J. C., Jr. (1978). The repressed issues in sentencing: Accountability, predictability, and equality in the era of the sentencing commission. *Georgetown Law Journal, 66,* 975-1107.

Cohen, J., & Cohen, P. (1983). *Applied multiple regression/correlation analysis for the behavioral sciences.* Hillsdale, NJ: Lawrence Erlbaum.

Cohen, L. E., & Kluegel, J. R. (1978). Determinants of juvenile court dispositions: Ascriptive and achieved factors in two metropolitan courts. *American Sociological Review, 43,* 162-176.

Cohen, L. E., & Kluegel, J. R. (1979a). The detention decision: A study of the impact of social characteristics and legal factors in two metropolitan juvenile courts. *Social Forces, 58,* 146-161.

Cohen, L. E., & Kluegel, J. R. (1979b). Selecting delinquents for adjudication. *Journal of Research in Crime and Delinquency, 16,* 143-163.

Crutchfield, R. D., & Bridges, G. S. (1986). *Racial and ethnic disparities in imprisonment: Final report.* Seattle: University of Washington, Institute for Public Policy and Management.

Dannefer, D., & Schutt, R. (1982). Race and juvenile justice processing in court and police agencies. *American Journal of Sociology, 87,* 1113-1132.

Duncan, O. D. (1966). Path analysis: Sociological examples. *American Journal of Sociology, 72,* 1-16.

Duster, T. (1987). Crime, youth unemployment and the black urban underclass. *Crime & Delinquency, 33,* 300-316.

Eisenstein, J., & Jacob, H. (1977). *Felony justice.* Boston: Little, Brown.

Elliott, D. S., & Agetan, S. (1980). Reconciling race and class differences in self-reported and official estimates of delinquency. *American Sociological Review, 45,* 95-110.

Emerson, R. M. (1969). *Judging delinquents: Context and process in juvenile court.* Chicago: Aldine.

Emerson, R. M. (1974). Role determinants in juvenile court. In D. Glaser (Ed.), *Handbook of criminology* (pp. 621-650). Chicago: Rand McNally.

Empey, L. T. (1983). *American delinquency.* Homewood, IL: Dorsey.

Fagan, J., Piper, E., & Moore, M. (1986). Violent delinquents and urban youth *Criminology, 24,* 439-471.

Fagan, J. A., Slaughter, E., & Hartstone, E. (1987). Blind justice? The impact of race on the juvenile justice process. *Crime & Delinquency, 33,* 224-258.

Farnworth, M., Frazier, C. E., & Neuberger, A. (1988). Orientations to juvenile justice: Exploratory notes from a statewide survey of justice officials. *Journal of Criminal Justice, 16*(6), 477-491.

Farrell, R., & Swigert, V. (1978). Prior offense as a self-fulfilling prophecy. *Law and Society Review, 12,* 437-453.

Federal Bureau of Investigation. (1987). *Uniform crime reports.* Washington, DC: U.S. Government Printing Office.

Federal Bureau of Investigation. (1990). *Uniform crime reports.* Washington, DC: U.S. Government Printing Office.

Feld, B. C. (1978). Reference of juvenile offenders for adult prosecution: The legislative alternative to asking unanswerable questions. *Minnesota Law Review, 62,* 515-618.

Feld, B. C. (1984). Criminalizing juvenile justice: Rules of procedure for juvenile court. *Minnesota Law Review, 69,* 141-276.

Feld, B. C. (1987). Juvenile court meets principle of offense: Legislative changes in juvenile waiver statutes. *Journal of Criminal Law and Criminology, 78,* 471-533.

Feld, B. C. (1988a). *In re Gault* revisited: A cross-state comparison of the right to counsel in juvenile court. *Crime & Delinquency, 34,* 393-424.

Feld, B. C. (1988b). Juvenile court meets principle of offense: Punishment, treatment, and the difference it makes. *Boston University Law Review, 68,* 821-915.

Feld, B. C. (1989). The right to counsel in juvenile court: An empirical study of when lawyers appear and the difference they make. *Journal of Criminal Law and Criminology, 79,* 1185-1346.

Feld, B. C. (1991). Justice by geography: Urban, suburban, and rural variations in juvenile justice administration. *Journal of Criminal Law and Criminology, 82,* 156-210.

Feld, B. C. (1993). *Justice for children: The right to counsel and the juvenile courts.* Boston: Northeastern University Press.

Fenwick, C. R. (1982). Juvenile court intake decision-making: The importance of family affiliation. *Journal of Criminal Justice, 10*(6), 443-453.

Ferdinand, T., & Luchterhand, E. (1970). Inner city youth, the police, the juvenile court, and justice. *Social Problems, 17,* 510-527.

Feyerherm, W. (1981). Juvenile court dispositions of status offenders: An analysis of case decisions. In R. L. McNeely & C. E. Pope (Eds.), *Race, crime, and criminal justice* (pp. 127-144). Beverly Hills, CA: Sage.

Feyerherm, W. (1993, February). *The status of the states: A report to OJJDP on the DMC initiative.* Paper presented at the annual OJJDP Formula Grants Conference, Seattle, WA.

Fisher, G. A., & Doyle-Martin, S. M. (1981). The effects of ethnic prejudice on police referrals to the juvenile court. *Californian Sociologist, 4*(2), 189-205.

Flowers, R. B. (Ed.). (1988). *Minorities and criminality.* New York: Greenwood.

Forslund, M. A., & Cranston, V. A. (1975). A self-report comparison of Indian and Anglo delinquency in Wyoming. *Criminology, 13,* 193-197.

Forslund, M. A., & Meyers, R. E. (1974). Delinquency among Wind River Indian Reservation youth. *Criminology, 12,* 97-107.

Frazier, C. E., & Bishop, D. (1985). The pretrial detention of juveniles and its impact on case dispositions. *Journal of Criminal Law and Criminology, 76,* 1132-1152.

Frazier, C. E., & Bishop, D. M. (1990). Obstacles to reform in juvenile corrections: A case study. *Journal of Contemporary Criminal Justice, 6*(3), 157-166.

Frazier, C. E., Bishop, D. M., & Henretta, J. (1992). The social context of race differentials in juvenile justice dispositions. *Sociological Quarterly, 33,* 554-562.

Frazier, C. E., & Cochran, J. K. (1986). Detention of juveniles: Its effects on subsequent juvenile court processing decisions. *Youth & Society, 17*(3), 286-385.

French, L. (1982). *Indians and criminal justice.* Totowa, NJ: Allanheld, Osmun.

Greene, W. (1981). Sample selection bias as a specification error: Comment. *Econometrica, 49,* 795-798.

Greene, W. (1990). *Econometric analysis.* New York: Macmillan.

Hagan, J. (1974). Extralegal attributes and sentencing: An assessment of a sociological viewpoint. *Law and Society Review, 8,* 357-384.

Hagan, J. (1979). Criminal justice in rural and urban communities: A study of the bureaucratization of justice. In S. L. Messinger & E. Bittner (Eds.), *Criminology review yearbook* (pp. 505-519). Beverly Hills, CA: Sage.

Hagedorn, J. (1988). *People and folks: Gangs, crime and the underclass in a rustbelt city.* Chicago: Lakeview.

Hall, E. L., & Simkus, A. A. (1975). Inequality in the types of sentences received by Native Americans and whites. *Criminology, 13,* 199-222.

Hanushek, E., & Jackson, J. (1977). *Statistical methods of social scientists.* San Diego, CA: Academic Press.

Harring, S. (1982). Native American crime in the U.S. In L. French (Ed.), *Indians and criminal justice* (pp. 93-108). Totowa, NJ: Allanheld, Osmun.

Hawkins, D., & Jones, N. E. (1989). Black adolescents and the criminal justice system. In R. L. Jones (Ed.), *Black adolescents.* Berkeley, CA: Cobb and Henry.

Heckman, J. (1979). Sample selection bias as a specification error. *Econometrica, 47,* 153-161.

Heckman, J. (1980). Sample selection bias as a specification error with an application to the estimation of labor supply functions. In J. P. Smith (Ed.), *Female labor supply: Theory and estimation* (pp. 206-239). Princeton, NJ: Princeton University Press.

Heerman, C. E. (1975). The Poncas and community control. *Integrated Education, 13* (4), 32-36.

Henretta, J. C., Frazier, C. E., & Bishop, D. M. (1986). The effects of prior case outcomes on juvenile justice decision-making. *Social Forces, 65,* 554-562.

Hindelang, M. (1978). Race and involvement in common law personal crimes. *American Sociological Review, 43,* 93-109.

Hindelang, M. J. (1982). Race and crime. In L. D. Savitz & H. Johnson (Eds.), *Contemporary criminology* (pp. 168-184). New York: John Wiley.

Horowitz, A., & Wasserman, M. (1980). Some misleading conceptions in sentencing research: An example and reformulation in the juvenile court. *Criminology, 18,* 411-424.

Huff, C. R. (1990). Denial, overreaction, and misidentification: A postscript on public policy. In C. R. Huff (Ed.), *Gangs in America* (pp. 310-317). Newbury Park, CA: Sage.

Huizinga, D., & Elliott, D. S. (1987). Juvenile offenders: Prevalence, offender incidence, and arrest rates by race. *Crime & Delinquency, 33,* 206-223.

Hutton, C. F., Pommersheim, F., & Feimer, S. (1989). I fought the law and the law won: A report on women and disparate sentencing in South Dakota. *New England Journal on Criminal and Civil Confinement, 15*(2), 177-201.

Jensen, G. F., Strauss, J. H., & Harris, V. W. (1977). Crime, delinquency and the American Indian. *Human Organization, 3,* 252-257.

Johnson, J., & Secret, P. (1992). Race and juvenile court decision making revisited. *Criminal Justice Policy Review, 4*(2), 124-139.

Kempf, K. (1982). *Racial discrimination in sentencing: An empirical assessment of the situation in Pennsylvania.* Unpublished master's thesis, Pennsylvania State University.

Kempf, K., & Austin, R. (1986). Older and more recent evidence on racial discrimination in sentencing. *Journal of Quantitative Criminology, 2*(10), 29-47.

Kempf, K., Decker, S. H., & Bing, R. L. (1990). *An analysis of apparent disparities in the handling of black youth within Missouri's juvenile justice systems* (Tech. Rep.). St. Louis: University of Missouri–St. Louis, Department of Administration of Justice.

Killingsworth, M. R. (1983). *Labor supply.* Cambridge, UK: Cambridge University Press.

Kleck, G. (1981). Racial discrimination in criminal sentencing: A critical evaluation of the evidence with additional evidence on the death penalty. *American Sociological Review, 46,* 783-805.

Kowalski, G., & Rickicki, J. (1982). Determinants of juvenile postadjudication dispositions. *Journal of Research in Crime and Delinquency, 19,* 66-83.

Krisberg, B. (1988, February 18). *Testimony before the House Subcommittee on Human Resources.*

Krisberg, B., & Schwartz, I. (1983). Rethinking juvenile justice. *Crime & Delinquency, 29,* 333-364.

Krisberg, B., Schwartz, I., Fishman, G., Eisikovits, Z., Guttman, E., & Joe, K. (1987). The incarceration of minority youth. *Crime & Delinquency, 33,* 173-205.

Krisberg, B., Schwartz, I. M., Litsky, P., & Austin, J. (1986). The watershed of juvenile justice reform. *Crime & Delinquency, 32,* 5-38.

Langan, P. (1985). Racism on trial: New evidence to explain the racial composition of prisons in the United States. *Journal of Criminal Law and Criminology, 76,* 666-683.

Laub, J. (1983). Urbanism, race, and crime. *Journal of Research in Crime and Delinquency, 20,* 183-198.

Laub, J., & Hindelang, M. (1980). *Juvenile criminal behavior in urban, suburban and rural areas.* Washington, DC: Government Printing Office.

Leiber, M. (1992). *Juvenile justice decision making in Iowa: An analysis of the influences of race on case processing in three counties* (Tech. Rep.). Cedar Falls: University of Northern Iowa.

Leman, N. (1986, June-July). The origins of the underclass. *Atlantic Monthly,* 31-55, 54-68.

Levy, J. E., Kunitz, S. J., & Everett, M. (1969). Navajo criminal homicide. *Southwestern Journal of Anthropology, 25,* 124-152.

Liska, A. E., & Chamlin, M. B. (1984). Social structure and crime control among macrosocial units. *American Journal of Sociology, 90,* 383-395.

Liska, A. E., & Tausig, M. (1979). Theoretical interpretations of social and class differentials in legal decision-making for juveniles. *Sociological Quarterly, 20,* 197-207.

Lockhart, L., Kurtz, P., Sutphen, R., & Gauger, K. (1991). *Georgia's juvenile justice system: A retrospective investigation of racial disparity* (Tech. Rep.). Athens: University of Georgia Press.

Lovell, R., & Pope, C. E. (1993). Recreational interventions. In A. P. Goldstein & C. R. Huff (Eds.), *The gang intervention handbook* (pp. 319-332). Champaign, IL: Research Press.

Maddala, G. (1987). *Limited-dependent and qualitative variables in econometrics.* Cambridge, UK: Cambridge University Press.

Manski, C. F. (1989). Anatomy of the selection problem. *Journal of Human Resources, 24*(3), 341-360.

Marshall, I. H., & Thomas, C. W. (1983). Discretionary decision-making and the juvenile court. *Juvenile and Family Court Journal, 34*(3), 47-59.

Matza, D. (1964). *Delinquency and drift.* New York: John Wiley.

May, P. A. (1982). Contemporary crime and the American Indian. *Plains Anthropologist, 27,* 225-238.

McCarthy, B. R. (1987). Preventive detention and pretrial custody in the juvenile court. *Journal of Criminal Justice, 15*(3), 185-200.

McCarthy, B. R., & Smith, B. L. (1986). The conceptualization of discrimination in the juvenile justice process: The impact of administrative factors and screening decisions on juvenile court dispositions. *Criminology, 24,* 41-64.

McNeely, R. L., & Pope, C. E. (1981). *Race, crime, and criminal justice.* Beverly Hills, CA: Sage.

Miller, E. (1986). *Street women.* Philadelphia, PA: Temple University Press.

Minnesota Supreme Court Task Force on Racial Bias in the Judicial System. (1993, May). *Final report.* St. Paul, MN: Supreme Court Administration.

Minnis, M. S. (1963). The relationship of the social structure of an Indian community to adult and juvenile delinquency. *Social Focus, 41,* 395-403.

Morash, M. (1984). Establishment of a juvenile record. *Criminology, 22,* 97-111.

Myers, M. A. (1990). Economic threat and racial disparities in incarceration: The case of postbellum Georgia. *Criminology, 28,* 627-656.

Myers, M., & Talarico, S. (1986). Urban justice, rural injustice? Urbanization and its effect on sentencing. *Criminology, 24,* 367-392.

Myers, M., & Talarico, S. (1987). *The social contexts of criminal sentencing.* New York: Springer-Verlag.

National Coalition of State Juvenile Justice Advisory Groups. (1987). *An act of empowerment.* Bethesda, MD: Author.

National Coalition of State Juvenile Justice Advisory Groups. (1989). *A report on the delicate balance.* Bethesda, MD: Author.

National Council of Juvenile and Family Court Judges. (1990). Minority youth in the juvenile justice system: A judicial response. *Juvenile and Family Court Journal, 41*(3A).

Native American Rights Fund in the Inequality of Justice. (1982). *The inequality of justice: A report on crime and the administration of justice in the minority community.* Washington, DC: U.S. Department of Justice.

North Dakota Advisory Committee to the U.S. Commission on Civil Rights. (1978). *Native American justice issues in North Dakota.* Washington, DC: U.S. Government Printing Office.

O'Brien, M. (1977). Indian juveniles in the state and tribal courts of Oregon. *American Indian Review, 5,* 343-367.

Office of Juvenile Justice and Delinquency Prevention. (1991). *Children in custody 1989* (NCJ-127189). Washington, DC: U.S. Department of Justice.

Olsen, L. (1982). Services for minority children in out of home care. *Social Service Review, 56*, 572-585.

Parry, D. L. (1987). Juvenile offense patterns in Alaska—1985. *Alaska Justice Forum, 4*(2). (University of Alaska, Anchorage, Justice Center, School of Justice)

Pawlak, E. (1977). Differential selection of juveniles for detention. *Journal of Research in Crime and Delinquency, 14*, 152-165.

Pennsylvania Commission on Sentencing. (1981). *Sentencing in Pennsylvania: A review of 1977 sentencing patterns.* Unpublished report, State College, Pennsylvania.

Petersilia, J. (1983). *Racial disparities in the criminal justice system.* Santa Monica, CA: RAND.

Peterson, R. (1988). Youthful offender designations and sentencing in New York criminal courts. *Social Problems, 32*, 111-130.

Phillips, C. D., & Dinitz, S. (1982). Labelling and juvenile court dispositions: Official responses to a cohort of violent juveniles. *Sociological Quarterly, 23*, 267-278.

Piliavin, I., & Briar, S. (1964). Police encounters with juveniles. *American Sociological Review, 51*, 101-119.

Pinkney, A. (1984). *The myth of black progress.* New York: Cambridge University Press.

Platt, A. (1969). *The child savers.* Chicago: University of Chicago Press.

Pommersheim F., & Wise, S. (1989). Going to the penitentiary: A study of disparate sentencing in South Dakota. *Justice and Behavior, 16*(2), 155-165.

Pope, C. E. (1979). Race and crime revisited. *Crime & Delinquency, 25*, 347-357.

Pope, C. E., & Clear, T. (Eds.). (1994). Race and punishment [Special issue]. *Journal of Research in Crime and Delinquency, 31*(2).

Pope, C. E., & Feyerherm, W. H. (1990a). Minority status and juvenile justice processing: An assessment of the research literature (Part 1). *Criminal Justice Abstracts, 22*, 327-335.

Pope, C. E., & Feyerherm, W. H. (1990b). Minority status and juvenile justice processing: An assessment of the research literature (Part 2). *Criminal Justice Abstracts, 22*, 527-542.

Pope, C. E., & Feyerherm, W. H. (1991). *Minorities in the juvenile justice system.* Washington, DC: U.S. Department of Justice, Office of Juvenile Justice and Delinquency Prevention.

Pope, C. E., & Feyerherm, W. (1992). *Minorities and the juvenile justice system: Full report.* Rockville, MD: U.S. Department of Justice, Office of Juvenile Justice and Delinquency Prevention, Juvenile Justice Clearing House.

Pope, C. E., & McNeely, R. L. (1981). Race and juvenile court disposition: An empirical analysis of initial screening decisions. *Criminal Justice and Behavior, 8*, 287-301.

Reasons, C. (1972). Crime and the Native American. In C. E. Reasons & J. L. Kuykendall (Eds.), *Race, crime and justice* (pp. 79-95). Santa Monica, CA: Goodyear.

Reasons, C. (1974). Racism, prisons and prisoners' rights. *Issues in Criminology, 9*(2), 3-21.

Reid, S. (1984). Cultural differences and child abuse intervention with undocumented Spanish-speaking families in Los Angeles. *Child Abuse and Neglect, 8*(1), 109-112.

Rhoden, E. (1994). Disproportionate minority representation: First steps to a solution. *Juvenile Justice, 2*, 9-14.

Robbins, S. P. (1985). Anglo concepts and Indian reality: A study of juvenile delinquency. *Human Organization, 44,* 57-62.

Rothman, D. J. (1980). *Conscience and convenience: The asylum and its alternatives in Progressive America.* Boston: Little, Brown.

Rusche, G., & Kirchheimer, O. (1968). *Punishment and social structure.* New York: Russell Sage.

Sampson, R. (1986). Effects of socioeconomic context on official reaction to juvenile delinquency. *American Sociological Review, 51,* 876-885.

Sampson, R. J., & Laub, J. H. (1993). Structural variations in juvenile court processing: Inequality, the underclass, and social control. *Law and Society Review, 27*(2), 285-311.

Schwartz, I. (1986, June 19). *Testimony before the House Subcommittee on Human Resources.*

Schwartz, I. M., Harris, L., & Levi, L. (1988). The jailing of juveniles in Minnesota: A case study. *Crime & Delinquency, 34,* 133-149.

Silberman, C. E. (1978). *Criminal violence, criminal justice.* New York: Vantage.

Slaughter, E., Hartstone, E., & Fagan, J. (1986). *Minority youth in the Colorado juvenile justice system: Final report.* Denver: Colorado Division of Criminal Justice.

Smith, D., & Visher, C. (1981). Street-level justice: Situational determinants of police arrest decisions. *Social Problems, 29,* 167-178.

Snyder, H. N. (1990, March). *Growth in minority detention attributed to drug law violators* (Juvenile Justice Bulletin). Washington, DC: Office of Juvenile Justice and Delinquency Prevention.

Spitzer, S. (1975). Toward a Marxian theory of deviance. *Social Problems, 22,* 638-651.

Spitzer, S. (1981). Notes toward a theory of punishment and social change. In S. Spitzer & R. Simon (Eds.), *Research in law and sociology* (Vol. 2, pp. 207-229). Greenwich, CT: JAI.

Stewart, O. (1964). Questions regarding American Indian criminality. *Human Organization, 23,* 61-66.

Tauke, T. (1987, September 11). *Comments in a hearing of the House Subcommittee on Human Resources.*

Terry, R. M. (1967). Discrimination in the handling of juvenile offenders by social control agencies. *Journal of Research in Crime and Delinquency, 4,* 218-230.

Thomas, C. W., & Cage, R. (1977). The effects of social characteristics on juvenile court dispositions. *Sociological Quarterly, 18,* 237-252.

Thomas, C. W., & Fitch, W. A. (1975). An inquiry into the association between respondents' personal characteristics and juvenile court dispositions. *William and Mary Law Review, 17,* 61-83.

Thornberry, T. P. (1973). Race, socioeconomic status and sentencing in the juvenile justice system. *Journal of Criminal Law and Criminology, 64,* 90-98.

Thornberry, T. P. (1979). Sentencing disparities in the juvenile justice system. *Journal of Criminal Law and Criminology, 70,* 164-171.

Thornberry, T. P., & Christenson, R. L. (1984). Juvenile justice decision-making as longitudinal process. *Social Forces, 63,* 433-444.

Tittle, C. (1994). The theoretical bases for inequality in formal social control. In G. S. Bridges & M. A. Myers (Eds.), *Inequality, crime, and social control* (pp. 21-52). Boulder, CO: Westview.

23% of young black males in penal system. (1990, February 27). *Milwaukee Journal,* p. A1.

Tracy, P. E., Wolfgang, M. E., & Figlio, R. M. (1990). *Delinquency careers in two birth cohorts.* New York: Plenum.

U.S. Bureau of the Census. (1982). *1980 census of population: General population characteristics Minnesota.* Washington, DC: U.S. Government Printing Office.

U.S. Bureau of the Census. (1989). *National data book and guide to sources: Statistical abstract of the U.S. (109th edition).* Washington, DC: U.S. Government Printing Office.

Velde, R. W. (1977). Racial justice: Black judges and defendants in an urban trial court. Lexington, MA: D. C. Heath.

Wacquant, L. J. D., & Wilson, W. J. (1989). The cost of racial and class exclusion in the inner city. *Annals of the American Academy of Political and Social Science, 501,* 8-25.

Wallace, D., & Humphries, D. (1981). Urban crime and capitalist accumulation: 1950-1971. In D. Greenberg (Ed.), *Crime and capitalism* (pp. 140-157). Mountain View, CA: Mayfield.

Weiner, N. L., & Willie, C. V. (1971). Decisions by juvenile officers. *American Journal of Sociology, 77,* 199-209.

Wilbanks, W. (1987). *The myth of a racist criminal justice system.* Belmont, CA: Wadsworth.

Wilson, J. Q. (1968). *Varieties of police behavior: The management of law and order in eight communities.* Cambridge, MA: Harvard University Press.

Wilson, W. J. (1978). *The declining significance of race.* Chicago: University of Chicago Press.

Wilson, W. J. (1987). *The truly disadvantaged: The inner city, the underclass and public policy.* Chicago: University of Chicago Press.

Wilson, W. J. (Ed.). (1989). The ghetto underclass: Social science perspectives [Special issue]. *Annals of the American Academy of Political and Social Science, 501.*

Winfree, T. L., & Griffiths, C. T. (1975). An examination of factors related to the parole survival of American Indians. *Plains Anthropologist, 20,* 311-319.

Wolfgang, M. E. (1966). *Patterns in criminal homicide* (2nd ed.). New York: John Wiley.

Wolfgang, M. E., Figlio, R. M., & Sellin, T. (1972). *Delinquency in a birth cohort.* Chicago: University of Chicago Press.

Wordes, M., Bynum, T. S., & Corley, C. J. (1994). Locking up youth: The impact of race on detention decisions. *Journal of Research in Crime and Delinquency, 31,* 149-165.

Zatz, M. S. (1982). Dynamic modeling of criminal processing histories. In J. Hagan (Ed.), *Quantitative criminology: Innovations and applications* (pp. 91-114). Beverly Hills, CA: Sage.

Zatz, M. S. (1987). The changing forms of racial/ethnic biases in sentencing. *Journal of Research in Crime and Delinquency, 24,* 69-92.

Index

Accountability, juvenile court
    philosophy and, 99
Aday, D., 102
Adult court, waiver to, 22
Adult defendants, separation from, 3
Advocacy groups, 167
African American families, 35, 171
African American males:
    incarceration rates, 161, 162
    percentage of U.S. population, 179
African American underclass, 213-214
African American youths:
    adjudication factors, 113-116
    arrest rates, 156, 182
    attorney services and, 78, 87
    California detention and, 153,
        161-164, 167
    crime rates and, 130
    delinquency rates, 117
    detention decisions and, 61, 73
    detention rates, 84, 88, 117-118, 120,
        201-202
    drug offenses and, 56
    drug use and, 172
    felonies and, 101
    Florida's juvenile justice system
        and, 19
    formal processing and, 119
    home removal and, 92
    intake factors, 113
    misinformation about, 42

    offense patterns and, 76
    Pennsylvania courts and, 108-121
    placement factors, 116
    police decisions and, 48, 51-52
    progression beyond referral, 110
    rates of delinquency, 72
    referral decisions and, 59
    secure detention and, 61
    self-esteem and, 174
    violent crimes and, 156, 164
Age:
    custody decisions and, 61
    first arrest and, 55
    informal processing and, 61
    processing decisions and, 24, 61
    urban court charges and, 67
Akers, R. L., 42
Alaska, American Indian delinquency
    in, 185
Alcohol-related offenses, American
    Indians and, 181, 182, 185
Alcohol treatment, 120
American Correctional Association, 13
American Indian adults, in criminal
    justice system, 181-184
American Indian youths:
    arrest rates, 184
    crime rates, 186-187
    detention and, 194-195
    disposition and, 195-197
    intake and, 194

juvenile justice processing of, 179-200
petition and, 195
recidivism and, 185
sentencing and, 188
Amplification effects, in case processing, 155
Annie B. Casey Foundation, 13
Appearance, police decisions and, 48, 55
Apprehension phase, police bias and, 47-65
Arab youths:
police decisions and, 52-53
weapons and, 56
Arizona, minority-serving services in, 12
Arnold, W. R., 73, 179
Arrest(s), 10
accumulation of, 101
African American youths and, 156
age of, 55
American Indian rates, 181, 182, 184
chance of, 8
community rates of, 130, 132
confinement rates and, 140-144
neighborhood context and, 101
police bias and, 47-65
rates of, 10
Asian families, values and, 170-171
Asian/Pacific Islander youth, California detention and, 154, 161, 162, 164, 167
Assessment process, 12, 175
Attorneys:
case processing decisions and, 92
private, 32, 78-80
urban courts and, 68
use of, 78-80, 87
Austin, J., 84, 153-178, 203, 212
Austin, R., 103

Bailey, W. C., 69, 84
Barth, E. A. T., 131
Barton, W. H., 70, 73
Behavior, rates of, 72-73
Bell, D., Jr., 70
Beretta, G., 128, 148

Bing, R. L., 68, 69, 100, 103, 128, 129, 179
Bishop, D., 73, 84, 91, 92, 100, 128, 179, 203
Bishop, D. M., 16-46, 48, 90
Bittner, E., 70
Black, D. J., 48, 70
Blalock, H. M., 131
Blau, J. R., 132
Blau, P. M., 132
Blumberg, A. S., 135
Blumstein, A., 135
Bogan, W., 8-9
Bookin-Weiner, H., 84
Bortner, M. A., 70, 71, 73
Briar, S., 48
Bridges, G. S., 128-152
Bynum, T. S., 47-65, 86, 188-189, 201-202
Byrne, J., 102

Cage, R., 73
California, overrepresentation of minority youth and, 153-178
Carter, T. J., 73
Case closure without action, 22
Case dispositions:
alternative, 171-172
American Indian youth and, 195-197
factors related to, 59-62, 89-91, 99, 100
private treatment and, 44-45
Case processing, 5, 99, 100, 201
age and, 61
American Indian youths, 179-200
amplification effects, 155
attorney services and, 92
discretionary decisions and, 133
economic status and, 101-102
evaluations of, 70-71
factors in Pennsylvania, 110-117
Florida's system and, 19-46
legal variables and, 80-83
multiple stages in, 19-20
police and, 47-48
policy recommendations, 121-124
pretrial detention and, 91-92
outcomes, 23, 24-27

recommendations for future, 204-212
referral rates and, 112
rural areas, 102-103
urban areas, 67, 102-103
See also Formal processing; Informal processing
Census data, 159
Center for the Study of Youth Policy, 7
Chamlin, M. B., 135
Charges, rates of, 10
Charging bias, 101
Checks-and-balances system, 210
Child, best interests of, 70, 71
Child abuse referrals, 102
Children and Adolescent Service System Projects, 9
Children in Custody data, 5, 7, 9, 158, 185
Child welfare services, 5
Christenson, R. L., 90
Cicourel, A. V., 70, 71
Civil rights suit, 42
Clarke, S. H., 73, 84, 91
Clear, T., 201
Clelland, D., 73
Cochran, J. K., 18, 73, 156
Coffee, J. C., Jr., 93
Cohen, L. E., 69, 84
Communities:
demographic changes and, 149-150
local business involvement and, 173-174
policy involvement and, 174
punishment effects, 128-152
safety in, 98, 122, 148
Community-based prevention efforts, 12
Community-based sanctions, 22
Community-based solutions, 122
Community corrections programs, 176
Community recreation centers, 172
Community service, 196
Confinement:
penetration versus, 5
racial disparities in, 128-152
See also Detention; Pretrial detention
Congress, 5, 8-9
Conley, D. J., 128-152

Contacts, police record of, 51
Contempt charge, 23
Control, formal, 84
Control variables, 10, 20, 100
Corley, C. J., 86, 201-202
Corley, E., 62
Counseling:
family, 172
informal, 5
private, 32, 44-45
County Justice System Subvention (AB 90) funds, 177
County unit of analysis, 135-136, 139, 167-177
Court(s):
caseload of, 120, 146-147
ethnic staffing balance and, 17, 1730
philosophy of, 99
referral to, 22, 27
rural versus urban, 102
See also Judicial decisions
Court outcomes, 102, 112
Court processing, factors associated with, 113-116
Cranston, V. A., 186-187
Crime:
American Indian rates, 186-187
community levels of, 130-131, 132, 134
economic factors and, 213-214
proportion committed by minority youth, 8, 9
root causes of, 173
social context, 212-215
Crutchfield, R. D., 131, 133, 135, 136, 139, 148
Cultural bias, 123
Cultural diversity curriculum, 43
Culturally appropriate treatment, 12
Cultural sensitivity, 123, 124, 173
Cultural values, 170-171
Custody decisions, 51, 59-61. *See also* Detention

Dannefer, D., 69, 73, 101
DeBurle, L., 129
Decker, S. H., 68, 69, 100, 103, 128, 129, 179

Deinstitutionalization, of status
        offenders, 3
Delinquency:
    American Indian youths, 185
    "other," 76
    prevention programs, 177
    rates of, 117
    urban areas, 102
Delinquents, official, 72
Demeanor, police decisions and, 48
Demographic changes, community
        problems and, 149-150
Demographic data, 159
Detention, 99, 201-202
    American Indian youth and,
        194-195
    decisions about, 22
    discretionary decisions and, 73
    expenditures for, 176
    factors associated with, 117-118,
        119-120
    Florida's system and, 22
    likelihood of, 24
    local rates of, 7
    offense seriousness and, 88
    police effects on, 51, 122
    prior record and, 88
    racial differences in, 8, 9, 83-86,
        128-152
    separate from adults, 3
Detention facilities:
    availability of, 83-84
    design of, 3
    See also Pretrial detention; Secure
        confinement
Dinitz, S., 70, 73
Discipline, 54
Dispositions. See Case dispositions
Disproportionate minority
        confinement, 1-15
    current status of, 4-5
    development of mandate, 7-10
    implementation of mandate, 5-7
    policy context for, 2-4
    research requirements of, 10-13
    See also Minority
        overrepresentation/differentials
Diversion, 70, 171-172
    eligibility for, 43-44

family considerations and, 33-34
    policy recommendations, 122
Doyle-Martin, S. M., 189
Drop outs, 175
Drug offenses:
    African American youths and, 56
    custody decisions and, 61
    minor, 76
    referral decisions and, 59
Drug-related offenses, 110
Drug treatment, 120
Drug use:
    African American youths and, 56,
        172
    policies and, 11
Duncan, O. D., 135
Dutton, T., 129

Economic conditions, improving, 173
Economic factors:
    attorney representation and, 80
    case processing and, 101-102
    crime and, 213-214
    police decisions and, 54
    punishment disparities and, 131-132
    racial differences attributable to,
        31-33, 101-102
    treatment choices and, 44-45
    Washington state confinement rates
        and, 145-146
Eisenstein, J., 136
Eisikovits, Z., 69, 72-73, 84, 156, 157,
        185-186
Elliott, D. S., 72, 177
Emerson, R. M., 70, 71
Empey, L. T., 35
Engen, R. L., 128-152
English as second language, 108, 171
Ethnic bias, Florida's justice system
        and, 16-46
Everett, M., 181

Fagan, J. A., 69, 72, 73, 74, 78, 80, 86,
        101, 155, 213
Families:
    attachments to, 187
    delinquency in, 102

differing values in, 124, 170-171
diversion programs and, 43
economic resources of, 31-33
intake process and, 44
police decisions and, 48, 54, 55
poverty and, 116
processing outcomes and, 120
racial differences attributable to, 33-35
single-parent, 54, 67, 102, 108
support services for, 174
Farnworth, M., 29
Farrell, R., 135
Fathers, absentee, 108
Feld, B. C., 66-97, 102, 129, 133
Felonies:
    African Americans charged with, 76, 101
    attorney presence and, 68
    factors influencing referral decisions, 59
    removal from home and, 82
    sentencing and, 81-82
    violent, 164
Felonies against the person, 80, 85
Felony involving property, 80
Females, custody decision and, 61
Fenwick, C. R., 155
Ferdinand, T., 101
Feyerherm, W., 1-15, 69, 72, 73, 99-100, 102, 133, 156, 179, 190, 192-193, 201, 202, 204
Figlio, R. M., 72, 102, 148, 181
Fisher, G. A., 189
Fishman, G., 69, 72-73, 84, 156, 157, 185-186
Fitch, W. A., 73, 93
Florida:
    juvenile assessment center, 12
    juvenile justice personnel interviews and, 20, 28-40
    racial differences in case processing in, 16-46
Florida Supreme Court, Commission on Race and Ethnic Bias, 16-46
Flowers, R. B., 182, 183, 184, 187
Formal processing, 22
    factors in Pennsylvania, 113-116
    likelihood of, 119

police effects on, 120
referral for, 24, 112
urban courts and, 67-68, 132-133
urban police and, 54
urban versus rural areas, 67-68, 102-103, 132-133
Formal social control, 77
Forslund, M. A., 184, 186-187
Foster care, 122
Foundations, 13
Frazier, C. E., 16-46, 48, 73, 84, 90, 91, 92, 100, 128, 156, 179, 203
French, L., 187
Funding, 3-4, 11-12, 176

Gangs, 101, 215
Gauger, K., 100, 102
Gender:
    California incarceration and, 161
    case processing and, 24, 101
    custody decision and, 61
Geography, justice by, 11
Georgia, decentralized courts and, 102
Ghettos, 133, 214-215
Greene, W., 107
Griffiths, C. T., 188
Guttman, E., 69, 72-73, 84, 156, 157, 185-186

Hagan, J., 102
Hall, E. L., 188
Harring, S., 182
Harris, L., 189
Harris, V. W., 182
Hartstone, E., 48, 69, 72, 73, 74, 78, 80, 86, 101, 155
Hawkins, D., 215
Heckman, J., 107
Heerman, C. E., 189
Henretta, J. C., 90
Hindelang, M. J., 72, 135, 156
Hispanic youths. *See* Latino youths
Homes:
    broken, 54
    removal from, 81-82, 88, 90, 92
Horowitz, A., 71, 73, 93
Huff, C. R., 101

Huizinga, D., 72, 177
Hyperghettoization, 214-215

Incarceration. *See* Detention
Individual prejudices, policy
    recommendations and, 41-42
Individuals, decisions tailored to, 98
Informal processing, 5, 22, 69, 117
    age and, 61
    police and, 47-48
    rural courts and, 67, 68
    urban versus rural areas, 102-103
Informal social control, 67
Information:
    congressional sources, 5
    quality of, 14, 15, 17-18
In-home supervision, 196
Institutional racism, 35-36, 169
Intake, 70
    American Indian youth and, 194
    factors in Pennsylvania, 113
    family and, 44
    formal processing beyond, 116
    offense seriousness and, 24
    policy recommendations, 122-123
Intake screening, 22
Intake workers, 5
    interviews with, 20, 28, 29
Intervention processes, 12
Interviews:
    Florida's juvenile justice system
        and, 20, 28-40
    police and, 49-50
Investigation, of individual racial bias,
    41-42, 124
Iowa, community-based prevention
    efforts in, 12

Jacob, H., 136
Jail removal, 3
Jane Boyd House, 12
Jensen, G. F., 182
JJDPA. *See* Juvenile Justice and
    Delinquency Prevention Act
Joblessness, 170
Joe, K., 69, 72-73, 84, 156, 157, 185-186
Jones, N. E., 215

Judicial decision making, 99
    characteristics affecting, 100-103
    discretionary, 69-74
    urban courts, 66-97
Judicial disposition, 22, 23, 27
Justice:
    by geography, 11
    individualized, 69-70, 71, 72, 99
    social context of, 212-215
Justice Department, 158-159
Justice philosophy, geographical
    differences, 11
Juvenile(s):
    "contamination" of, 3
    definitions of, 159-150
    police bias and, 47-65
    protecting rights of, 3
    social circumstances and, 35-36
Juvenile court. *See* Court(s)
Juvenile court judges:
    discretionary decisions and, 133
    interviews with, 20, 28
    policy recommendations, 123
Juvenile justice:
    early stages of, 122
    inequality in administration of,
        130-134
    in Pennsylvania, 98-124
    outcomes and, 123, 201, 211-212
Juvenile justice administration, social
    context of, 66-97
Juvenile Justice and Delinquency
    Prevention Act of 1974
    (amended 1988), 2-4, 157-158
Juvenile justice system:
    Florida's, 16-46
    future directions, 201-216
    goals of, 98-99
    stages in, 206-207

Kempf, K., 68, 69, 100, 103, 128, 129,
    179
Killingsworth, M. R., 106, 107
Kluegel, J. R., 69, 84
Koch, G. G., 73, 84, 91
Krisberg, B., 8, 9-10, 69, 72-73, 84, 91,
    156, 157, 185-186
Kunitz, S. J., 181

Kurtz, P., 100, 102

Lang, K., 70
Langan, P., 135
Language barriers, 108, 171
Latino families, values and, 170-171
Latino males:
  incarceration rates, 8
  percentage of U.S. population, 179
Latino youths:
  adjudication factors, 113-116
  California detention and, 154,
    161-164, 167
  crime rates and, 130
  delinquency rates, 117
  demographic changes and, 149-150
  detention rates, 117-118, 120, 202
  formal processing and, 119
  intake factors, 113
  nonurban areas, 102
  Pennsylvania courts and, 108-121
  placement factors, 116
  police decisions and, 52-53
  progression beyond referral, 110
  school and, 108
  weapons and, 56
Law enforcement agencies, ethnic
    staffing balance and, 170, 173
Legal variables, dispositional decisions
    and, 80-83, 93
Leman, N., 213-214
Leonard, K. K., 98-124
Levi, L., 189
Levy, J. E., 181
Liska, A. E., 135, 191
Litsky, P., 84
Local agencies, partnerships with, 14
Local politics, 6-7
Lockhart, L., 100, 102
Logistic regression analysis, 59-62
Logit analysis, 104-106
Lovell, R., 215
Luchterhand, E., 101

Males, processing decisions and, 24.
    See also African American males;
    Gender; Latino males

Manski, C. F., 121
Marshall, I. H., 71
Matza, D., 70, 71, 72
May, P. A., 187
McCarthy, B. R., 69, 70, 72, 78, 84, 86,
    95, 155, 179
McNeely, R. L., 103, 155
Mental health services, 5, 9, 44
Meyers, R. E., 184
Miller, E., 213
Minnesota:
  American Indians in prisons in,
    183, 189
  rural courts in, 102
  urban juvenile courts and, 66-97,
    102
Minnis, M. S., 184
Minorities, misperceptions of, 42-43,
    149
Minority concentration, degree of, 131,
    135
Minority family, 33-35, 43
Minority groups, definitions of, 159-160
Minority overrepresentation/
    differentials:
  attorney representation and, 78
  California juvenile justice system
    and, 153-178
  confinement and, 128-152
  critical issues in, 5
  detention and, 83-86
  economic factors and, 31-33
  extent of, 12
  family considerations, 33-35
  Florida's justice system and, 16-46
  incarceration rates and, 7-10, 83-86,
    128-152
  institutional racism and, 35-36
  offense patterns and, 76
  Pennsylvania and, 98-124
  perceptions of, 29, 169-172
  police and, 47-65
  possible explanations for, 11
  prejudiced individuals and, 30-31
  racial bias and, 29-30
  racial differences attributable to,
    29-30
  sentencing and, 81
  state plans to reduce, 4

urban juvenile courts and, 66-97
Minority proportion index, 160-161
Minority youths:
    adjudication factors, 113-116
    attorney services and, 87
    California detention and, 153-178
    case-processing outcomes and, 23,
        24-27
    court referrals and, 27
    crime rates, 8, 9
    detention rates and, 7-10, 84-86,
        117-118, 120, 201-202
    intake factors, 113
    interests of, 119
    judicial disposition and, 27
    misinformation about, 42
    offense history and, 24
    Pennsylvania courts and, 108-121
    placement factors, 116
    police and, 47-65
    prior delinquency and, 77
    rates of delinquency, 72
    uncooperative, 43
    Washington state confinement and,
        139-152
    welfare of, 150
Misdemeanors:
    African Americans charged with, 76
    against person, 24
    attorney presence and, 68
    custody decisions and, 61
    factors influencing referral
        decisions, 59
Misperceptions, prejudice based on,
    42-43, 149
Missouri:
    attorney presence and, 68
    urban versus rural courts in, 103
Monitoring, 13, 124, 204
Montana, American Indians in prisons
    in, 183
Moore, M., 213
Moral values, threats to prevailing, 149
Multivariate analysis, 100
Myers, M., 102, 136, 137
Myths, prejudice based on, 42-43

National Center for Juvenile Justice, 11

National Coalition of Hispanic Mental
    Health and Social Service
    Organizations, 8
National Coalition of State Juvenile
    Justice Advisory Groups, 1, 6, 9,
    10, 15
National Council of Juvenile and
    Family Court Judges, 9, 13, 47,
    202-203
National Council on Crime and
    Delinquency, 8
National Youth Survey, 9-10
Native American youths:
    attorney representation and, 80, 87
    detention rates and, 88
    home removal and, 92
    nonurban areas, 102
    police decisions and, 53
    status offenses and, 76
Nebraska, American Indian
    delinquency in, 189
Neglect referrals, 102
Neighborhood context, arrest decisions
    and, 101
Neuberger, A., 29
Noel, D. L., 131
North Carolina, community groups
    and, 12
North Dakota, American Indians in
    prisons in, 183

O'Brien, M., 185
Offenders, social characteristics of, 22
Offense(s):
    against the person, 76, 80, 85, 110
    characteristics of, 22, 56
    history of. See Prior record
    multiple, 112, 117-118
    number of, 108
    principle of, 70, 73
Offense patterns, racial disparities and,
    76
Offense seriousness, 22-23, 101, 130
    attorney services and, 78, 87
    custody decisions and, 61
    detention and, 69, 84, 88
    dispositional decisions and, 93
    intake decisions and, 24

judicial decision making and, 27, 72
police decisions and, 54-55, 56
referral decisions and, 59
sentencing and, 73, 91
urban areas and, 67
Offense type, 101
secure confinement and, 80-81
Office of Juvenile Justice and
Delinquency Prevention
(OJJDP), 2-4, 8, 11, 99, 160
Oregon, culturally appropriate
treatment and, 12
Organizational practices, differential
effects on minorities, 43
Out-of-home placement, 80, 89-91, 112
Out-of-home supervision, 196
Overrepresentation. *See* Minority
overrepresentation/differentials

Parens patriae objectives, 98, 119, 122
Parental neglect, 123-124
Parental supervision, 33-34
police decisions and, 54, 55
Parole, American Indians and, 188-189
Parry, D. L., 185
Paternoster, R., 188-189
Peers, attachment to, 187
Penetration, confinement versus, 5
Pennsylvania, role of race in juvenile
justice in, 98-124
Personal demoralization offenses, 184
Personal observations, racial/ethnic
bias and, 36-40
Personal problems, 108
Petitioned cases, 116-117, 195
Phillips, C. D., 70, 73
Piliavin, I., 48
Pinkney, A., 213
Piper, E., 213
Placement outcomes, 116
Platt, A., 35
Police, 47-65
cultural awareness training and, 173
custody decisions and, 59-61
dispositional decision making and,
70, 101
ethnic-staffing balance and, 170, 173
formal-processing effects, 120, 122

patrolling patterns, 101
referrals and, 122
urban areas and, 132
Police case files, 49
Police contacts, accumulation of, 101
Policies:
community involvement in, 174
convergence with research themes,
1-15
differential effects on minorities,
43-45
drugs and, 11
future directions, 202-204
future roles, 13-15
individual prejudices and, 41-42
recommendations for, 40-45,
121-124, 176
success of, 14
Political attention, avoidance of, 71
Political order, inequality in, 132
Politics:
local, 6-7
research environment and, 17-18
Pommersheim, F., 188
Pope, C. E., 10, 69, 72, 73, 99-100, 102,
103, 133, 155, 156, 179, 190,
192-193, 201-216
Poupart, L. M., 179-200
Poverty, 123, 133, 170, 213
placement outcomes and, 116
processing effects and, 120
social service workers reacting to,
102
Prejudice, based on myths and
misperceptions, 42-43
Prejudiced individuals, racial
differences attributable to, 30-31
Pretrial detention:
disposition and, 84
influence on sentence, 91-92, 93
policy recommendations, 122
urban areas and, 69, 102
Prevention, 12, 177
Price-Spratlen, T., 128-152
Prior record, 22, 71, 76-78
custody decision and, 59
detention and, 88, 117-118
dispositional decision and, 90, 93
judicial disposition and, 27

measuring, 23
police and, 55-56
race and, 24
referral decisions and, 59
research controlling for, 101
sentencing and, 73, 82
Private residential care, 120
Probation, 70, 172, 196
Probation department, ethnic-staffing
    balance and, 170, 173
Probation violations, 76
Processing. *See* Case processing
Property misdemeanors, 56
Prosecutorial decisions, 22, 24-27
Prosecutors:
    discretionary decisions and, 133
    interviews with, 28
Public defenders:
    interviews with, 20, 28, 29
    use of, 78-80
Public hearing testimony, 17-19
Public order offenses, 76
Punishment:
    community effects, 128-152
    juvenile court philosophy and, 99
Punitive emphasis, 176

Race:
    case-processing outcomes and, 23,
        24-27, 124
    neighborhoods and, 101
Racial differentials. *See* Minority
    overrepresentation/differentials
Racial bias, Florida's justice system
    and, 16-46
Reasons, C., 181, 182
Recidivism, 91
    American Indian youths and, 185
    chronic, 77
Record, prior. *See* Prior record
Reed, W. L., 73
Referral(s), 70
    confinement rates and, 140-144
    discretionary decisions, 101
    factors influencing, 59
    likelihood of, 189
    police effects on, 49, 51, 122
    policy recommendations, 122

rates in Pennsylvania, 110-112
typical, 24
Washington state confinement
    rates, 140-144
Rehabilitation, 69-70, 71, 90, 176
Reiss, A. J., Jr., 48, 70
Reporting, of individual racial bias,
    41-42
Research:
    convergence with policy themes,
        1-15
    Florida's juvenile justice system
        and, 16-46
    future directions, 207-208
    future roles, 13-15
    inconsistent findings of, 100
    language used, 18
    police decisions and, 49-65
    political environment and, 17-18
    quality data and, 17-18
Residential facilities, commitment to,
    22
Resources, 3-4, 11-12, 176
    constrained set of, 98, 171
Rhoden, E., 12
Ride-alongs, 50
Risk screening, 175
Robbins, S. P., 187
Rothman, D. J., 69
Runaways, 56
Rural areas, American Indian youths
    in, 179-200
Rural courts:
    attorney presence and, 68
    centralized procedures in, 102
    detention and, 69
    informal controls and, 67, 68
    sentencing and, 66, 68, 69-74

Sampson, R., 102
Sanctions, 42
Schools:
    difficulties with, 108, 112
    failure of, 172
    policies of, 175
Schutt, R., 69, 73, 101
Schwartz, I., 7, 8, 9, 15, 69, 72-73, 84,
    91, 156, 157, 185-186, 189

Secure confinement, 59, 61, 89-91, 117
  equitable usage, 6
  probability of being held in, 24, 26,
    80-82
  policy recommendations, 122
Self-esteem, African American youths
    and, 174
Sellin, T., 72, 102, 148, 181
Sentencing:
  American Indian youth and, 188
  discretionary, 72, 73, 74
  effects of prior sentences on, 90-91
  offense seriousness and, 91
  offense type and, 81
  pretrial detention effects on, 91-92,
    93
  prior records and, 82
  rural courts and, 66
  urban versus rural areas, 68, 69-74,
    102
Shelter care, 117, 122
Sibling delinquency, 102
Sight and sound separation, 3
Silberman, C. E., 214
Simkus, A. A., 188
Simpson, E. E., 131, 133, 136
Slaughter, E., 48, 69, 72, 73, 74, 78, 80,
    86, 101, 155
Slums, 133
Smith, B. L., 69, 70, 72, 73, 78, 86, 155
Smith, D., 48
Social changes, community problems
    and, 149-150
Social characteristics, 22
Social conditions, improving, 173
Social context:
  of crime and justice, 212-215
  of juvenile justice administration,
    66-97
Social control:
  formal, 77
  informal, 67
Social factors, 35-36, 93
  individualized justice and, 71
  police decisions and, 48, 54
  poverty and, 214-215
  sentencing and, 72
  treatment choices and, 44-45
Social resources, access to, 31-32

Social service workers, poverty and,
    102
Social services, 150-151
Social structure, 68, 130-131
Social welfare orientation, 150-151
Sontheimer, H., 98-124
South Dakota, American Indian
    incarceration in, 188
Spitzer, S., 131
State(s), compliance with JJDPA
    mandates, 2-4, 11-12
State agencies, partnerships with, 14
State attorneys, interviews with, 20
Status offenses, 23, 56
  attorney presence and, 68
  deinstitutionalization and, 3
  factors influencing referral
    decisions, 59
  Native Americans and, 76
  referral decision and, 61
Stereotypes, 169
Stewart, O., 181, 182, 187
Strauss, J. H., 182
Substance abuse:
  police decisions and, 54
  prevention and treatment, 172, 175
Suburban areas, intake factors and, 113
Suburban courts:
  detention and, 69
  formal processing and, 120
  sentencing and, 68, 103
Supervision, 5
  informal, 70
  parental, 33-34, 54, 55
  status offenders and, 3
Sutphen, R., 100, 102
Swigert, V., 135
Systems, tendency toward
    homeostasis, 6
Systems perspective,
    overrepresentation and, 5

Talarico, S., 102, 136, 137
Tausig, M., 191
Thomas, C. W., 71, 73, 93
Thornberry, T. P., 48, 73, 90, 101, 179
Tittle, C., 149
Town meetings, 158, 167-169

Tracy, P. E., 148
Training personnel, 123, 173, 208
Training schools, 5, 70

Underclass, 213-214
Urban areas:
    delinquency rates and, 102
    Washington state confinement rates
        and, 147
Urban courts, 66-97
    formal processing and, 67-68,
        132-133
    pretrial detention and, 69
    sentencing and, 68, 69-74, 102
Urbanization:
    crime and, 213-214
    punishment disparities and, 132
    Washington state confinement rates
        and, 146
Urban police, formal practices and, 54

Variables:
    control, 10, 20, 100
    race-related, 11
Velde, R. W., 155
Vermont, 12
Victims:
    injured, 110
    wishes of, 55
Violence, 130-131, 134, 213
    African American youths and, 156,
        164
    Washington state confinement rates
        and, 144, 148
Visher, C., 48

Wacquant, L. J. D., 214-215

Waiver, 196
Washington State, racial disparities in
    punishment in, 134-152
Wasserman, M., 71, 73, 93
Weapon use, 56, 59, 61
White families, 35
White males, incarceration rates of, 8
Whites, social hegemony and, 131
White youths:
    adjudication factors, 116
    attorney representation and, 78, 87
    California detention and, 153,
        161-164, 167
    court referrals and, 27
    delinquency rates, 72, 117
    detention decisions and, 73
    detention rates and, 8, 84, 117-118,
        120, 202
    informal processing and, 61
    intake factors, 113
    interests of, 119
    judicial disposition and, 27
    offense patterns and, 76
    Pennsylvania courts and, 108-121
    placement factors, 116
    prior delinquency and, 24, 77
    Washington state confinement and,
        139-152
Wilson, J. Q., 101, 212-213, 214-215
Winfree, T. L., 188
Wise, S., 188
Wolfgang, M. E., 72, 102, 148, 181
Wordes, M., 47-65, 86, 201-202

Youth training schools, 176

Zatz, M. S., 7, 10, 11, 13, 191

About the Contributors

James Austin is Executive Vice President of the National Council on Crime and Delinquency (NCCD). He received his Ph.D. in sociology from the University of California, Davis. He directs NCCD's national research and publication program, and his current projects include evaluation of drug treatment programs in local correctional agencies and the national evaluation of the multistate correctional options program for the National Institute of Justice. He is the author of numerous articles and books, including *Reinventing Juvenile Justice* (with Barry Krisberg, 1993).

Donna M. Bishop is Senior Research Associate, Center for the Studies in Criminology and Law, University of Florida. Her major research interests include juvenile justice processing and, more recently, causes and consequences of child abuse. She is currently completing a study (with Charles E. Frazier, Lonn Lanza-Kaduce, and Larry Winner) for the Florida legislature on the effect of new permissive and mandatory legislation for the transfer of juveniles to criminal court jurisdiction.

George S. Bridges is Associate Professor of Sociology at the University of Washington. His ongoing research interests include crime, inequality, and social control. He is currently studying the relation-

239

ship between race, involvement in crime, and racial disparities in punishment.

Timothy S. Bynum is Professor in the School of Criminal Justice and Associate Director of the Institute for Public Policy and Social Research at Michigan State University. He has recently directed several research projects studying the impact of interventions in drug enforcement and juvenile justice. He also served as Principal Investigator of the study of disproportionate representation of minorities in juvenile justice in Michigan.

Darlene J. Conley is Assistant Professor of Sociology at the University of Washington. In addition to her research on racial disproportionality in the juvenile justice system, she is currently conducting ethnographic research on syringe exchange programs and the prevention of AIDS.

Rodney L. Engen is a doctoral candidate in sociology at the University of Washington. His current research interests include the roles of race, social class, and school contexts in the etiology of delinquency and also the impact of offender race and social contexts on juvenile justice processes in Washington State.

Barry C. Feld is Centennial Professor of Law at the University of Minnesota Law School. He received his J.D. from the University of Minnesota Law School in 1969 and his Ph.D. in sociology from Harvard University in 1973. He has written four books and more than two dozen major law review and criminology articles on juvenile justice administration, with a special emphasis on serious young offenders, procedural justice in juvenile court, and sentencing policy. He chaired the Due Process Committee of the Minnesota Juvenile Justice Task Force, helping to shape the state's revision of the juvenile code in 1994.

William H. Feyerherm is Director of the Regional Research Institute at Portland State University. He received his Ph.D. in criminal justice from the State University of New York at Albany. He served as coinvestigator (with Carl Pope) of the OJJDP Technical Assistance

Program to address minority overrepresentation. Other recent work includes a process evaluation of the gang prevention and intervention efforts of the Boys' and Girls' Clubs of America and an evaluation of Boys' and Girls' Club programming in public housing as part of the national "weed-and-seed" efforts. He has numerous publications on various aspects of criminal and juvenile justice processing.

Charles E. Frazier is Professor of Sociology and Associate Dean of the College of Liberal Arts and Sciences at the University of Florida. His general research area is the sociology of juvenile and criminal justice and evaluation research, with particular focus on race and gender inequality and the social dynamics and effects of state and federal reform initiatives. He is currently completing a study (with Donna Bishop, Lonn Lanza-Kaduce, and Larry Winner) for the Florida legislature on the effect of new permissive and mandatory legislation for the transfer of juveniles to criminal court jurisdiction.

Kimberly Kempf Leonard is Associate Professor of Criminology and Criminal Justice at the University of Missouri–St. Louis. She received her Ph.D. in criminology and criminal law from the University of Pennsylvania. She directed research on minority overrepresentation in juvenile justice for Missouri and Pennsylvania. Her general research areas include equal application of criminal and juvenile justice policies and patterns of offending. She is currently writing a book (with Paul Tracy) on offending over the life course among the 1958 Philadelphia birth cohort.

Carl E. Pope is Professor of Criminal Justice at the University of Wisconsin–Milwaukee. He received his Ph.D. in criminal justice from the State University of New York at Albany. He is author of numerous publications on criminal and juvenile justice processing, confinement, and race-related issues. He served as coinvestigator of the OJJDP Technical Assistance Program to address minority overrepresentation and is currently analyzing processing differences based on race within the juvenile justice systems of Wisconsin. Other recent work includes a process evaluation of the gang prevention and intervention efforts of the Boys' and Girls' Clubs of America and an evaluation of Boys' and Girls' Club programming in public housing as part of the national "weed and seed" efforts.

Lisa M. Poupart is a member of the Lac Du Flambeau band of Lake Superior Chippewa Indians. She is currently a doctoral candidate in the School of Justice Studies at Arizona State University. She received her M.S. in 1991 from the Criminal Justice Program at the University of Wisconsin–Milwaukee.

Townsand Price-Spratlen is Assistant Professor of Sociology at Ohio State University. He has been a postdoctoral research fellow at Pennsylvania State University. His current research interests focus on the effects of social ties and community development on residential mobility and neighborhood change, and the relationship between criminal sanctioning and individual and community marginalization.

Henry Sontheimer is Senior Evaluation Analyst with the Pennsylvania Commission on Crime and Delinquency. He was formerly a Juvenile Court Consultant with the Center for Juvenile Justice Training and Research at Shippensburg University of Pennsylvania. He received his Ph.D. from Pennsylvania State University. His articles have appeared in *Justice Quarterly, Juvenile and Family Court Journal,* and the *Journal of Offender Counseling, Service and Rehabilitation.*

Madeline Wordes is a doctoral candidate in ecological/community psychology at Michigan State University. She served as the Project Coordinator of the study of disproportionate representation of females and youths of color in the juvenile justice system in Michigan. She currently directs a study of community alternatives for stateward delinquent youths.